THE unofficial RECIPES OF THE HUNGER GAMES

THE UNOFFICAL

RECIPES OF THE HUNGER GAMES

187 RECIPES INSPIRED BY

THE HUNGER GAMES, CATCHING FIRE,

AND MOCKINGJAY

ROCKRIDGE UNIVERSITY PRESS ⬤ BERKELEY, CALIFORNIA

CONTENTS

INTRODUCTION   XIII

SECTION ONE   **THE HUNGER GAMES**   XIV

1 THE WOODS AND THE HEARTH   3

Prim's Goat Cheese Gifts   4
Tesserae Hearth Bread   5
Catfish Stew With Greens   6
Katniss Mint Tea   7
Hope Springs Eternal Dandelion Salad   8
Fried Catfish and Roasted Katniss Tubers   9

2 THE SEAM AND DISTRICT 12   11

Real Bakery Loaf Bread   12
Greasy Sae's Call It Beef Soup   13
Peeta's Burnt Raisin Nut Bread   14
Mr. Mellark's Farewell Cookies   15

3 THE TRAIN   17

Thick and Creamy Carrot Soup   18
Fresh Green Salad   19
Tribute Lamb Chops   20
Creamy Mashed Potatoes   21
Finger Licking Chocolate Cake   22
New Day Dawning Coddled Eggs With Glazed Ham Steaks   23
Golden Fried Potatoes   24
Irresistible Hot Chocolate   25
Peeta's Sweet Breakfast Rolls   26

4 THE CAPITOL   29

Orange Chicken in Cream Sauce   30
Flower-Shaped Rolls   31

Sweet Peas With Tiny Onions   32
Golden Honey Custard   33
Goose Liver and Puffy Bread   34
Creamy Mixed Mushroom Soup   35
Bitter Greens With Pea-Sized Tomatoes   36
Noodles in Green Sauce   37
Fiery Spirits Banana Rum Cake   38
Batter Cakes With Thick Orange Preserves   39
Gamemakers' Suckling Pig   40
Salty Tears Fish Soup   41
Beloved Lamb Stew With Dried Plums   42
Haymitch's Pork Chops and Smashed Potatoes   43

5 THE ARENA 45

District 4's Loaves and Fishes   46
All for Rue Groosling Legs   47
District 11's Seeded Crescent Loaf   48
Arena Beef Strips   49
One Fine Spit-Roasted Rabbit   50
Peeta's Healing Groosling Soup With Sweet Root Vegetables   51
Roasted Rabbit Legs With Egg Sauce   52
Deceptively Sweet Berry Syrup Soda   53
Goat Cheese Toasts With Fresh Apple   54
Mellark Bakery's Goat Cheese and Apple Tarts   55

6 RECIPES INSPIRED BY THE HUNGER GAMES 57

Mrs. Everdeen's Sugar Berry Jam   58
Prim's Birthday Venison Steaks   59
Tesserae Cereal With Mixed Berries   60
Golden Cornucopia Cake   61
Cake on Fire   62
President Snow's Snowy Rose Cupcakes   63
Venison Stew With Sweet Roots for Rue   64
Peeta's Hot Chocolate Pudding   65
Creamy Roasted Katniss Soup   66

7 AUTHENTICITY FOR THE ADVENTUROUS 69

Greasy Sae's Special Winter Soup   70
Mom Everdeen's Breakfast of Mush   71
Mrs. Everdeen's Rabbit Stew With Wild Greens   72
Rich Goose Liver and Puffy Bread   73
Pale Purple Melon   74
Backpack Treasure Dried Fruits   75
District 12 Jerky   76

Campfire Bony Fish on a Stick   77
Goat Trader's Stew   78

SECTION TWO   **CATCHING FIRE**   80

8 RETURN TO DISTRICT 12 AND TOURING PANEM   83

Hazelle's Hearty Beaver Stew   84
Finger Thawing Herb Tea   85
Greasy Sae's Gourd and Bean Soup   86
Haymitch-Style Boiled Cabbage and Burnt Meat   87
Lavender Cookies Fit for a President   88
Paprika Duck and Rosemary Tubers With Gravy   89
Haymitch's Hangover Muffins   90
Peeta's Multigrain Bread   91
Soothe My Soul Tea   92
Mellark's Cinnamon Bread   93
Bittersweet Memories Dill Bread   94
Prim's Hearty Beef Stew   95
Mrs. Everdeen's Simple Broth   96

9 THE TRAIN TO QUARTER QUELL   99

Silent, Cold Soup of Beet Puree   100
Fish Cakes With Wasabi-Lime Mayo   101
Cornish Hens Stuffed With Oranges Over Rice   102
Watercress and Almond Salad   103
Chocolate Covered Cherry Custard   104
Soothing Honey and Spiced Milk   105

10 THE QUARTER QUELL FESTIVITIES AND TRAINING   107

Homesick Cheese Buns   108
Snow's Suckling Pig   109
Capitol Lamb Stew With Plum Dumplings   110
Presidential Stuffed Fowl   112
Ocean Creatures and Cocktail Sauce   113
Savory Pumpkin Soup With Nuts   114
Taste of Spring Soup   115
Cold Raspberry Soup With Fresh Berries   116
No Manners Needed Chocolate Cake   117
Blood Orange Quail   118
Disappearing Mints   120
Sweet Pheasant With Cranberry Jewels   121
Baby Vegetables in Lemon Butter Sauce   122
Parsley Mashed Potatoes   123

Fruit Kebabs and a Fountain of Chocolate   124
Mashed on the Floor Peas   125
Breakfast Through a Mouthpiece   126
Plutarch's Roasted Turkey Leg   127

11 THE 75TH HUNGER GAMES   129

Fence-Roasted Tree Nuts   130
Chestnut and Apple Salad With Toasted Bread Croutons   131
Burnt "Tree Rat" for the Timid   132

12 RECIPES INSPIRED BY CATCHING FIRE   135

Peppermint Ice Cream   136
Lamb Chops With a Balsamic Plum Reduction   137
Lamb's Neck With Sweet Roots and Greens   138
Fruit-and-Herb-Stuffed Portobello Caps   139
Orange and Sweet Berry Coolers   140
Fresh Orange Vanilla Rice Pudding   141
Rue's Cold Carrot and Yam Puree   142
Easy Apple Tart   143
Mellark's Whole Wheat Cinnamon Raisin Bread   144
Pumpkin Pie With Slivered Nuts   145
Potato Leek Soup   146
Haymitch-Inspired Cabbage Casserole   147
Sweet Asian Watercress Salad   148
Stewed Yams and Plums With Orange Juice   149
Juicy Chocolate Citrus Cake   150
Chicken With Orange Sauce   151
Tiny Plum Tarts   152
Sautéed Apples With Brown Sugar and Cinnamon   153
Catching Fire Lamb Puffs   154
Jewel-Colored Mosaic Gelatin   155
Pepper Jack and Chive Muffins   156
Skewered Bird   157

13 AUTHENTICITY FOR THE ADVENTUROUS   159

Charred Tree Rat   160
Sweet Raw Shellfish   161
Authentic Arena Clambake   162
District 4 Shellfish in a Spicy Chile Sauce   163
Hazelle's Authentic Beaver Stew   164
Spit-Roasted Goat   165

SECTION THREE   **MOCKINGJAY**   168

14 ESCAPE TO DISTRICT 13   171

Get You Through 'Til Lunch Hot Breakfast Grain   172
District 13's Mashed Breakfast Turnips   173
"Wish There Was Meat" Bean and Onion Stew   174
District 13's Bread   175
Slightly Slimy but Delicious Gray Fish and Okra Stew   176
Feel Better Fast Bread Soaked in Warm Milk   177
Say It Isn't So Bread and Cabbage   178
Peeta's Minced Venison Stew   179
Hot Under the Collar Grain and Milk   180
Mushier Than Mud Beets   181
Good for Your Soul Pea Soup   182

15 HUNTING ONCE MORE WITH GALE   185

Wind in Your Hare Pie   186
Crispy Juicy Roasted Turkey   187
It's Not Really Dog and Rhubarb Stew   188
Deliciously Simple Grilled Groosling Kebabs   189

16 THE MISSIONS AND VICTORS' VILLAGE   191

Greasy Sae's Chicken Fried Slop   192
Greasy Sae's Seriously Beef Stew   193
Not From a Can Cod Chowder   194
Fancy Capitol Cream-Filled Cookies   195
Greasy Sae's Plum Lamb Stew   196
Better Than Nothing Bread With Moldy Cheese and Mustard Sauce   197
Capitol Living Liver Pate   198
Capitol Fig Cookies   199
Tigris' Ham and Potato Hash   200
Greasy Sae's Eggs and Toast   201
Buttercup's Bacon and French Toast   202
Finnick and Annie's Wedding Cider   203
Finnick and Annie's Wedding Cake   204

17 RECIPES INSPIRED BY MOCKINGJAY   207

Panem Biscuits   208
District 13's Sausage Gravy   209
Stick to Your Ribs   210
Gale's Venison Pot Roast   211
Greasy Sae's Black Walnut Cookies   212
District 13's Hoe Cakes   213

Appalachian Homestead Cornbread   214
Greasy Sae's Fried Ham and Red-Eye Gravy   215
Greasy Sae's Pickled Crab Apples   216
Katniss' Favorite Fried Okra   217
Prim's Blackberry Cobbler   218
Cole Slaw Salad for Haymitch   219
Eat It on the Go Deer Jerky   220
Greasy Sae's 5-Bean Soup   221
Prim's Pickled Beets   222
Dry Land Fish Fry   223
District Dumplings   224
Potato Biscuits   225
Greasy Sae's Zucchini and Corn Medley   226

18 AUTHENTICITY FOR THE ADVENTUROUS 229

Greasy Sae's Holiday Stuffed Possum   230
Peeta's Positively Awesome Roasted Raccoon   231
Capitol Fried Squirrel Wings   232
Greasy Sae's Baked Groundhog   233
Gale's Rat on a Stick   234
Keep You Going Possum Entrails Stew   235
Fried Snake Steak   236
Katniss' Baked Pigeon   237
Greasy Sae's Badger Stew   238
Grilled Minnow Hash   239
Fried Snail Scampi   240

SECTION FOUR CELEBRATING THE HUNGER GAMES 242

19 LET THE GAMES BEGIN 243

Deceptively Sweet Party for Kids   244
Children at the Capitol   245
Cornucopia Buffet for Kids   246
A Rustic Menu for Adventurous Teens   247
Teens Partying at the Capitol   248
Cornucopia Buffet for Adults   249
Dining With President Snow   250

CONCLUSION 251

INDEX 252

INTRODUCTION

IN the *Hunger Games* trilogy, the characters fought, salivated, and sacrificed, all in the name of food. So what better way to immerse yourself back into the world of Panem than through your taste buds?

Food, or lack thereof, serves as both symbol and sustenance throughout the trilogy. Panem occupied its own post-apocalyptic world and, in a sense, also had its own food groups: foods hunted or foraged for basic survival, humble dishes made in the District homes, and Capitol foods that were meant to impress more than nourish. The foods presented in *The Hunger Games, Catching Fire,* and *Mockingjay* ranged from simple game meats to elaborate and uncommon party fare; all of those varieties, from the modest to the ostentatious, are represented in *The Unofficial Recipes of The Hunger Games.*

Many dishes presented, such as the Gamemakers' Suckling Pig, are directly mentioned in the trilogy, while others are merely inspired by the different scenes that transpire. And for more adventurous fans—those who don't mind hunting for their meal—the cookbook offers recipes that are literally on the wild side, with fare such as Katniss' Baked Pigeon or Capitol Fried Squirrel Wings. These dishes would be a tantalizing feast for most of the inhabitants of Panem, although they are unusual by today's standards.

Cooking and eating *The Unofficial Recipes of The Hunger Games* allows fans to delve back into each book of the trilogy in a whole new way. When a craving for the world of *Hunger Games* strikes, tear off a piece of Peeta's Burnt Raisin Nut Bread or slurp a spoonful of Greasy Sae's Special Winter Soup, and transport all of your senses back into the world of Panem.

The Unofficial Recipes of The Hunger Games desires to emulate some of the adventures of the Hunger Games trilogy, however, it is not our desire to place anyone—tribute or otherwise—in danger. If you decide to follow in the footsteps of Katniss and forage some of the ingredients in the recipes, please properly educate yourself before consuming or handling any ingredient. The recipes within "Authenticity for the Adventurous" require safe handling precautions; please adhere to wild game safety practices when catching or preparing any game meat. We suggest consulting Dressing and Cooking Wild Game, or another book on the subject, as a safety companion when preparing any of the "Adventurous" recipes.

The Unofficial Recipes of The Hunger Games does not endorse the killing of any small animals, or other game. It is the reader's responsibility to follow all laws and legislation relating to hunting, fishing and other gaming concerns. Enjoy the adventure!

SECTION ONE

THE HUNGER GAMES

1 THE WOODS AND THE HEARTH

2 THE SEAM AND DISTRICT 12

3 THE TRAIN

4 THE CAPITOL

5 THE ARENA

6 RECIPES INSPIRED BY THE HUNGER GAMES

7 AUTHENTICITY FOR THE ADVENTUROUS

THE first book of the trilogy, *The Hunger Games,* introduced readers to Katniss, Peeta, Gale and the other characters of the story. The world of *Hunger Games* was very different from the 21st-century; in this new world, food was a commodity, a tool and a sign of wealth. For most of the characters, food was scarce and valued very highly when it was available, no matter how simple it might be. The contrast between the scarcity and simplicity of the District foods and the extravagance of the Capitol tables is a metaphor for the poverty of the Districts and the ease and superficiality of life in the Capitol.

The first portion of this section is devoted to the foods directly mentioned in *The Hunger Games* and follows the book as closely as possible in terms of chronology.

Chapter 1 (The Woods and the Hearth), features recipes for foods made in the homes of District 12, many of them from the ingredients Katniss and Gale were able to hunt or find. Many of these foods, like Prim's Goat Cheese Gifts, have special significance to the story that unfolds. Chapter 2 (The Seam and District 12) boasts the famous dishes from District 12, such as Greasy Sae's Call It Beef Soup.

In Chapter 3 (The Train), you'll find the foods that introduced Katniss and Peeta to the world of plenty, with dishes such as Peeta's favorite: Irresistible Hot Chocolate. Chapter 4 (The Capitol) is full of recipes for the wildly extravagant and includes unusual foods the tributes were introduced to on their arrival, such as Orange Chicken in Cream Sauce and Gamemakers' Suckling Pig, whereas Chapter 5 (The Arena) features foods that the tributes either made themselves or were given by sponsors, such as District 4's Loaves and Fishes.

Chapter 6 (Recipes Inspired by *The Hunger Games*) is a collection of recipes that use the story or the foods found in the books as inspiration and evoke the spirit and the memory of this first book in the trilogy. Finally, this section closes with Chapter 7 (Authenticity for the Adventurous), where you'll find unusual dishes like Mrs. Everdeen's Rabbit Stew With Wild Greens.

All of the recipes are deliciously different, and all are a trip back into the story that started it all.

1

THE WOODS AND THE HEARTH

*"In the woods waits the only person with whom
I can be myself: Gale."*

KATNISS, *THE HUNGER GAMES* BY SUZANNE COLLINS, CHAPTER 1

IN THE WOODS, Katniss was able to be herself with Gale, but she was also able to find food with which to feed herself and the family that depended on her. The recipes in Chapter 1 are the peasant foods of the futuristic world in which *The Hunger Games* is set.

In the 19th, 18th and earlier centuries, the rural poor hunted, fished and foraged for whatever they could use to fill their stomachs and ward off starvation for one more day. They became very adept at making those foods taste good, and many of the recipes they created are now popular dishes in restaurants and gourmet kitchens.

In Chapter 1, we try to do the same with the ingredients that Katniss and Gale were able to gather or obtain through trade.

PRIM'S GOAT CHEESE GIFTS

SERVES 4

On the first morning of the trilogy, Prim left a gift of goat cheese wrapped in fresh basil for her sister, Katniss. Like many foods in the trilogy, this one was poetically symbolic. Goats are common sacrificial animals in many cultures. Prim left this symbol of sacrifice for Katniss very quietly, without fanfare. Soon, Katniss would make a very real sacrifice for Prim.

Unique presentation and refined flavors make this dish an excellent appetizer for a party, while also enjoyable as a light snack.

8 OUNCES CHEVRE GOAT CHEESE, AT ROOM TEMPERATURE
5 TABLESPOONS OLIVE OIL
4 TABLESPOONS FRESH LEMON JUICE
2 TEASPOONS FRESHLY GROUND BLACK PEPPER
1 TABLESPOON WHITE WINE VINEGAR
8 (9-INCH) PIECES COOKING TWINE (UNTREATED, UNBLEACHED) SUCH AS YOU'D USE FOR TRUSSING A CHICKEN
1-2 LARGE BUNCHES FRESH BASIL, ABOUT 16 (6-INCH LONG) STEMS WITH LEAVES INTACT

In a small, non-metallic mixing bowl, use a fork to mash up the goat cheese.

In a separate bowl, combine the olive oil, lemon juice, pepper and vinegar.

Add the olive oil, lemon juice, vinegar and pepper mixture to the goat cheese and mix well. Put in the fridge to chill while you assemble the basil stem "gift wrap."

Take 2 pieces of twine; lay them in a cross pattern (one vertical, one horizontal) and tie a knot in the center. Repeat for the other 3 sets of 2.

Remove cheese from fridge and divide into 4 equal portions.

One at a time, roll each portion into a ball and set aside.

Take 3 or 4 basil stems, depending on size, place in an asterisk pattern (like slicing a pizza) and then place 1 ball of cheese in the center.

Carefully wrap the cheese ball with the basil stems.

Holding the ball tightly together, place onto the knot of the first twine "cross." Tie the first 2 pieces tightly at the top of the ball, then weave the second pair of strings through that and knot again. Repeat for the other 3 balls.

Refrigerate in a covered container until ready to use.

To serve, let the packets come to room temperature, open them and spread the cheese onto sliced Real Bakery Loaf Bread.

With your fingers, tear a few of the basil leaves and place them on top of the cheese and bread.

Serve with bowls of fresh blackberries, blueberries or raspberries.

TESSERAE HEARTH BREAD

MAKES 1 LOAF

In The Hunger Games, *rations of grain and oil came at a high price for the children in the districts of Panem. The stakes were high for second helpings, as additional tesserae equated to an increased number of reaping entries.*

In this book, we're using barley and barley flour to stand in for the unnamed grain given out in the tesserae. This bread is darker and heavier than that which was enjoyed by those who could afford bakery bread.

2 TABLESPOONS OLIVE OIL
2 CUPS BARLEY FLOUR
2 TEASPOONS BAKING POWDER
1 TEASPOON SALT
¾ CUP WARM (110-DEGREE) WATER
2 TABLESPOONS GOAT'S MILK

Preheat oven to 400 degrees.

Lightly oil a baking sheet and set aside.

Sift together the barley flour, baking powder and salt in a large mixing bowl. Set aside.

Combine water, olive oil and milk in a blender and lightly blend until well emulsified.

Add to the flour mixture and stir with a wooden spoon until all the dry ingredients are thoroughly mixed and dough is formed.

Turn the dough out onto a lightly floured cutting board or table and, using your hands or a rolling pin, shape the dough into a flat, round circle about ½-inch thick.

Place onto the baking sheet, lightly cut a cross into the top with a wet knife and put into oven.

Bake for 15 minutes or until golden.

CATFISH STEW WITH GREENS

SERVES 4

We can only guess at what type of fish Gale and Katniss caught on their fishing trip, but since District 12 resides in what used to be Appalachia, catfish is a safe assumption.

This stew is hearty, but the distinct flavors of the catfish and the greens give it a nice freshness as well.

6 TABLESPOONS OLIVE OIL
1 CUP WHITE ONIONS, CHOPPED
2 LARGE CLOVES GARLIC, CRUSHED
½ CUP FRESH PARSLEY, CHOPPED
1 TEASPOON OREGANO
1 TEASPOON ROSEMARY
1 CUP FRESH KALE OR SPINACH
2 TEASPOONS TOMATO PASTE
12 OUNCES FISH STOCK
1½ POUNDS CATFISH NUGGETS OR FILETS CUT
    INTO 2-INCH CHUNKS
SALT AND PEPPER TO TASTE

In a large soup pot, heat the olive oil on medium heat.

Add the onions and garlic and cook for 5 minutes, until the onions are soft and translucent, stirring occasionally.

Add parsley, oregano, rosemary and kale or spinach, and cook for 5 more minutes.

Stir in tomato paste and cook for 1 minute, then add fish stock and bring just to a boil.

Add fish and lower heat immediately to medium-low.

Simmer fish slowly for about 10–15 minutes. Season with salt and pepper.

Serve with crusty bread and bowls of fresh strawberries for dessert.

KATNISS MINT TEA

MAKES 2 MUGS OR 4 TEACUPS

Until Peeta's gift of burnt bread, tea made of old mint leaves was all Katniss had to give her mother and sister. Later in the series, she chewed mint as a way of staving off hunger when she had nothing to eat.

Mint tea can be very refreshing and comforting. Here we use fresh mint, and you can add a touch of honey if you'd like.

2 CUPS COLD WATER
2 TEASPOONS FRESH MINT LEAVES

Warm a teapot by filling it with boiling water and set aside.

Bring 2 cups cold water to boil in a pot.

Meanwhile, crush the mint leaves by tearing them and then, using a mortar and pestle, mash them up to extract the oils somewhat. If you do not have a mortar and pestle you can use a wooden spoon and a small mixing bowl.

Once the cold water comes to a boil, turn off the heat.

Dump the old water from the teapot and drop in the mint leaves.

Pour the fresh boiled water over the leaves, put the lid on the teapot and let it steep for at least 15–20 minutes.

Place a fresh mint leaf in the bottom of a cup and gently pour the tea over it.

HOPE SPRINGS ETERNAL DANDELION SALAD

SERVES 4

On the life-changing day that Peeta snuck Katniss the Burnt Raisin Nut Bread, she spied some dandelions growing wild and remembered that they can be eaten. It's poetic that her first foraging expedition was for this springtime green, as it represented the beginning of a new life and a new hope for her family's survival.

This is a traditional Appalachian recipe for the dish, using warm bacon dressing. The dandelion greens should be picked fresh and rinsed several times to remove any dirt.

4 SLICES BACON
¼ CUP WHITE GRANULATED SUGAR
¼ CUP CIDER VINEGAR
**2 CUPS WASHED AND TORN DANDELION
    GREENS, DRIED THOROUGHLY**

Cut bacon slices into 8 pieces.

Cook the bacon pieces over medium heat in a sauté pan.

Remove bacon from pan and drain on a paper towel.

Reserve ¼ cup of the bacon drippings and return sauté pan to low heat.

Add drippings, sugar and cook, stirring, until melted.

Stir in cider vinegar, add bacon pieces and then pour warm dressing over dandelion greens.

Toss and serve.

Dandelion greens are considered a weed by most gardeners and landscapers, but they're actually quite delicious if you harvest them at the right time. The key is to pick them before they've gone to flower. Once they've flowered, they become too tough and quite bitter. Be sure to soak them in cold water and rinse at least once in order to remove any bugs.

FRIED CATFISH AND ROASTED KATNISS TUBERS

SERVES 4

Katniss fondly remembered the day she was at the creek and noticed tall plants growing in the water close to the creek bed. They were katniss tubers, the plant for which her father had named her. She told us that when boiled or baked they're as good as any potato. The katniss plant is also known as swan potato, tule potato, or (more fittingly as a metaphor) arrowhead, due to the shape of its leaf.

Native Americans have used tubers of katniss, a nourishing root, as a food source for many generations. You can order the tubers from specialty sites online or substitute cassava or yucca, widely available in grocery store produce sections. Just peel the rough skin before using.

FOR ROASTED KATNISS TUBERS:
4 ROOTS OR TUBERS, SCRUBBED, PEELED AND
    QUARTERED
2 TABLESPOONS OLIVE OIL
2 TABLESPOONS FRESH PARSLEY, CHOPPED
1 TEASPOON SALT
½ TEASPOON FRESHLY GROUND BLACK PEPPER
½ TEASPOON PAPRIKA

FOR CATFISH:
4 (6-8 OUNCE) CATFISH FILETS
1 CUP WHOLE MILK
1 CUP YELLOW CORNMEAL (NOT SELF-RISING)
2 TEASPOONS SALT
1 TEASPOON FRESHLY GROUND BLACK PEPPER
¼ CUP CANOLA OIL

Preheat oven to 400 degrees.

FOR ROASTED KATNISS TUBERS:

In large mixing bowl, toss Katniss tubers with olive oil, parsley, salt, pepper and paprika.

Place seasoned Katniss tubers on baking sheet and bake for 20 minutes. They should be golden and fork tender like a potato.

When done turn the oven off. Place the tubers in an oven safe baking dish and cover with aluminum foil. Place the tubers in the oven to keep warm while fish is cooked.

FOR CATFISH:

Rinse the catfish filets and dry thoroughly with paper towels. Place the filets in a casserole or baking pan and pour milk over the top.

On a plate, combine corn meal, salt and pepper. Mix until well combined.

Take filets 1 at a time from the milk and dredge them in the cornmeal to coat evenly. Set filets aside and allow to sit for 5-10 minutes.

Heat the oil over medium-high heat in a cast-iron skillet.

Add the coated catfish filets 1 or 2 at a time, depending on the size of your skillet. Add olive oil as necessary to keep fish from sticking to the bottom of the pan.

Cook for about 5 minutes on each side, until golden brown and the fish flakes easily with a fork. Once cooked, place each filet on a paper towel, sprinkle with salt, and allow it to drain.

If you're cooking in large batches, place the drained catfish in the oven with the Katniss tubers to keep warm until all the fish is done.

NOTES

THE SEAM AND DISTRICT 12

"To this day, I cannot shake the connection between this boy, Peeta Mellark, and the bread that gave me hope, and the dandelion that reminded me that I was not doomed."

KATNISS, *THE HUNGER GAMES* BY SUZANNE COLLINS, CHAPTER 2

THE FOODS AVAILABLE to the residents of the Seam and District 12 are largely a mystery. While we're pretty well informed about what Katniss and Gale were able to find, forage and hunt, it is unclear whether other residents of the District and the Seam were able to trade or barter for other ingredients. It is clear, however, that food was scarce and ingredients were simple throughout District 12. Most of the recipes in Chapter 2 are for foods that were meant to sustain more than tantalize, with a few rare treats that were probably only available to those such as the Peacekeepers and visiting officials.

REAL BAKERY LOAF BREAD

MAKES 2 LOAVES

This is the bread that appeared at the end of Gale's arrow on the first morning of the book. There were various types of bread in The Hunger Games, *and each represented a different way of life and different chance of surviving. The books don't specify what type of grain was given out in the rations, but it's understood that the Capitol breads were better than the bakery breads, and that the bakery breads were better than those made from grain rations.*

Since there was little technology or gadgetry in District 12, it's safe to assume that the breads sold at Mellark's Bakery were probably much like the artisanal breads popular today. For those breads, we suggest a mixture of white, whole wheat and barley flours. For grain rations, we'll use barley and whole wheat, but it's likely that the Mellarks had to use whatever they could buy or obtain through trade.

2½ CUPS WHOLE WHEAT FLOUR
¾ CUP BARLEY FLOUR
2 TEASPOONS SALT
2 TEASPOONS YEAST
1½ CUPS WARM WATER (ABOUT 110 DEGREES)
OLIVE OIL

Using your hands or a whisk, mix together the flours, salt and yeast in a large bowl until well blended.

Add the water and mix with your hands or a stand mixer until smooth dough forms together.

Cover loosely with a clean damp towel and set in a warm place for at least 2 hours to rise. Rub a bit of olive oil over the surface to prevent dough from drying out.

After the dough has risen to about double, sprinkle the dough with a bit of flour, then divide into 2 equal-sized hunks.

Start forming the first hunk into a loaf. Roll into a ball shape and knead fairly gently for 5 minutes, folding it over from near side to far and turning as you go.

Use both hands to form the dough into an oval or round shape, set on a piece of parchment paper and cover with a mixing bowl. Repeat with the second loaf.

Let rise for 1 hour, or until roughly doubled again.

Put a baking stone or pizza stone on the middle rack of the oven and preheat to 450 degrees for about 15 minutes. (If you don't have a stone, you can substitute a heavy baking sheet—just skip the preheating and grease the pan with olive oil.)

Dust the tops of your loaves with a bit of all-purpose flour and use a wet knife to lightly score the dough diagonally along the tops.

Place dough and parchment directly onto the pizza stone or cast-iron pan. Fill an oven-safe casserole dish with 1 cup of hot water and place carefully on bottom rack of the oven.

Bake the loaves until golden brown and crusty, about 25–30 minutes. Place on a cooling rack and let cool to room temperature or a bit warmer before slicing.

GREASY SAE'S CALL IT BEEF SOUP

SERVES 4

Greasy Sae told Katniss that once it was in the soup, she'd call it beef. We'll start with beef and call it dog. After all, you'd like to eat the soup. If you want something a bit wilder, you can try one of the recipes in Chapter 7.

Greasy Sae had to work primarily with ingredients brought to her by traders. The ingredients in this soup include the greens and other wild things people like Katniss and Gale brought in.

---

1 TABLESPOON BUTTER

1 LARGE WHITE ONION, THINLY SLICED

½ CUP ALL-PURPOSE FLOUR

1 TABLESPOON SALT

1 TEASPOON FRESHLY GROUND BLACK PEPPER

2 POUNDS STEW BEEF, CUBED

2 CLOVES CRUSHED GARLIC

2 TABLESPOONS CANOLA OR OLIVE OIL

4 CUPS BEEF STOCK

2 CUPS WARM WATER

1 BAY LEAF

2 CUPS WASHED AND TORN DANDELION GREENS OR WATERCRESS

1 CUP QUICK-COOKING BARLEY

Heat a large, heavy pot on medium heat. Add butter and heat until completely melted and no longer frothy.

Add thinly sliced onions. Let onions brown and caramelize for about 10 minutes, stirring occasionally while you prepare beef and other ingredients.

Put flour, salt and pepper in a plastic bag, shake well and add beef in batches, shaking to coat. Set coated beef aside.

Add garlic to onions, then remove onions to a plate and set aside.

Add oil to the same pot and brown beef until well seared on all sides.

Put onions, garlic and any residual butter back into the pot.

Add beef stock, warm water and bay leaf and bring just to a boil, then reduce heat to low and cover. Let simmer for 1½ hours. Taste for seasoning and add salt or pepper as needed.

Add greens and barley and simmer covered for another 20–30 minutes, until barley and greens are just tender.

Serve with some crusty bread dipped in olive oil.

PEETA'S BURNT RAISIN NUT BREAD

MAKES 2 LOAVES

Peeta's gift of bread to 11-year-old Katniss was the first contact the two of them have. Giving her the bread cost him something, which made an impression on young Katniss, who had all but given up on feeding her starving family. Bread is called "the staff of life," and in this case two loaves of burnt bread did help save the lives of Katniss, Prim and their mother.

This recipe calls for goat's milk, as that is what Prim later traded for bread from Mr. Mellark. Feel free to use cow's milk if you like, but try this recipe with goat's milk at least once!

SHORTENING
2 CUPS PACKED LIGHT BROWN SUGAR
1½ CUPS WHOLE WHEAT FLOUR
1½ CUPS ALL-PURPOSE FLOUR
3 TEASPOONS BAKING POWDER
1 TEASPOON BAKING SODA
1 TEASPOON GROUND CINNAMON
1 TEASPOON GROUND NUTMEG
1 TEASPOON SALT
1½ CUPS PECAN PIECES
1½ CUPS WALNUT PIECES
1½ CUPS GOLDEN RAISINS
1½ CUPS REGULAR RAISINS
4 EGGS
1½ CUPS GOAT'S MILK
6 TABLESPOONS MELTED BUTTER, DIVIDED
2 TEASPOONS VANILLA

Preheat oven to 350 degrees. Grease 2 (8 x 4-inch) loaf pans with shortening or butter and set aside.

In a large bowl, mix together sugar, flours, baking powder, baking soda, spices and salt and stir with a wooden spoon or whisk until well blended.

Add the nuts and raisins to the mixture.

In another bowl beat eggs and add goat's milk, melted butter and vanilla. Whisk ingredients together until well blended.

Combine wet ingredients with the dry ingredients mixture until the dough is moist and consistent.

Divide evenly into the 2 loaf pans.

Bake for 1 hour, or until a wooden toothpick inserted into the middle comes out clean. Let bread cool to slightly warm before removing from pan. Once removed, turn out the loaves onto a rack to finish cooling.

If you do want to serve them burnt, wrap all but a corner of each loaf very well in foil, then place under a broiler for just a few minutes until the exposed corners are burnt.

MR. MELLARK'S FAREWELL COOKIES
MAKES 2 DOZEN

When Mr. Mellark brought a paper packet of cookies to Katniss after the reaping, it touched her, but not nearly as much as his promise to watch out for Prim.

Here's a recipe for spicy cookies using ingredients the Mellarks appear to have had. These are tasty snacks and would hold up well on a train journey, too.

2 CUPS ALL-PURPOSE FLOUR
3 TEASPOONS CINNAMON
1 TEASPOON GROUND GINGER
1 TEASPOON BAKING POWDER
½ TEASPOON SALT
½ TEASPOON GROUND ALLSPICE
½ TEASPOON NUTMEG
1 STICK UNSALTED BUTTER AT ROOM
    TEMPERATURE
¾ CUP DARK BROWN SUGAR
1 EGG
1 TEASPOON VANILLA

In a large bowl, combine all of the dry ingredients, except the brown sugar, with a whisk or wooden spoon. Mix until well blended and set aside.

In a medium bowl, use a hand mixer to cream together the butter and brown sugar until it is light and fluffy. Add the egg and vanilla and mix until well combined.

Add the dry ingredients a cup at a time and mix just until blended and the dough is smooth.

Cover the dough with plastic wrap and refrigerate for at least 3 hours, or overnight.

Preheat your oven to 350 degrees.

Lightly dust a large, clean work surface with flour and roll the dough out to about ¼-inch thick.

Use a cookie cutter or a cup to cut the cookies, re-rolling the scraps as you go.

Place the cookies about 1 inch apart on a lightly greased baking sheet and bake for 10 minutes, or until golden.

Let cool on the pan before removing with a spatula.

NOTES

3

THE TRAIN

"The pair last year were two kids from the Seam who'd never, not one day in their lives, had enough to eat."

KATNISS, *THE HUNGER GAMES* BY SUZANNE COLLINS, CHAPTER 3

THE TRAIN TO THE CAPITOL was Peeta and Katniss' introduction to the way the more fortunate eat. To young people who had lived their whole lives without ever having enough food, the meals experienced on the train may as well have been from another planet altogether. Their minds could barely take it all in; in fact, even Peeta and Katniss' bodies had trouble accepting such plenty. These foods weren't as lavish as what awaited the tributes in the Capitol, but they certainly weren't the simple fare of home.

THICK AND CREAMY CARROT SOUP

SERVES 4

For her first dinner aboard the train, Katniss had this rich and creamy soup made of carrots, a vegetable that probably hadn't been seen very often back home. It was just one of many courses on the train, but in Katniss' world it would have been a filling meal by itself.

This soup is wonderful with crusty bread and a green salad. It tastes even better after sitting, so make it a day ahead to allow the flavors to intensify.

1 TABLESPOON OLIVE OIL

1½ CUPS SWEET ONIONS (SUCH AS VIDALIA), CHOPPED

2 POUNDS CARROTS, PEELED AND CUT INTO 1-INCH PIECES

1 TEASPOON SALT

1 TEASPOON BLACK PEPPER

½ TEASPOON GROUND GINGER

½ TEASPOON TARRAGON

3 CUPS FAT-FREE CHICKEN OR VEGETABLE BROTH

1 CUP WATER

2 TABLESPOONS HALF-AND-HALF

1 BUNCH PARSLEY (FOR GARNISH)

Heat olive oil in a large heavy pot over medium heat.

Add onion and carrots to pan and sauté for 15 minutes, stirring frequently until the onions are soft and translucent.

Stir in the salt, pepper, ground ginger and the tarragon, and cook for 1 more minute.

Turn the heat on high and add the broth and water to the pot. Bring to a boil and cover, then turn the heat to low and simmer 30 minutes, or just until carrots are tender.

Remove from the burner and allow to cool to room temperature. You can speed up the cooling process by placing the mixture into a large bowl or baking pan.

Once cooled, put carrot mixture in batches into a food processor or blender and blend until smooth. (You can skip this step and use a hand blender if you have one.)

Pour blended batches back into the original pot. Add the half-and-half and stir well, then warm over low heat, stirring frequently until serving temperature.

Garnish with parsley if desired and serve with Fresh Green Salad, Tribute Lamb Chops and Creamy Mashed Potatoes.

FRESH GREEN SALAD
SERVES 4

While Katniss and Gale often had greens for their meals, they were usually cooked and used to make a meal more nutritious and filling. A fresh green salad such as this would have probably been something new to them in the Capitol. Since the residents of the Capitol were known for their love of sweets, this may have been served with a sweet dressing such as poppy seed or balsamic vinaigrette.

1 CUP FRESH SPINACH LEAVES RINSED
1 CUP MESCLUN GREENS RINSED
1 CUP ROMAINE LETTUCE, WASHED AND
   CHOPPED
¼ CUP SWEET POPPY SEED OR BALSAMIC
   DRESSING

In a large salad bowl, toss all of the greens with clean hands until well mixed.

Pour a little of the dressing over the greens and use two wooden spoons to turn greens until lightly coated. Add more dressing as needed.

Serve immediately.

TRIBUTE LAMB CHOPS

SERVES 4

The highlight of Katniss and Peeta's first meal on the train was these tender lamb chops. A rich dish for anyone, it was incredibly decadent to these young people who rarely had meat on the table.

Lamb absorbs the flavors of herbs beautifully, so use fresh herbs to get the best results. Allowing the meat to rest for 10 minutes after cooking will ensure that it's moist and flavorful.

2 TABLESPOONS PLUS 1 TEASPOON OLIVE OIL
1 TEASPOON FRESH ROSEMARY
1 TEASPOON FRESH TARRAGON
1 TEASPOON FRESH THYME
1 TEASPOON FRESH PARSLEY
2 CLOVES PEELED GARLIC
4 LAMB CHOPS CUT 1-INCH THICK
SALT AND PEPPER

Place olive oil, rosemary, tarragon, thyme, parsley and garlic in food processor until a fine puree is achieved. Set aside.

Salt and pepper both sides of each lamb chop.

Take ¼ of the herb mixture and rub onto both sides of each lamb chop, then place the herbed chops onto a plate.

Once all of the chops are covered with the mixture, cover the plate with plastic wrap and allow them to marinate in the fridge for 1 hour. Remove plastic wrap and let it to come to room temperature.

Set oven to broil and allow to heat.

Heat a cast-iron or other heavy, large skillet over high heat.

Add 1 teaspoon olive oil and sear chops for 2–3 minutes per side until nicely browned.

Remove pan from heat and place in the oven. Broil for about 7 minutes or until medium rare.
(This recipe works great on the grill too!)

Let meat rest 10 minutes so the juices recede.

Serve with Creamy Mashed Potatoes.

CREAMY MASHED POTATOES

SERVES 4

Potatoes were often featured on Capitol tables, so it's not surprising that they were served during the first meal on the train. The Capitol folks loved their potatoes and served them several ways throughout the series.

These potatoes are perfect with the Tribute Lamb Chops and any other roasted or grilled meats.

Use Yukon Gold potatoes for the richest flavor.

2 QUARTS WATER

8 MEDIUM YUKON GOLD POTATOES, PEELED AND QUARTERED

½ STICK BUTTER

¼ CUP HALF-AND-HALF

1 TEASPOON SALT

½ TEASPOON WHITE PEPPER

2 TEASPOONS FRESH PARSLEY, CHOPPED

Place 2 quarts water into a large, heavy pot and bring to a boil.

Add potatoes, return to a boil and then reduce heat to medium-low and simmer for 15 minutes, or until potatoes are tender.

Drain potatoes into a colander and set aside.

In the same pot, combine butter, half-and-half, salt and pepper and place over very low heat just until butter is melted and liquid is warmed through.

Place drained potatoes back into heavy pot and use a potato masher to mash the potatoes until smooth and creamy.

Turn off heat, stir in chopped parsley and serve.

FINGER LICKING CHOCOLATE CAKE

SERVES 12

During the first meal on the train, Katniss was so offended by Effie's commentary on the table manners of past tributes that she ate the rest of her meal with her fingers. Katniss made her point and, just to be sure, wiped her fingers on the tablecloth when she was through with the meal. A rich chocolate cake, similar to this one, was served for dessert at that meal.

CAKE:
2¾ CUPS SEMISWEET CHOCOLATE CHIPS
1 CUP BUTTER
1 CUP SUGAR
1 CUP HALF-AND-HALF
1 TEASPOON CINNAMON
8 EGGS
2 TABLESPOONS VANILLA EXTRACT

GLAZE:
1 CUP SEMISWEET CHOCOLATE CHIPS
3 TABLESPOONS HALF-AND-HALF
2 TABLESPOONS BUTTER, SOFTENED
2 TABLESPOONS DARK CORN SYRUP
1 TEASPOON VANILLA
2 TEASPOONS COCOA POWDER

Preheat oven to 350 degrees.

Grease a 10-inch round springform pan generously and set aside.

CAKE:

In a double boiler, combine the semi-sweet chocolate chips, butter, sugar, half-and-half and cinnamon and cook over very low heat, stirring frequently.

Cook until all chips are melted and smooth. Remove from heat and pour into shallow bowl to cool.

In a large bowl, beat eggs on high for 2 minutes until fluffy but not stiff.

Fold into cooled chocolate mixture until well blended and stir in vanilla.

Pour into greased pan and place on a baking sheet. Bake for 45–50 minutes, or until a toothpick poked into the center comes out with a few moist crumbs. Do not over bake!

Let cake cool and don't be alarmed if it settles a bit.

Once cooled to room temperature, cover and chill for 1 hour. Use a knife to loosen cake around the edge of the pan and remove.

GLAZE:

To make the glaze, combine the chips, half-and-half, butter, corn syrup and vanilla in a double boiler and stir over low heat until the chocolate chips are melted.

Remove from the heat and stir until very smooth.

Pour some of the glaze over the top and sides of cake to cover very thinly and spread with a rubber spatula to smooth the surface a bit.

Chill for 15 minutes, and then use the spatula to apply another coat with the rest of the glaze. Chill overnight.

NEW DAY DAWNING CODDLED EGGS WITH GLAZED HAM STEAKS

SERVES 4

Upon awakening on the train, Peeta and Katniss were greeted by a lavish breakfast. For young people who often had nothing at all for breakfast, this meal must have seemed extremely luxurious.

For our recipe, we continue the theme of richness with creamy coddled eggs, while the Capitol sweet tooth is well represented with this simple glazed breakfast ham.

FOR THE CODDLED EGGS:
4 TABLESPOONS ROOM TEMPERATURE BUTTER, DIVIDED
1 CUP HALF-AND-HALF, DIVIDED
4 WHOLE EGGS
SALT AND FRESHLY GROUND PEPPER
1 TEASPOON FRESH PARSLEY, CHOPPED

FOR THE GLAZED HAM STEAKS:
4 (6-OUNCE) SLICES OF BREAKFAST HAM STEAK
4 TABLESPOONS LIGHT MOLASSES
1 TABLESPOON DARK BROWN SUGAR
½ TEASPOON DRY MUSTARD

FOR THE CODDLED EGGS:

Preheat oven to 375 degrees.

Rub ¼ of the softened butter into each of 4 small, oven-safe ramekins or custard dishes, being sure to coat the bottoms as well as the sides. Place the ramekins onto a 9 x 13-inch baking pan.

Pour ¼ cup of half-and-half into each ramekin and then add 1 egg to each without stirring. Sprinkle with salt and pepper to taste.

Place baking pan onto middle rack of the oven and pour in enough hot tap water to reach halfway up the ramekins.

Bake for 15–20 minutes, or until yolks are still runny but have a thin white coating. Remove from the oven and set aside. Leave the ramekins in the pan to keep them warm.

FOR THE GLAZED HAM STEAKS:

As the eggs are baking, place ham steaks into a large, heavy skillet and cook over medium heat, turning after 5 minutes.

While ham cooks, combine molasses, brown sugar and dry mustard in a microwave safe bowl, stir well and heat for 1 minute. When ham is done, place onto plates and drizzle with glaze.

Sprinkle fresh chopped parsley over coddled eggs and serve with the ham.

GOLDEN FRIED POTATOES

SERVES 4

Katniss enjoyed piles of delicious fried potatoes with her eggs and ham. She seemed to favor this "home-style" version of potatoes more than any other.

Use a cast-iron skillet for the best results, but if you don't have one, a heavy skillet will do. Some recipes use leftover baked potatoes, but using raw potatoes results in a wonderful flavor.

4 RAW YUKON GOLD POTATOES, WASHED
2 TABLESPOONS CANOLA OIL
½ CUP SWEET ONION (SUCH AS VIDALIA), CHOPPED
2 TABLESPOONS BUTTER
½ TEASPOON SALT
½ TEASPOON FRESHLY GROUND BLACK PEPPER

Slice potatoes into ½-inch slices. Do not remove the skin.

Heat canola oil in a skillet over high heat. Add potatoes and brown on all sides about 5 minutes.

Add onions and butter and continue to cook for an additional 3 minutes or until onions are soft.

Season potatoes and onions with salt and pepper then reduce heat to medium-low.

Place lid over top and continue cooking for an additional 10 minutes or until tender

IRRESISTIBLE HOT CHOCOLATE

SERVES 2

Katniss had never seen hot chocolate before breakfast on the train, but the hot chocolate she was served was so irresistible that she ignored the array of foods until she'd drunk the last drop. Later in the story, Katniss emulated Peeta, dipping her roll into the hot chocolate as she saw him do this first morning on the train.

For this recipe, buy the best chocolate you can afford. It doesn't take much, and the resulting drink is so irresistibly worthwhile.

1¼ CUPS WHOLE MILK
½ CUP HEAVY CREAM OR HALF-AND-HALF
½ OF ONE REAL CINNAMON STICK
½ TEASPOON HIGH-QUALITY VANILLA EXTRACT
¼ CUP LIGHT BROWN SUGAR
4 OUNCES (ABOUT 4 SQUARES) OF GOOD
   BITTERSWEET CHOCOLATE, FINELY GRATED

In a medium saucepan, combine the milk, cream, cinnamon stick and vanilla. Heat on medium to low heat until slightly frothy.

Add brown sugar and stir, cooking until dissolved.

Remove pan from heat and stir in chocolate a little at a time, stirring constantly until all is melted.

Let sit for 10 minutes off the heat, and then remove the cinnamon stick. Return to heat just until warmed through and serve.

PEETA'S SWEET BREAKFAST ROLLS

MAKES 2 DOZEN

The book doesn't tell us whether the rolls served for breakfast were sweet or not, but these slightly sweet yeast rolls are perfect for dipping into Irresistible Hot Chocolate.

Dip these in hot chocolate or slather them with butter and honey for a delicious breakfast meal. They'll keep for 2–3 days in a well-sealed container.

½ CUP WARM WATER, 110 DEGREES
2 PACKAGES ACTIVE DRY YEAST
1½ CUPS ROOM TEMPERATURE MILK
½ CUP SUGAR
2 TEASPOONS SALT
2 BEATEN EGGS
½ CUP BUTTER-FLAVORED SHORTENING
7–7½ CUPS FLOUR

Mix water and yeast in a large mixing bowl and stir with a wooden spoon until dissolved.

Add the milk, sugar, salt, eggs, shortening and about half of the flour.

Mix until smooth and then liberally flour a clean surface or large cutting board with some of the remaining flour.

Turn out the dough onto the floured surface and knead, adding additional flour as needed until dough stops sticking. Knead for about 5 minutes, or until it's smooth and elastic.

Place dough in a large bowl greased with butter-flavored shortening and turn to grease other side as well. Cover with a clean, damp cloth and let rise for about 1½–2 hours, until doubled.

Punch the dough down and then let rise again until almost doubled.

Preheat oven to 350 degrees and spray 2 (12-muffin) pans with cooking spray, or grease with shortening. As oven preheats, pinch off pieces of dough (about golf-ball size), roll into balls and place 1 in each muffin cup.

Bake for 10–12 minutes, or just until lightly golden.

Dip into your hot chocolate or spread with butter.

NOTES

NOTES

THE CAPITOL

"As long as you can find yourself, you'll never starve."

KATNISS, *THE HUNGER GAMES* BY SUZANNE COLLINS, CHAPTER 4

TO SAY THAT THE CAPITOL was an entirely new world to Katniss, Peeta and the other tributes would be a serious understatement. Although the different Districts had varying degrees of technology and sophistication, first-timers to the Capitol wouldn't have ever seen anything like it before. The city itself was spectacular, and the residents, at first, were like another species. The food was no different.

Katniss and the other tributes were overwhelmed by a smorgasbord of foods they may had only heard of and never seen. Most of them couldn't have dreamed of eating these things back home, and most of them would never eat them again, either. For a time, though, the tributes were treated to an array of rich, glamorous and often whimsical dishes.

ORANGE CHICKEN IN CREAM SAUCE

SERVES 6

This dish enchanted Katniss soon after she arrived in the Capitol, so much so that she mused on how to recreate it back home using wild turkey.

The recipe looks more complicated than it really is and the flavor makes the preparation worthwhile. Be sure to use fresh orange juice, as frozen would be too sweet.

FOR THE CHICKEN:
2 TABLESPOONS OLIVE OIL
4 POUNDS CUT-UP CHICKEN, BONE IN
2 CUPS CHICKEN STOCK OR WATER
2 TEASPOONS SALT
½ TEASPOON FRESHLY GROUND BLACK PEPPER
½ TEASPOON PAPRIKA
½ TEASPOON GRATED ORANGE ZEST
1 LARGE ORANGE, HALVED
1 MEDIUM ORANGE, PEELED
2 TABLESPOONS FRESH PARSLEY
3 CUPS COOKED RICE, KEPT WARM

FOR THE CREAM SAUCE:
4 TABLESPOONS BUTTER
4 TABLESPOONS ALL-PURPOSE FLOUR
2 CUPS CREAM
½ TEASPOON SALT
2 TABLESPOONS JUICE FROM A FRESH ORANGE
½ TEASPOON PAPRIKA

FOR THE CHICKEN:

In a large, heavy soup pot, heat the olive oil over medium-high heat.

In batches, brown each piece of chicken skin side down, just until nicely golden.

Set each aside on a plate until all of the chicken has been browned.

Drain all but a tablespoon or so of the drippings, return the chicken to the pot and add chicken stock.

Sprinkle with salt, pepper and paprika and turn heat to low.

Grate orange zest and sprinkle over chicken, and then squeeze both halves of the large orange over the chicken, catching any pits in the palm of one hand. Reserve the last squeeze to save 2 tablespoons of juice for the sauce.

Cover chicken tightly and allow it to simmer on low for 45 minutes. Meanwhile, slice the other peeled orange thinly into rounds and set aside.

FOR THE CREAM SAUCE:

When chicken has been cooking for 35 minutes, melt butter in a medium skillet over medium-high heat.

Once it turns frothy, quickly whisk in the flour all at once and cook, stirring constantly, until it forms a golden paste, about 2 minutes.

Slowly stir in the cream, whisking constantly to make sure it is smooth, and then add the reserved orange juice, paprika and salt.

Reduce heat to medium and cook for 4–5 minutes, stirring frequently until smooth and slightly thickened.

To serve, place 1 piece of chicken onto a scoop of rice, add a few slices of orange, pour the sauce over and sprinkle with fresh parsley to garnish.

Serve with Flower-Shaped Rolls and Sweet Peas With Tiny Onions.

FLOWER-SHAPED ROLLS
MAKES 1 DOZEN

Both decorative and festive, the Flower-Shaped Rolls have an artistic Capitol touch. Fortunately, these rolls are simpler to make than they might appear.

---

1 RECIPE REAL BAKERY LOAF BREAD
2 EGGS, BEATEN WITH 1 TEASPOON WATER FOR EGG WASH

Grease 2 muffin pans (6 cups each) generously.

Follow the instructions for preparing the bread through the first rising.

Once the dough has doubled in bulk for the first time, gently punch it down and divide into 14 roughly even pieces.

Put 2 of the pieces in a bowl, set aside, and cover with a damp cloth.

Working with the other 12 pieces, very gently form into balls (golf ball size) and place each one in the greased muffin cups.

Set aside with a damp cloth to cover and let rise again until almost doubled.

Preheat oven to 350 degrees.

Take the two reserved pieces of dough and form them into 12 balls the size of a gumball. Discard remaining dough.

Using clean, sharp scissors, snip into each of the 12 rolls, first vertically and then horizontally. Gently pull each piece back and over so that it rests on the edges of the cup, like the petals of a flower.

Brush each roll generously with the egg wash, then dip each of the small balls you made into the egg wash, coating completely, before pressing them into the center of each roll.

Bake for 8–10 minutes, or just until golden.

SWEET PEAS WITH TINY ONIONS

SERVES 6

Katniss enjoyed these delicate peas and onions with her Orange Chicken in Cream Sauce. Peas aren't something that Katniss would have had access to back in District 12, which probably made them even more delicious.

Fresh peas are wonderful for this recipe if you have access to them, but thawed and well-drained frozen peas will work just fine.

**4 TABLESPOONS BUTTER
1 CUP OF PEARL ONIONS, PEELED
½ TEASPOON SALT
½ TEASPOON SUGAR
1 POUND OF TINY SPRING PEAS**

Melt the butter over medium heat until frothy, and then add the pearl onions.

Sauté, turning occasionally, until the onions are golden and the butter is slightly brown. Do not allow to burn.

Add the salt and sugar, and then stir well.

Add the peas and stir again to coat them with the butter sauce.

Heat through, stirring occasionally, for about 5 minutes.

GOLDEN HONEY CUSTARD

Desserts were almost unheard of in District 12, unless you had something to trade for a precious and expensive sweet. For Katniss, a pudding or custard such as the one she eats on the train would have seemed incredibly rich and introduced her to flavors she could have only dreamed about.

These individual custards are just the right blend of simple and fancy. This dish is easy to make, but tastes like something far more involved than it really is.

¾ **CUP OF WHOLE MILK**
¼ **CUP OF HEAVY WHIPPING CREAM**
½ **CUP OF HONEY**
1 **TEASPOON OF PURE VANILLA EXTRACT**
½ **TEASPOON OF NUTMEG**
2 **WHOLE EGGS**
NON-STICK COOKING SPRAY

Preheat the oven to 350 degrees.

In a double boiler, heat the milk, cream, honey, vanilla and nutmeg, whisking frequently to keep it from sticking. Heat just until frothy and set aside, off the heat.

In a medium bowl, beat the eggs well. Ladle just a few tablespoons of the milk mixture into the eggs to temper them and keep them from scrambling, and then pour the eggs into the milk mixture. Whisk well.

Spray 6 ramekins or custard dishes (about 6-ounce capacity) lightly with cooking spray and set into a 9 x 13-inch pan. Use 2 pans if 1 isn't large enough.

Divide the custard evenly among the 6 ramekins.

Put pan onto the middle rack of the oven and then pour enough hot water into the pan to come almost to the top of the ramekins.

Bake for 30–40 minutes, or until a knife inserted into 1 of the custards comes out clean.

Let cool nearly to room temperature and serve.

GOOSE LIVER AND PUFFY BREAD

MAKES 16

Katniss snacked on filling "goose liver and puffy bread" before attending a lavish dinner. Even though the snack was very rich for her, it was still a tempting novelty.

This is a simple recipe that will let you experience similar flavors, though we use chicken livers here. In Chapter 7 you'll find a more complex recipe using goose liver.

1 TABLESPOON OLIVE OIL
1 SMALL WHITE ONION, DICED
1 CLOVE CRUSHED GARLIC
½ TEASPOON SALT
½ TEASPOON FRESHLY GROUND BLACK PEPPER
½ TEASPOON DRIED SAGE
½ TEASPOON DRIED THYME
1 POUND CHICKEN LIVERS, WELL DRAINED ON
     PAPER TOWELS
2 CANS REFRIGERATED CRESCENT ROLLS
     (16 ROLLS)

Preheat oven to 375 degrees and line a baking sheet with parchment paper.

In a large skillet, heat the olive oil over medium heat.

Add onion, garlic, salt, pepper, sage and thyme. Sauté just until onions are transparent and soft.

Add the chicken livers and use a spatula to roughly chop them as they cook. Sauté for about 15 minutes, until slightly firm and cooked through.

Line a colander with paper towels and pour livers in to drain off water, oil and cooking juices.

Blend mixture in a food processor or blender until fairly smooth and set aside to cool to room temperature.

Unroll each crescent and place 1–2 tablespoons of filling onto each one. Roll up gently, pinching ends shut once rolled.

Bake for 8–10 minutes, or until golden.

CREAMY MIXED MUSHROOM SOUP

SERVES 6

While Cinna, Portia, Haymitch and Effie talked strategy at dinner, Katniss was focused on tasting new foods. This recipe pays homage to Katniss and her forest foraging while maintaining the Capitol's theme of very rich foods.

---

6 OUNCES SLICED FRESH SHIITAKE MUSHROOMS (OR DRIED MUSHROOMS, SOAKED IN WARM WATER FOR 1 HOUR)

6 OUNCES FRESH BABY PORTOBELLO MUSHROOMS, CUT IN HALF

6 OUNCES FRESH WHITE BUTTON MUSHROOMS, SLICED

1 TABLESPOON OLIVE OIL

1 TEASPOON SALT

FRESHLY GROUND BLACK PEPPER TO TASTE

1 TABLESPOON OF FRESH THYME, CHOPPED

1 STICK (8 TABLESPOONS) BUTTER

1 CUP DICED WHITE ONION

¼ CUP GREEN ONIONS, CHOPPED

¼ CUP ALL-PURPOSE FLOUR

4 CUPS GOOD VEGETABLE, MUSHROOM OR BEEF STOCK

1 CUP DRY WHITE WINE

2 CUPS HALF-AND-HALF AT ROOM TEMPERATURE

¼ CUP FRESH PARSLEY, CHOPPED

Rinse all mushrooms in cold water to remove any dirt and grit. Dry mushrooms with paper towels, cut as directed and set aside.

In a large skillet, heat the olive oil over medium heat; add the mushrooms, salt, pepper and thyme and sauté for 10 minutes, stirring occasionally.

In a large, heavy pot, melt butter over medium-high heat.

Add the white and green onions and turn heat to low, allowing them to cook for 15 minutes.

Quickly stir in the flour, using a whisk to help the flour soak up the butter and juices.

Slowly add the stock and wine, stirring well to make sure there are no lumps.

Add the mushrooms and add salt and pepper to taste. Cover and let simmer on low heat for another 10 minutes.

Remove from heat, add in the half-and-half and stir until warmed through.

Pour into soup bowls, garnish with sprinkles of fresh parsley and serve.

Wild mushrooms are a true delicacy and many people gladly spend all day searching them out. However, foraging for mushrooms is not as simple as picking mushrooms that "look harmless." Many edible mushrooms have a similar-looking poisonous counterpart. Invest in a good wild mushroom guide or, better yet, take one of the many classes available through community colleges or a local foraging group.

BITTER GREENS WITH PEA-SIZED TOMATOES

SERVES 6

Greens were an ingredient that Katniss and Gale often brought home from their trips through the woods. It's easy to imagine that greens were sometimes the only thing they brought home.

There are many varieties of wild or cultivated greens that could have been used for this dish. We're using a combination of kale and chard for a slightly bitter yet delicious flavor.

1 SMALL BUNCH OF FRESH KALE
1 BUNCH OF FRESH SWISS CHARD
1 TABLESPOON OF OLIVE OIL
1 CLOVE CRUSHED GARLIC
2 TABLESPOONS COOKED BACON, CRUMBLED
1 TABLESPOON OF BUTTER
1 TABLESPOON OF WATER
½ PINT OF RED OR ORANGE GRAPE TOMATOES
    (CHERRY TOMATOES WORK WELL TOO!)
SALT AND PEPPER TO TASTE
½ TEASPOON APPLE CIDER VINEGAR

Remove the kale leaves from their stems and rinse the leaves well in a bowl of fresh water to allow any sand to settle.

Cut off the toughest parts of the stems from the Swiss chard, roughly chop the rest of the stems and leaves and rinse well in a colander.

Add the kale to the colander and let sit for 30 minutes to drain, or spin in a salad spinner.

In a heavy skillet, heat the olive oil on medium-high heat.

Add the garlic and sauté for 1 minute.

Add the bacon crumbles and butter, and once butter is melted add the greens and 1 tablespoon of water.

Cover and cook for 10 minutes, stirring occasionally.

Add the tomatoes, stir well and cover and cook for 5 more minutes.

Salt and pepper to taste.

Spoon onto plates or into soup bowls, drizzle with apple cider vinegar and serve.

NOODLES IN GREEN SAUCE

SERVES 6

In the book, Katniss didn't tell readers how this dish tasted. In fact, we aren't even sure if she tasted it herself. What we do know is that she thought it was yet another culinary oddity from the Capitol.

For this dish, we'll use a flavorful pesto sauce. For added fun, use spinach fettuccine noodles for the pasta. This is a great dish to serve with fish.

1 CUP FRESH ITALIAN BASIL
¾ CUP OF EXTRA VIRGIN OLIVE OIL
½ CUP OF TOASTED PINE NUTS (OPTIONAL)
2 CLOVES OF GARLIC
½ TEASPOON SALT
¼ CUP GRATED PECORINO CHEESE
¼ CUP GRATED FRESH PARMESAN CHEESE
    (INCREASE THIS TO ¾ CUP IF YOU CANNOT
    FIND THE PECORINO)
1 POUND OF SPINACH FETTUCCINE

In a food processor, add basil, olive oil, pine nuts, garlic and salt.

Pulse mixture until finely chopped.

Don't let the mixture get so smooth that it becomes a paste or liquid. Scrape the mixture into a bowl and stir in the grated cheeses.

Slowly add the oil a quarter cup at a time, stirring well after each addition of oil.

Bring a large pot of salted water to a boil, add the pasta and cook just until al dente.

Remove 2 tablespoons of the pasta water and add to the sauce.

Drain the pasta well, and then return it to the pot and place over medium-low heat. Add the sauce, stir in the pasta and cook until heated through.

FIERY SPIRITS BANANA RUM CAKE

SERVES 12

Katniss had trouble dealing with feelings that resulted from drinking a glass of wine. While she might like the drama of eating a cake on fire, she probably wouldn't care for the alcoholic effects of eating it.

Between the flambéed bananas and the rum in the cake batter, this is a very spirited cake. You may want to reserve it for adults only.

CAKE:

1 CUP WALNUTS, CHOPPED
1 (18½-OUNCE) BOX YELLOW CAKE MIX
1 (1¾-OUNCE [4-SERVING SIZE]) BOX OF
    INSTANT VANILLA PUDDING MIX
4 EGGS
½ CUP COLD MILK
½ CUP VEGETABLE OIL
½ CUP DARK RUM

FLAMBÉED BANANAS:

6 TABLESPOONS BUTTER
4 TABLESPOONS BROWN SUGAR
½ TEASPOON NUTMEG
8 FIRM BANANAS, CUT INTO QUARTERS
½ CUP DARK RUM, WARMED

CAKE:

Preheat oven to 325 degrees.

Grease and flour a 12-cup Bundt pan.

Sprinkle the nuts on the bottom of the pan.

Combine all of the cake ingredients and mix for 2 minutes on high with an electric mixer.

Pour into the Bundt pan and bake for 1 hour. Cool the cake in the pan and then invert onto a serving plate.

Prick the top all over with a fork.

FLAMBÉED BANANAS:

Melt butter in a large heavy skillet on medium-high heat until no longer frothy.

Add sugar and nutmeg.

Stir until sugar is mostly melted, then lay bananas into the pan in a single layer. Cook for 2 minutes, turn and cook until golden on the other side, about another 2 minutes.

Using tongs or a fork, arrange bananas in a ring around the top of the cake, with the curved edges facing the center.

Warm the rum in the microwave for 10 seconds just before serving.

Pour rum around the top of the cake and light using a wand type lighter. Please use caution when doing this, making sure that your sleeves are not in the way and that everyone stands back a bit. The flames only last a moment.

Slice the cake and serve.

BATTER CAKES WITH THICK ORANGE PRESERVES

makes 8 LARGE CAKES

Katniss didn't seem to care all that much for this dish, probably because of the cloying bittersweet flavor that orange preserves lend. Her tastes remained fairly simple, even in the Capitol.

Here's a version using apricot preserves and a bit of orange zest that Katniss probably would have liked better. It has just the right blend of sweet and tart.

PANCAKES:
1¼ CUPS ALL-PURPOSE FLOUR
1 TEASPOON SALT
1 TEASPOON BAKING SODA
1¼ CUPS BUTTERMILK
1 EGG
2 TABLESPOONS MELTED BUTTER

ORANGE PRESERVES:
¾ CUP APRICOT PRESERVES
1 TEASPOON MELTED BUTTER
½ TEASPOON GRATED ORANGE ZEST

PANCAKES:

Mix all of the dry ingredients in a large bowl.

Add the buttermilk, egg and melted butter.

Stir with a fork but do not over-mix. The batter should be a bit lumpy. Let sit for 5 minutes before using.

Very lightly grease or spray with vegetable spray a non-stick skillet or griddle and heat on medium heat. Add more grease as necessary.

Ladle batter onto skillet and turn once bubbles form around the edges.

Cook other side for 1 minute, then remove to a plate and cook the rest of the cakes.

ORANGE PRESERVES:

While the cakes are being made, combine all of the thick orange preserves ingredients in a small sauce pan and heat on low just until warmed through.

To serve, top the pancakes with a pad of butter and pour the warm preserves over the top.

GAMEMAKERS' SUCKLING PIG

SERVES 24

Katniss expressed her frustration and anger with the Gamemakers by shooting an arrow at the suckling pig they were about to enjoy. It's doubtful that they got the true point, but she did make an impression.

You can purchase a suckling pig from many butchers, but you'll likely need to call ahead. Try to find one that's between 15–20 pounds, as this recipe calls for roasting the pig in the oven. Traditionally, this would be prepared on a spit over an open fire; as this option may be difficult for most people to undertake, we'll stick with the oven-roasting method. Brining the pig makes this roast especially moist and tender.

**1 SUCKLING PIG OF 15-20 POUNDS, DRESSED
    AND CLEANED**
15 QUARTS WATER
6½ CUPS KOSHER SALT
4½ CUPS GRANULATED SUGAR
1 FIRM RED APPLE
½ CUP OLIVE OIL, FOR BASTING

Rinse the pig in cold water and set aside.

Put three 33-gallon heavy-duty trash bags inside of each other to make a triple-layer trash bag. To make the next step easier, you may want to put the trash bags into a clean 30-gallon trash can so that the bags will stand up as you fill them.

Place water, salt and sugar in the tripled-up garbage bags and stir to dissolve. Use a wooden spoon to lessen the chances of tearing.

Place the pig in the bags, remove all excess air and tie them tightly, 1 bag at a time, starting with the innermost bag.

Place onto a bus pan or other large container and refrigerate overnight, or for at least 12 hours.

Heat the oven to 275 degrees and put the rack on the lowest level.

Remove the pig from the brine, pat dry with paper towels or a clean towel and throw out the brine.

Lay the pig on its side and stuff the interior with 15–20 large balls of lightly crumpled aluminum foil until it's filled out. (This will help the pig keep its shape during cooking.)

Transfer the pig onto a baking sheet with a roasting rack. Place it stomach down, with the back legs tucked underneath and pointing forward and the front legs tucked underneath and toward its sides.

Prop up the head with a large, oven-safe bowl. Place a large, firm red apple in its mouth; cover the pig tightly with more aluminum foil and place in the oven.

Roast the pig, rotating once, until it reaches 130 degrees, about 2–3 hours. Remove the foil, brush with olive oil and turn the oven up to 400 degrees.

Baste with oil every 15 minutes and rotate once more, cooking for another 45–60 minutes, or until the internal temperature (at the center of the pig's thigh) reaches 160 degrees.

Remove the pig from the oven and let rest 20–30 minutes before carving.

SALTY TEARS FISH SOUP

SERVES 4

After making her point to the Gamemakers, Katniss worried that her temper had cost her sponsors, and that being without sponsorship would cost her life. That night at dinner, the saltiness of her fish soup reminded her of tears. This recipe is a version of a traditional Italian soup made with salt cod.

¼ CUP OLIVE OIL
1 LARGE RED ONION, SLICED
1 BULB FENNEL, CUT INTO QUARTERS
5 CLOVES GARLIC, CHOPPED
1 CUP ROMA TOMATOES, DICED
¼ CUP FENNEL GREENS, CHOPPED
4 TABLESPOONS TOMATO PASTE
½ CUP FRESH PARSLEY
¼ CUP FRESH BASIL
1 BAY LEAF
1 CUP DRY WHITE WINE
6 RED POTATOES, PEELED AND CUT INTO
    EIGHTHS
2 CUPS OF FISH STOCK OR VEGETABLE STOCK
1 POUND SALT COD FILLETS, SOAKED IN COLD
    WATER FOR 24 HOURS (CHANGE THE WATER
    SEVERAL TIMES DURING SOAKING)
2 TEASPOONS SALT
1 TEASPOON FRESHLY GROUND BLACK PEPPER

In a large, heavy stockpot, heat the olive oil over medium heat.

Add the onions, fennel bulb and garlic and cook for 4 minutes, just until the onion is translucent and soft.

Add the tomatoes, fennel greens, tomato paste, fresh parsley, fresh basil, and bay leaf and stir well.

Add the wine and stir again to mix evenly.

Add in the potatoes and fish stock and bring to a boil, then reduce heat to medium and simmer for 10 minutes.

Meanwhile, cut cod into chunks of about 2 inches. After the potatoes have been cooking for 10 minutes, add the fish to the pot, turn heat to low and cook another 30 minutes.

Taste for salt and pepper and ladle into bowls.

Garnish with fresh parsley if you like.

BELOVED LAMB STEW WITH DRIED PLUMS

Lamb stew may not sound like a breakfast dish, but Katniss loved it when it was served the morning before her televised interview. Later on in the trilogy, she was thrilled to find a canned version. Perhaps it was a traditional dish in Panem.

This stew is a wonderful dish for cooler weather. All you need is some good bread and you'll have true comfort food, Capitol style.

½ CUP ALL-PURPOSE FLOUR
2 TEASPOONS SALT
1 TEASPOON GROUND BLACK PEPPER
2 TABLESPOONS OLIVE OIL
5 POUNDS LAMB STEW MEAT, CUT INTO
    2-INCH PIECES
1 LARGE ONION, CHOPPED
4 CLOVES GARLIC, CHOPPED
½ CUP RED WINE
5 CUPS BEEF STOCK
4 TEASPOONS BROWN SUGAR
1 TEASPOON MILD CURRY POWDER
3 CUPS CARROTS, CHOPPED
3 CUPS DRIED PLUMS OR PRUNES
1 CUP THINLY SLICED CELERY
2 TABLESPOONS FRESH THYME
3 TEASPOONS FRESH ROSEMARY
1 TEASPOON FRESH PARSLEY
2 BAY LEAVES
6 CUPS COOKED WILD RICE

In a large re-sealable plastic bag, combine the flour, salt and pepper. Add the stew meat and shake well to lightly coat the meat.

In a large, heavy pot (ceramic coated would be best), heat the oil over medium-high heat and brown the lamb in batches until well-seared on all sides, removing the meat to a plate as it's done. Don't worry about the brown residue sticking to the bottom of the pot.

Remove any excess oil from pot, reserving about ¼ cup in the pot.

Add the onion and garlic, and sauté on high medium-high heat until the onion turns a golden brown. Be careful not to burn the garlic.

Deglaze the pot with the wine and scrape the bottoms and sides to loosen all of the browned bits for rich flavor.

Simmer and reduce slowly for 5 minutes.

Add the stock, lamb, brown sugar and curry powder.

Bring to a boil, reduce heat, cover the pot and simmer slowly for 90 minutes.

Add the vegetables, plums and herbs to the pot, taste for salt and pepper and simmer for another 30 minutes, or until the meat is fork tender.

Spoon over hot wild rice and garnish with fresh parsley.

HAYMITCH'S PORK CHOPS AND SMASHED POTATOES

SERVES 4

On the night that Katniss disclosed her impulsive attack on a suckling pig, Haymitch was feasting on a pig of his own.

These delicious and moist pork chops are flavored with the orange juice Katniss found so remarkable. Since Haymitch would typically spend a good part of his day smashed, he'd probably like his potatoes that way, too.

---

1 TABLESPOON OLIVE OIL
1 MEDIUM SWEET ONION, SLICED THINLY
1 CLOVE GARLIC, CHOPPED
4 (½-INCH THICK) BONE-IN PORK LOIN CHOPS
1½ TEASPOON SALT, DIVIDED
½ TEASPOON FRESHLY GROUND BLACK PEPPER
3 TABLESPOONS ORANGE JUICE CONCENTRATE
1 TEASPOON FRESH ROSEMARY
6 MEDIUM RED POTATOES, PEEL ON AND CUT
   INTO QUARTERS
¼ CUP MILK
4 TABLESPOONS BUTTER
½ TEASPOON FRESH ROSEMARY, CHOPPED
BLACK PEPPER TO TASTE

In a large, heavy skillet on medium-high heat, heat the olive oil and sauté the onion and garlic just until they are translucent.

Sprinkle chops with salt and pepper and brown on both sides.

Add orange juice concentrate and rosemary, reduce heat to low and cover. Simmer for 30 minutes.

Meanwhile, bring a large pot of lightly salted water to boil and add potatoes.

Boil for 15 minutes, or until potatoes are fork tender. Drain well in a colander.

Reduce heat to medium and add milk and butter. Cook until the butter is melted.

Return potatoes to the pot and, using a potato masher or a meat tenderizer, roughly smash the potatoes. They should be quite chunky and lumpy; do not over-mash.

Add salt and fresh rosemary, pour in milk mixture and stir until milk is well incorporated. Taste for seasoning.

Place pork chops on plates, spoon onion mixture over top and serve with a large spoonful of the smashed potatoes.

NOTES

THE ARENA

"That the Careers have been better fed growing up is actually to their disadvantage, because they don't know how to be hungry. Not the way Rue and I do."

KATNISS, *THE HUNGER GAMES* BY SUZANNE COLLINS, CHAPTER 16

THE FOODS THAT WERE AVAILABLE to the tributes in the Arena were a strange mix. The tributes had to hunt and forage for whatever they could find while sponsors gifted them with foods—both basic and frivolous. Added into the mix were foods supplied by the government—foods that the tributes fight to get and fight to keep.

This section is a motley collection of the plain and the fancy, the luxurious and the basic.

DISTRICT 4'S LOAVES AND FISHES

MAKES 1 LOAF

District 4 was known for its fishing, but we're left to wonder if the fish-shaped loaf they contributed to the Arena was only coincidentally reminiscent of the Biblical tale of provision.

You could shape this loaf by hand if you're a born sculptor. If not, you can find copper or aluminum pans in the shape of a fish in gourmet markets and cookware stores. They're designed for making terrines, but work just as well for this bread, and there's no artistic skill needed.

½ CUP MILK

1 TABLESPOON VEGETABLE SHORTENING

1½ TABLESPOONS SUGAR

1 TEASPOON SALT

½ TEASPOON EACH OF BLUE AND GREEN FOOD COLORING

¾ CUP WARM WATER, ABOUT 110 DEGREES.

1 PACKAGE ACTIVE DRY YEAST (2¼ TEASPOONS)

3 CUPS ALL-PURPOSE FLOUR, MORE AS NEEDED

1 EGG MIXED WITH 1 TABLESPOON WATER

For people who love to bake homemade bread, kneading is part of the fun. For others, kneading is hard work with an unclear purpose. The reason bread dough must be kneaded is to develop the gluten in the bread. Without this step, bread would be very heavy and lack the chewy texture we so enjoy. You'll know your dough is ready if you can pinch off a small piece and stretch it almost paper-thin before it finally breaks.

In a small saucepan over low heat, combine the milk, shortening, sugar, salt and food coloring, and stir until the shortening has melted.

Adjust the food coloring as needed to make a deep greenish-blue color. Set aside and allow to cool.

In a large bowl, dissolve the yeast in the warm water, whisking to mix well. Add milk mixture.

Add in the first 2 cups of flour 1 cup at a time, stirring with each addition. You may need to add flour a small amount at a time until the dough follows the spoon around your bowl.

Turn the dough out onto a lightly floured surface and knead, turning and folding the dough, adding small amounts of flour if needed, until the dough is soft and smooth and no longer sticks to your fingers.

Place the dough in a lightly greased bowl and turn over once to coat both sides.

Cover with a clean cloth and set in a warm place to rise for 30 minutes.

Preheat oven to 375 degrees and grease the fish pan or baking pan generously.

Turn risen dough onto a clean surface and knead for 5 minutes.

Mold into a roughly rectangular shape and mold into the form of a fish, or place into fish pan and gently work dough until it is flush with all parts of the pan.

Use a fork to mix egg and water and then brush the bread all over with the egg wash.

Bake on the middle rack of the oven for 30–40 minutes, depending on the thickness of the loaf.

When the top is golden and the bread sounds hollow when thumped, it's done. Let cool on a rack for 30 minutes, then gently turn out of pan.

ALL FOR RUE GROOSLING LEGS

SERVES 4

Rue was Katniss' friend and ally, and not only helped her stay human but also helped her stay alive. Still, she was amazed when Katniss gave her a whole groosling leg, all for herself.

Since we don't have groosling roaming around, in this recipe we use turkey drumsticks, which you can often find in the supermarket during the holidays.

2 TABLESPOONS OF MELTED BUTTER
4 LARGE, RAW TURKEY LEGS
1 TEASPOON SALT
½ TEASPOON FRESHLY GROUND PEPPER
½ TEASPOON DRIED SAGE

Preheat oven to 350 degrees.

Melt the butter in the microwave, and then set aside.

Place the turkey legs onto a baking pan and brush with the melted butter, then season each leg on all sides with the salt, pepper and sage, turning to get both sides.

Place in the hot oven and bake for 1 hour, turning frequently. Serve warm and eat off of the bone.

DISTRICT 11'S SEEDED CRESCENT LOAF

MAKES 1 LOAF

District 11's bread was a yeasty, light loaf that could be easily formed into the shape of a crescent moon. For Katniss and her friends, this bread wasn't a treat but a means of survival in the Arena.

If you can find black sesame seeds at your local gourmet or health food store, they make a more dramatic appearance on the top of the bread. Otherwise, generously coating the loaf with poppy seeds works just fine.

½ CUP MILK
1 TABLESPOON VEGETABLE SHORTENING
1½ TABLESPOONS SUGAR
1 TEASPOON SALT
¾ CUP WARM WATER, ABOUT 110 DEGREES.
1 PACKAGE ACTIVE DRY YEAST (2¼ TEASPOONS)
2 TABLESPOONS TOASTED POPPY SEEDS
3 CUPS ALL-PURPOSE FLOUR, MORE AS NEEDED
1 EGG MIXED WITH 1 TABLESPOON WATER
ADDITIONAL 2 TABLESPOONS OF POPPY SEEDS
    OR 1 TABLESPOON OF BLACK SESAME SEEDS

In a small saucepan over low heat, combine the milk, shortening, sugar and salt. Stir until the shortening has melted. Set aside and allow to cool to 110 degrees.

In a large bowl, dissolve the yeast in the warm water, whisking to mix well. Add milk mixture.

Combine 2 tablespoons of poppy seeds with the flour, stirring well. Add in the first 2 cups of flour 1 cup at a time, stirring with each addition. You may need to add flour a small amount at a time until the dough follows the spoon around your bowl.

Turn the dough out onto a lightly floured surface and knead, adding small amounts of flour if needed, until the dough is soft and smooth and no longer sticks to your fingers.

Place the dough in a lightly greased bowl and turn over once to coat both sides. Cover with a clean cloth and set in a warm place to rise for 30 minutes.

Preheat oven to 375 degrees and lightly grease a baking sheet.

Turn dough out and knead for 5 minutes. Then form a slightly oval mound and gently roll back and forth with your hands close to both ends of the dough to make them just slightly thinner than the center.

Lift the dough to the baking sheet and pull each end toward the center in a crescent moon shape.

Use a fork to mix the egg and water and generously brush egg wash over the surface of the bread.

Sprinkle with remaining seeds and bake on the middle rack for 35–45 minutes, until the bread is golden and sounds hollow when thumped.

ARENA BEEF STRIPS
YIELDS ABOUT 40 SERVINGS

The dried beef strips found in the Arena were probably less flavorful than the ones in this recipe. They would mostly likely have been seasoned simply, with salt and pepper, and dried to a hard jerky.

This recipe is adapted from a traditional Hawaiian dish called pipi kaula and has a slightly sweet, Asian flavor. It is oven-dried and the results are chewier and moister than beef jerky. These will keep well in an airtight re-sealable plastic bag in the fridge.

4 POUNDS FLANK STEAK
2 CUPS TERIYAKI SAUCE
¼ CUP SEA SALT
1 TABLESPOON BROWN SUGAR
1 TABLESPOON GRATED FRESH GINGER
2 SMALL CHILI PEPPERS, CRUSHED
2 CLOVES GARLIC, CRUSHED
¼ TEASPOON PEPPER

Trim some but not all of the fat from the steak and slice meat against the grain into long strips, about 2 inches wide.

Whisk together the remaining ingredients in a bowl until well mixed. In a rectangular, glass baking dish, pour a little marinade and arrange a single layer of meat; add more marinade and meat layers until all meat is covered.

Let marinate overnight.

Preheat oven to 165 degrees. Drain the steak strips and reserve marinade in a bowl.

Place the meat on cooling racks set on foil-lined baking sheets.

Oven-dry 6–7 hours, until meat resembles jerky, basting every hour with the marinade.

Cover and refrigerate for up to 1 week, or freeze in airtight re-sealable plastic bags for up to 6 months.

To serve, broil 3 minutes on each side, and then slice the meat on the diagonal, in slices about ¼-inch thick. Place each slice on a small piece of bread or whole wheat cracker.

ONE FINE SPIT-ROASTED RABBIT

SERVES 4

While nestled in a tree to sleep, Katniss overheard Peeta and the Careers as they killed one of the female tributes nearby. She was surprised and felt betrayed by Peeta and his apparent collusion with the Careers, but "one fine rabbit" caught in her snare was at least some consolation.

If you use a campfire and simple rod, you'll need to turn the spit manually every five minutes or so. You can also use the spit attachment on a barbecue grill.

5–7 POUND FRESH DRESSED RABBIT
1 TEASPOON DRIED SAGE
1 TEASPOON DRIED THYME
1 TEASPOON SALT
½ TEASPOON FRESHLY GROUND BLACK PEPPER
2 TABLESPOONS OLIVE OIL
ONE WHITE ONION, CUT IN HALF
4 TABLESPOONS MELTED BUTTER

Thoroughly rinse the rabbit inside and out and dry very well with paper towels or a clean dishcloth.

Combine sage, thyme, salt and pepper very well. Rub the rabbit all over with the olive oil, and then rub in herb mixture.

Place the rabbit into a small trash bag, close tightly and leave in fridge overnight to marinate.

Prepare your spit and build a fire about 30 minutes before you are ready to roast. Make sure you keep the fire at a nice even heat. If you are using charcoal, wait until the coals are glowing and covered in a light ash before cooking. If you are using a gas grill, turn the burners onto medium-low heat and let the grill heat for about 15 minutes.

Remove the rabbit from the re-sealable plastic bag, insert onion into rear cavity and slide onto spit through both rear cavity and mouth.

Tie front legs together in front of the rabbit and tie back legs together to the spit itself (use wet twine or thin wire).

Place spit so that it is about 8 inches above the flame, and rotate every 5 minutes.

Baste rabbit well with melted butter and roast for about 45 minutes, or until a meat thermometer inserted between the thigh and body registers 160 degrees.

Allow the rabbit to rest on a platter for 30 minutes before carving.

PEETA'S HEALING GROOSLING SOUP WITH SWEET ROOT VEGETABLES

SERVES 6

Based on the description Katniss gave of wild groosling, it may be something of a cross between a young goose (called a gosling) and a duck. Katniss fed this soup to Peeta in the cave in an effort to heal his body, but their time there together started healing their relationship as well.

Goose can be hard to find, so feel free to substitute duck if you need to. The flavor is similar, but not quite as rich.

4 TABLESPOONS BUTTER
1½ TABLESPOONS OLIVE OIL, DIVIDED
3 POUNDS VERY YOUNG GOOSE OR DUCK CUT
   INTO SERVING-SIZE PIECES
1 CUP ONION, CHOPPED
2 STALKS DICED CELERY
1 LARGE CARROT, PEELED AND DICED
1 MEDIUM LEEK, RINSED AND DICED
2 TABLESPOONS PARSLEY
1 TEASPOON SEA SALT
1 TEASPOON FRESHLY GROUND PEPPER
½ TEASPOON THYME
6 CUPS CHICKEN OR DUCK STOCK, DIVIDED
2 TEASPOONS TOMATO PASTE
1 BAY LEAF
3 SWEET POTATOES, PEELED AND CUT
   INTO 1-INCH CHUNKS
3 CARROTS, PEELED AND CUT INTO
   1-INCH CHUNKS
2 TURNIPS, PEELED AND CUT INTO
   1-INCH CHUNKS
½ TEASPOON COARSE SEA SALT
½ TEASPOON FRESH SAGE

Heat a large, heavy stockpot over medium-high heat and add the butter and ½ tablespoon olive oil.

Once butter is melted, add meat in batches and brown on both sides.

Place cooked meat on a paper towel to drain while you cook the rest.

Once all the meat is browned, add the onions, diced celery, carrot and leek. Then add the parsley, salt, pepper, and thyme and sauté for 10 minutes.

Add in ½ cup of the stock to deglaze the pan, scraping the browned bits loose to flavor the soup with a wooden spoon.

Put the meat back into the pot and pour in the rest of the stock and add the tomato paste and bay leaf, stirring well to mix in the tomato paste.

Cover and simmer on low for 2 hours and 15 minutes.

While soup is cooking, preheat oven to 400 degrees

Combine the sweet potatoes, chopped carrots and turnips on the pan. Pour the tablespoon of olive oil right over the vegetables.

Add sea salt and sage and toss with your hands to coat. Place in oven and roast for 20–30 minutes, until just tender. Set aside.

Once soup has finished cooking and duck is tender, add the root vegetables in, stir well to heat through and taste for salt and pepper.

Pour into bowls and garnish with fresh sage leaf.

ROASTED RABBIT LEGS WITH EGG SAUCE

Katniss was able to keep herself going in the Arena because of her extensive hunting and foraging skills. During the Hunger Games, she nourished herself with raw eggs and rabbit legs. Here, we combine the two by using soft-poached yolks as a rich sauce. It may sound strange, but it lends a creamy, rich balance to the salty, slightly gamey rabbit.

If possible, buy two fresh rabbits and have the butcher package the four legs separately. Put the rest of the meat in the freezer to use for Mrs. Everdeen's Rabbit Stew With Greens. If you can only get frozen cut-up rabbit, pull the legs out without thawing the meat and rewrap, then freeze the rest.

4 RABBIT LEGS, RINSED AND DRIED
1 TABLESPOON OLIVE OIL
1 TEASPOON SALT, DIVIDED
½ TEASPOON FRESHLY GROUND BLACK PEPPER
1 TABLESPOON BUTTER
1 TABLESPOON DRIED PARSLEY
2 CUPS WATER
4 LARGE WHOLE EGGS

Preheat oven to 375 degrees.

Lightly grease a baking sheet or baking pan.

Rub the rabbit legs with olive oil and season with salt and pepper.

Bake for 20 minutes, then baste with butter and sprinkle with parsley.

Continue baking for another 15 minutes, or until thigh registers at 160 degrees on a meat thermometer.

Set aside to rest for 10 minutes.

As the rabbit rests, bring salted water to a boil in a medium saucepan.

Drop in eggs 1 at a time. Don't worry about swirling the whites as you would with poached eggs.

Boil 1 minute, then remove from heat and take yolks out with a slotted spoon and place on a saucer or plate. Use your fingers to pull off any white strings.

Dump the yolks into a mug or measuring cup and pierce each one. Place a rabbit leg onto each plate and pour yolk over each.

DECEPTIVELY SWEET BERRY SYRUP SODA

MAKES 2 CUPS

When Katniss mixed up the sleep syrup Haymitch sent her with some wild berries, she fed it to Peeta with a spoon. It was a trick, but one meant to save his life.

You can use this simple syrup by adding a teaspoon to a glass of iced lemon-lime soda for a pretty and refreshing drink. It makes a nice beverage for Hunger Games parties, or just to revive you on a hot day. You can also serve a bit of this warm over vanilla ice cream.

1 CUP SUGAR
½ CUP WATER
1 CUP RED RASPBERRIES
2 CUPS LEMON-LIME SODA

In a medium saucepan, pour the sugar into the water and stir over low heat until all sugar is dissolved.

Put raspberries into a blender and blend until smooth. Add to the saucepan and cook over low heat until thick and smooth.

Cool the syrup in a closed container in the fridge.

To make the punch, pour lemon-lime soda over ice in an 8-ounce glass and top with 1 teaspoon syrup. Do not stir. Garnish with a fresh mint leaf, such as Katniss chewed in the Arena.

The syrup keeps well in the fridge for several weeks.

GOAT CHEESE TOASTS WITH FRESH APPLE

SERVES 4

Katniss and Peeta bonded in their cave over a simple meal of goat cheese on bread with slices of fresh apple. As is the case many times in the trilogy, this meal was a focal point for a pivotal change in the story.

A combination of Granny Smith and Pink Lady Apples will make this extra pretty, but you can substitute any firm, slightly tart apples that are available.

4 LARGE SLICES OF SOURDOUGH OR REAL BAKERY BREAD, CUT ½-INCH THICK
1 CUP OF GOAT CHEESE
1 SMALL GRANNY SMITH APPLE, SLICED THIN
1 SMALL PINK LADY APPLE, SLICED THIN

Preheat oven to 300 degrees. Place the sliced bread directly onto the rack and toast just until it starts to crisp, about 3 minutes.

Pull out rack, turn toast over and spread each slice with ¼ cup goat cheese.

Put back into the oven for 3–4 minutes, until cheese is melted and bubbly.

Top with alternating slices of Granny Smith and Pink Lady apples and serve.

MELLARK BAKERY'S GOAT CHEESE AND APPLE TARTS

SERVES 8

During the time Peeta and Katniss spent alone in their cave, Peeta told her about the goat cheese and apple tarts his father baked—tarts they couldn't afford to eat. It brought the two of them even closer, and Katniss realized that she and Peeta weren't really so different after all.

Frozen pastry shells make this elegant dessert a very simple dish to make. They should be eaten at room temperature for the best flavor.

8 PIE PASTRY TART SHELLS, THAWED
6 OUNCES GOAT CHEESE
6 OUNCES MASCARPONE CHEESE
¾ CUP SUGAR, DIVIDED
½ TEASPOON NUTMEG
2 PINK LADY APPLES, PEELED AND SLICED
    ½-INCH THICK
1 WHOLE EGG WHISKED WITH 1 TABLESPOON
    WATER

Preheat oven to 350 degrees. Prick each tart shell with a fork and place on a baking sheet.

Bake for 8 minutes in the center of the oven.

In a medium bowl, mix goat cheese, Mascarpone cheese and ½ cup sugar with an electric mixer until smooth.

In a separate bowl, mix the nutmeg and ¼ cup sugar, add the apples and toss to coat well.

Remove the tart shells from the oven and use a spoon to fill the shells with the cheese mixture, ¾ full. Smooth the surface with a rubber spatula.

Brush the edges of each tart shell with the egg wash, and then arrange apple slices on top to cover completely.

Return the pan to the oven and bake for 12–15 minutes, or until apples are golden brown.

Let cool to room temperature before garnishing with fresh mint and serving.

NOTES

RECIPES INSPIRED BY THE HUNGER GAMES

*"Happy Hunger Games! And may the odds
be ever in your favor!"*

EFFIE, *THE HUNGER GAMES* BY SUZANNE COLLINS, CHAPTER 1

THESE RECIPES FEATURE INGREDIENTS found throughout the first book of *The Hunger Games* and incorporate themes from the story. While these recipes don't exist in the book exactly as written here, they could be fun to include in a meal inspired by *The Hunger Games*.

MRS. EVERDEEN'S SUGAR BERRY JAM

MAKES 8 (8-OUNCE) JARS

When Katniss mixed up some sleep syrup for Peeta, she told him that she made it from "sugar berries" she found nearby, and that her mother used to make a jam from them.

For this recipe, we use a mixture of berries that might have been found growing wild in District 12, or in the Arena. They make a great gift for the Hunger Games *fans on your Christmas or birthday list.*

---

4 CUPS FRESH STRAWBERRIES, SLICED
2 CUPS FRESH RASPBERRIES
2 CUPS FRESH BLACKBERRIES
**1 (1.75-OUNCE) PACKAGE OF SWEETENED
   PECTIN POWDER (AVAILABLE IN THE
   CANNING GOODS SECTION)**
4 CUPS GRANULATED SUGAR, DIVIDED

Sterilize 8 (8-ounce) canning jars by running them through the dishwasher. Allow to air dry, or dry on the dishwasher's cycle. Heat a medium saucepan of water to a simmer and place lids inside. Turn off the heat and allow to sit.

In a medium, non-metallic bowl, crush all of the berries together with a wooden spoon. Don't puree them—you want to keep some fruit in larger pieces. Put in a large stockpot and set aside.

In a small bowl, whisk together the pectin powder and just ¼ cup of the sugar.

Place the stockpot of berries on medium-high heat and add the pectin and sugar mixture a little at a time, stirring constantly.

Use a whisk to keep the berries from burning on the bottom as you bring the mixture to a rolling boil.

Add the rest of the sugar, whisking constantly.

Cook and stir constantly for 1 minute, then immediately ladle the jam into your canning jars, leaving ¼ empty at the top to allow the lids to seal properly.

Wipe the rims of all jars carefully with a damp paper towel, put on the lids and then screw the rings on tightly.

In a clean stockpot, boil enough water to cover the jars completely. (You can also use a canner if you have one.)

Place the jars carefully into the pot using canning tongs and boil for 8–10 minutes. Do this process in batches if needed, being sure to replenish the water and bring back to a boil between batches.

Set the jars on a clean towel where they won't get too much light from nearby windows, and where they won't get bumped or knocked over, which could break the seal.

Leave them for about 10–12 hours, or until each of the lids has sunken in the center, which means they've sealed properly.

This jam will keep indefinitely while it's sealed, but needs to be refrigerated after opening.

PRIM'S BIRTHDAY VENISON STEAKS

SERVES 4

In the book, Katniss related that she bought her beloved Prim a goat for her birthday by selling some of the deer she and Gale had killed that day. The butcher let them keep a couple of venison steaks as well.

Here's one way that the family may have prepared venison steaks. It's flavorful and tender, and is a great way to try venison for the first time.

4 TABLESPOONS OLIVE OIL, DIVIDED
4 (½-POUND) VENISON STEAKS, CUT
    ½-INCH THICK
1 TEASPOON SALT
½ TEASPOON FRESHLY GROUND BLACK PEPPER
1 TEASPOON DRIED ROSEMARY

Heat a large cast-iron or very heavy skillet over high heat and add 2 tablespoons of the oil.

Season steaks with salt and pepper and let come to room temperature.

Fry for about 4 minutes. Turn and cook for another 2 minutes.

Baste the tops with the remaining olive oil and sprinkle with rosemary.

Cook for another 3–4 minutes, or until meat thermometer reads 155 degrees for medium doneness and 165 degrees for well-done meat.

TESSERAE CEREAL WITH MIXED BERRIES

SERVES 4

Grain was an integral ingredient throughout the three books. Grain is what the residents of District 12 received in the tesserae, and it was so important to their survival that many children risked going to the Hunger Games by requesting extra rations, which got them an extra entry in the lottery.

This grain cereal uses mixed hot cereal from the store, so it represents many types of grain. The berries represent those times when Katniss, Gale and Prim were able to find sweet berries growing wild. You can substitute cow's milk for milk from Prim's treasured goat.

2 CUPS WATER
½ TEASPOON SALT
1 CUP STEEL-CUT ROLLED OATS
1 CUP QUICK-COOKING BARLEY
1 TEASPOON FLAX SEED
2 TEASPOONS BROWN SUGAR
¼ CUP BLACKBERRIES OR RASPBERRIES
¼ CUP GOAT'S MILK
4 TEASPOONS BUTTER

Bring the water and salt to boil in a large saucepan.

Pour in the oats, barley and flax seed, stirring constantly.

Reduce heat and simmer on low for 10 minutes.

Stir in the brown sugar and berries and stir just until the sugar is melted and well incorporated.

Ladle into 4 bowls and top each with a pat of butter and a small bit of goat's milk.

GOLDEN CORNUCOPIA CAKE

The Cornucopia held coveted supplies, tools and food that the tributes needed during their time in the Arena. In American tradition, a cornucopia is also called the Horn of Plenty, but in The Hunger Games *it represented need more than plenty.*

This recipe is extremely easy as it uses a box cake mix and canned frosting. It's a great dessert for a Hunger Games *dinner or party. You can find the gold doilies in most baking supply stores or on superstore shelves during the holidays.*

⅓ CUP BUTTER

1 BOX MOIST YELLOW CAKE MIX

3 EGGS

3 CUPS BUGLE-SHAPED SNACK CHIPS

1 (8-INCH) GOLD FOIL PAPER DOILY

1 CAN GOLD SPRAY PAINT

HOT GLUE GUN AND GLUE STICK

1 CUP MRS. EVERDEEN'S SUGAR BERRY JAM OR
     OTHER BERRY JAM

1 CAN WHITE FROSTING AT ROOM TEMPERATURE

Preheat oven to 350 degrees and grease the bottoms of 2 (8-inch round) cake pans.

Melt the butter in the microwave for 30 seconds, or until fully melted. Put in a cool dish and allow it to cool to room temperature.

In a large bowl, combine cake mix, eggs and butter and mix with an electric mixer on high speed for 2 minutes.

Pour evenly into the 2 cake pans and bake as directed on the box.

Allow to cool in the pan for 30 minutes before turning out onto cooling racks.

Meanwhile, assemble the bugle-shaped snacks, spray paint, doily, hot glue gun and glue sticks on a table covered with newspapers.

Cover each snack with gold spray paint, using tweezers or pliers to hold them so that you can get the inside.

Set each cornucopia on the newspaper to thoroughly dry, about 30 minutes.

Using the hot glue gun, put a dot of glue on the underside of each snack and arrange the snacks around the edge of the doily, with the curved sides facing inward.

Next, take several snacks and glue them into the design of your choice in the center of the doily to create a centerpiece.

Allow the doily and cornucopia to dry for at least 15 minutes.

When cakes have cooled, turn out of pan. Place one cake on a platter or plate and spread a thick layer of jam on top.

Place the second cake upside down on top of the first, pressing down a bit to get it firmly placed.

Frost the cake as directed and allow to sit uncovered for a minimum of a couple of hours, until the frosting has crusted just a bit and is not as tacky.

Carefully lift the doily and center on top of the cake.

CAKE ON FIRE

SERVES 10

Katniss described a "cake on fire" being served during a Capitol celebration. It was probably a cake made with alcohol, then set aflame.

This version is decorated to look like it's on fire rather than actually being so, which makes it an excellent way to serve a "cake on fire" to kids and those that don't care for the flavor of alcohol.

This is also an excellent dessert to serve at a Hunger Games *theme party. Shortcuts make it easy to prepare, even with the kids.*

ONE BOX RED CAKE MIX
EGGS AND OIL AS DIRECTED ON PACKAGE
2 CANS BUTTER CREAM FROSTING
ORANGE FOOD COLORING
RED FOOD COLORING
YELLOW FOOD COLORING
2 ORANGE-FLAVORED FRUIT LEATHER ROLLS
2 CHERRY OR OTHER RED-FLAVORED FRUIT
    LEATHER ROLLS

Prepare the cake as directed on the package and bake in 2 (8-inch round) cake pans. Allow to cool on cooling racks.

Divide the first can of frosting into 3 small bowls.

Add enough food coloring into each bowl to make a red, orange or yellow frosting. The yellow requires quite a bit of food coloring. Stir gently to blend well without making too thin.

Open the plain can of frosting and stir until smooth. Place the first cake right side up on a plate and spread thinly with the white frosting, then place the second cake upside down on top.

Frost the rest of the cake fairly thinly with the butter cream frosting.

Using a frosting bag, make a circular pile of small "flames" reaching upward with the red frosting. Make a smaller one on top of it with the orange frosting and then another on top of that with the yellow frosting.

Lay the fruit leathers out flat on a cutting board and use a sharp knife to cut flame shapes.

Attach the fruit leather around the sides of the cake with dots of leftover icing, alternating between red and orange, with the tips of the flames pointing upward.

PRESIDENT SNOW'S SNOWY ROSE CUPCAKES

MAKES 1 DOZEN

Katniss will always remember President Snow as reeking of (likely genetically engineered) roses. These cupcakes represent him well.

They take a little bit of time to make, but these cupcakes are very showy and will be a big hit for both their flavor and their symbolism.

CUPCAKES:
1 CUP WHITE SUGAR
½ CUP BUTTER, ROOM TEMPERATURE
2 EGGS
2 TEASPOONS VANILLA EXTRACT
1½ CUPS ALL-PURPOSE FLOUR
1¾ TEASPOONS BAKING POWDER
½ CUP MILK

FROSTING:
4 CUPS CONFECTIONER'S SUGAR
1 CUP SHORTENING
2 TABLESPOONS WATER
1 TEASPOON GOOD VANILLA EXTRACT
2 CUPS MOIST COCONUT FLAKES
12 FRESH WHITE ROSES (NOT TREATED WITH ANY CHEMICALS OR PESTICIDES) STANDING IN ICE WATER

CUPCAKES:

Preheat oven to 350 degrees. Line one or two muffin pans with paper liners, enough for 12 cupcakes.

In a medium bowl, beat the sugar and butter with an electric mixer until fluffy and light.

Beat in the eggs, one at a time, and then stir in the vanilla.

Combine flour and baking powder, add to the creamed mixture and mix well on low speed.

Gently stir in the milk until the batter is smooth. Use an ice cream scoop or ladle to portion the batter into the muffin tins.

Bake for 20–25 minutes on the middle rack of the oven. Remove cupcakes from pan and allow them to cool on a rack.

FROSTING:

Mix together the sugar, shortening, water and vanilla and blend well with an electric mixer.

Add in all of the coconut and mix until well blended. It will be very coconut-y and lumpy.

Use a spatula to spread the frosting on each cupcake, mounding it up nice and big.

Just before serving, remove the roses from the water and snip the buds right at the very top of the stems. Place 1 rose firmly atop each cupcake.

VENISON STEW WITH SWEET ROOTS FOR RUE

SERVES 8

Venison, or deer meat, was a precious commodity in The Hunger Games. *So were true friends. This would have been a nice stew for Katniss and Rue to share—the hunter and the forager combining their skills to make a great meal.*

Venison has a rich flavor that takes seasoning very well and goes wonderfully with potatoes. Stewing makes it tender and moist.

3 TABLESPOONS CANOLA OIL
3 POUNDS VENISON STEW MEAT
3 ONIONS, CHOPPED
2 CLOVES GARLIC, CRUSHED
2½ CUPS WATER, DIVIDED
1 CUP BEEF STOCK
1 TABLESPOON SOY SAUCE
1 TABLESPOON SALT
½ TEASPOON DRIED SAGE
1 BAY LEAF
8 SMALL RED POTATOES, PEELED AND
    QUARTERED
8 CARROTS, PEELED AND CUT INTO 1-INCH
    PIECES
½ CUP ALL-PURPOSE FLOUR

In a large, heavy pot, heat the oil and brown the venison well on all sides.

Add the onions and garlic and cook for 1 minute.

Add 2 cups water, stock, soy sauce, salt, sage and bay leaf to the pot.

Bring to a boil and immediately reduce heat to low. Simmer, covered, for 1½ hours, or until meat is almost tender.

Add the potatoes and carrots and cook another 30 minutes, or until vegetables are tender.

Combine flour and ½ cup water and mix briskly with a whisk until smooth. Whisk slowly into the stew and cook until thickened, about 2 minutes.

Ladle into bowls and serve.

PEETA'S HOT CHOCOLATE PUDDING

SERVES 10

This is an extremely easy recipe and a fun take on Katniss' much-loved hot chocolate. It's another way to interpret the drink she and Peeta enjoyed so much on the train to the Capitol.

If you're cooking with Hunger Games-loving kids, this is a good recipe to let them try themselves.

1 CUP ALL-PURPOSE FLOUR

¾ CUP WHITE SUGAR

6 TABLESPOONS UNSWEETENED COCOA POWDER, DIVIDED

2 TEASPOONS BAKING POWDER

¼ TEASPOON SALT

½ CUP MILK

2 TABLESPOONS VEGETABLE OIL

1 TEASPOON VANILLA EXTRACT

1 CUP PACKED BROWN SUGAR

¾ CUPS HOT WATER

Preheat oven to 375 degrees.

In a medium bowl, combine the flour, white sugar, 2 tablespoons cocoa, baking powder and salt. Stir in the milk, oil and vanilla and blend well until smooth.

Pour into an ungreased 9-inch square baking pan.

In a small bowl, mix together the brown sugar and 4 tablespoons of cocoa. Sprinkle evenly over the batter.

Pour ¾ cup hot water over all. Do not stir!

Bake for 30 minutes. Cake is supposed to be very gooey and moist, so don't over bake.

Portion into deep bowls and serve warm.

CREAMY ROASTED KATNISS SOUP

SERVES 4

This soup is as rich in flavor and texture as anything served at the Capitol, but it's made with the humble katniss plant. Katniss fondly remembered her father teaching her to find and harvest these roots.

If you can't find katniss tubers, cassava or yucca will work just as well. Their flavor and texture is similar.

---

2 POUNDS KATNISS TUBERS OR YUCCA, PEELED AND CLEANED, CUT INTO 1-INCH PIECES
4 TABLESPOONS OLIVE OIL, DIVIDED
1 TEASPOON PAPRIKA
½ TEASPOON SALT
½ TEASPOON PEPPER
1 DICED WHITE ONION
2 CLOVES GARLIC, CRUSHED
½ TEASPOON MILD CURRY POWDER
2 CUPS VEGETABLE BROTH
1 CUP PLAIN YOGURT
½ CUP SOUR CREAM
½ CUP HEAVY CREAM
½ CUP SCALLIONS OR CHIVES, CHOPPED

Preheat oven to 375 degrees.

Place the katniss tubers onto a baking sheet; add 2 tablespoons of the olive oil and toss to coat.

Sprinkle with paprika, salt and pepper and roast for about 30 minutes, or until fork tender. Set aside.

Meanwhile, in a heavy saucepan, heat the remaining olive oil over medium-high heat.

Add the onions and cook until they are golden but not dark.

Add the garlic and curry powder and cook for 3 minutes more.

Combine the katniss and the onion mixture in a food processor or blender and blend until smooth. Return the mixture to the saucepan over medium heat.

Whisk in the broth, and then add the cold ingredients (yogurt, sour cream and cream).

Cook, stirring frequently, until heated through.

Taste for seasoning and add salt if needed.

Ladle into bowls and sprinkle with chopped scallions or chives to serve.

NOTES

NOTES

7

AUTHENTICITY FOR THE ADVENTUROUS

*"But I told Rue I'd be there. For both of us.
And somehow that seems even more important
than the vow I gave Prim."*

KATNISS, *THE HUNGER GAMES* BY SUZANNE COLLINS, CHAPTER 18

THE RECIPES IN THIS CHAPTER are for those of you who would like a bit more of the wild in your menu, or who are happy to go through a bit more trouble to replicate the foods and meals you've read about in *The Hunger Games*.

These recipes include foods found throughout the book, such as dishes from District 12, the Capitol and the Arena.

GREASY SAE'S SPECIAL WINTER SOUP

SERVES 6

While dining on the rich offerings of the Capitol, Katniss thought back almost fondly to this Seam specialty that uses a little of this and a little of that.

One of the ingredients is "pig entrails," which are commonly called chitterlings, a popular Appalachian ingredient. We'll forgo Greasy Sae's mice meat and use rabbit. Many spices are made of "tree bark," and we include some here.

2 POUNDS CLEANED CHITTERLINGS, THAWED
3 TEASPOONS SALT, DIVIDED
1½ TEASPOONS FRESHLY GROUND BLACK PEPPER, DIVIDED
½ TEASPOON RED PEPPER FLAKES
1 POUND RABBIT PIECES, THAWED
4 TABLESPOONS OLIVE OIL, DIVIDED
3 CARROTS, PEELED AND CUT INTO 1-INCH PIECES
2 STALKS CELERY, SLICED THINLY
1 ONION, ROUGHLY CHOPPED
1 TEASPOON CARDAMOM
½ TEASPOON CINNAMON
1 QUART BEEF STOCK OR BROTH

Wash and rinse the thawed chitterlings and cut into 2-inch pieces. Rinse again and place in a bowl of cold water to soak for 1 hour.

Rinse again, tossing out water.

Fill a pot with 2 quarts water, add chitterlings and bring to a boil.

Add 2 teaspoons salt, 1 teaspoon freshly ground pepper and ½ teaspoon pepper flakes.

Cook at a good simmer, covered, for 2 hours and drain.

After the chitterlings have been cooking for 1 hour, preheat the oven to 400 degrees.

Rub the thawed rabbit pieces with 2 tablespoons olive oil and season with 1 teaspoon salt and ½ teaspoon pepper.

Place on a baking sheet and roast for 20–25 minutes, until the juices run clear when poked with a fork. Set aside.

Meanwhile, in a second large pot, heat final 2 tablespoons olive oil over medium heat.

Add carrots, celery, onion, cardamom and cinnamon and stir.

Sauté about 15 minutes, until the carrots and celery are soft.

Add chitterlings and beef broth, bring to a boil and turn heat to low.

Simmer 25 minutes, then add rabbit and simmer on low for another 10 minutes.

Add salt and pepper to taste as needed.

MOM EVERDEEN'S BREAKFAST OF MUSH

SERVES 6

In the Capitol, Katniss remembered her mother's meal of breakfast mush made from ration grain. In the real Appalachia, breakfast mush was likely a type of fried mush, using up leftover cooked cereal. Mrs. Everdeen may have fried hers using tesserae oil, or a little leftover groosling fat if she had it.

You can use chicken or goose fat if you have it, or just use bacon drippings as we do here. It's a filling and delicious breakfast that is well suited to cool weather.

3 CUPS COW'S MILK OR GOAT'S MILK
¼ TEASPOON SALT
1¼ CUPS QUICK COOKING BARLEY
2 TABLESPOONS BACON DRIPPINGS
MOLASSES OR SYRUP IF DESIRED

In a medium saucepan, bring milk and salt to a boil.

Add barley and cook on medium heat, stirring frequently to prevent sticking, for about 5 minutes.

Pour into a large bowl and allow to congeal for 1 hour, or leave in fridge overnight.

Heat bacon drippings in a heavy skillet on medium-high heat, taking care not to let it burn.

Turn mush out onto a cutting board, roughly shape into a rectangle with your hands and slice ½-inch thick slices.

Fry each slice for 1–2 minutes on each side, until browned and crusty on the outside.

Serve with molasses or syrup if desired.

Mrs. Everdeen was the unofficial healer/doctor of District 12. We don't know if barley was the grain given out in rations, but if it was, she would have approved. Barley is not only high in fiber, but also rich in iron. That iron would likely have been very important to a community that existed largely without meat. Meats typically have a higher dose of iron than any plant-based sources, making barley a welcome addition to the District 12 diet.

MRS. EVERDEEN'S RABBIT STEW WITH WILD GREENS

SERVES 6

As Katniss taught herself to hunt and forage, she not only provided survival for her family, but also prepared herself to survive the Arena. The first time she brought home a rabbit, the family had been without meat for months. Her mother roused herself from her grief to skin the rabbit and cook it up with some greens.

Rabbit is a tender and moist meat when used in a stew. This dish is hearty and filling, and tastes even better the next day.

2 POUNDS CUT RABBIT, FRESH OR THAWED

1 TEASPOON SALT

4 TABLESPOONS BUTTER

1 TABLESPOON OLIVE OIL

2 CLOVES GARLIC, CRUSHED

2 LEEKS, CUT INTO 1-INCH PIECES (ALL BUT DARKEST GREEN TOPS)

1 TABLESPOON FRESH THYME, CHOPPED

1 TABLESPOON FRESH ROSEMARY, CHOPPED

6 CUPS CHICKEN STOCK

2 CUPS FRESH DANDELION GREENS

½ TEASPOON FRESHLY GROUND BLACK PEPPER

Salt the rabbit pieces and allow to sit for 15 minutes.

In a large, heavy pot, heat the butter and oil on medium-low heat and sweat the garlic, leeks, thyme and rosemary just until leeks are soft. Remove to a plate.

Turn heat up to medium high. Pat the rabbit pieces dry and place in the pot, adding more olive oil if needed. Working in batches, brown rabbit on all sides quite well. Do not crowd the pot because the rabbit won't brown properly.

Once all of the rabbit is browned, scrape the bits from the bottom and sides of the pot, leaving them in the pot to flavor your stew. You can use about ½ cup of stock to deglaze the pan.

Return rabbit to pot, add sautéed leek mixture and remaining stock, bring to a boil and then reduce heat to low and cover. Simmer for 1 hour.

Add dandelion greens to pot, taste for salt and pepper, cover and let simmer for 30 more minutes.

Ladle over rice if you like, or serve with crusty bread.

RICH GOOSE LIVER AND PUFFY BREAD

This is another variation of the goose liver and puffy bread that Katniss snacked on when she first got to the Capitol.

Foie gras, which is probably what the Capitol served, can be extremely expensive. Alternatively, you can use goose liver pate, which is much less expensive and is made from regular goose liver.

12 SHEETS OF PUFF PASTRY DOUGH, THAWED
3 TABLESPOONS MELTED BUTTER
½ CUP GOOSE LIVER PATE
2 EGGS, WELL BEATEN PLUS 1 TABLESPOON OF
   WATER

Preheat oven to 350 degrees and grease a large baking sheet.

On a clean surface, lay out 4 sheets of puff pastry dough, one on top of the other. Brush top sheet with melted butter.

Add another 4 sheets on top of this stack.

Use a spoon to make 6 small mounds of liver filling in 2 rows, 3 in each row, lengthwise along the pastry dough.

Brush the egg wash around these mounds, using about half of the egg wash.

Carefully lay 1 sheet of pastry over this stack and use your hands to gently mold the pastry over the mounds so that they're very visible.

Brush with more melted butter, covering the entire sheet.

Now lay the other 3 sheets on top, 1 at a time, being careful to keep the liver mounds rounded and visible.

Use a pizza wheel to cut the stack into 6 even squares.

There will be excess around each mound. One at a time, brush the outer edges of each square with more egg wash and use your hands to crimp the outer edges inward into a roughly round, almost pie-crust edging.

As each one is molded, place it on the baking sheet. Repeat for the remaining sections.

Baste with any remaining butter and bake for 15–17 minutes, or just until golden.

Serve warm.

PALE PURPLE MELON

SERVES 10—12

The pale purple melon Katniss spied on the lavish table in the Capitol was probably genetically engineered. It certainly doesn't exist in nature as we know it, but you can engineer it, too.

This recipe is very sweet, so it's best left for decorative purposes or the taste buds of very young kids. It does look remarkable, so it is great for a Hunger Games-themed party.

½ CUP SUGAR
1 PACKET UNSWEETENED GRAPE DRINK MIX
½ CUP HOT WATER
2 CUPS WATER
1 HONEYDEW MELON, SLICED INTO ½-INCH
  SLICES

In a large measuring cup, combine sugar and drink mix packet, and then add in hot water.

Stir well until sugar is melted.

Add cold water and pour into a 9 x 13-inch glass baking dish.

Place the melon slices in a single layer in the dish and let sit for 15 minutes.

Turn the slices over and let sit another 15 minutes.

Remove the slices and place into a re-sealable plastic bag.

Carefully pour the drink mixture into the bag and seal tightly.

Place back onto the baking dish and put in the fridge for at least 2 hours, shaking the bag up at least once.

To serve, remove the melon, drain on paper towels and then arrange on a platter.

BACKPACK TREASURE DRIED FRUITS

When Katniss is able to steal a backpack from one of the Careers, she finds a bounty of dried fruits to sustain her.

Drying fruits is easy, but takes some time. This recipe will keep well in a tightly closed jar or airtight re-sealable plastic bag for up to two weeks. Use very ripe fruits for the best flavor.

4 MEDIUM GRANNY SMITH APPLES, PEELED AND SLICED THINLY
4 BARTLETT PEARS, PEELED AND SLICE THINLY
6 WHOLE APRICOTS, UNPEELED, SLICED THINLY

Preheat oven to 150 degrees.

Line 3 baking sheets with parchment paper.

Spread the apples on the first, the pears on the second and the apricots on the third.

Place all of the pans in the oven and dry for about 10 hours.

The apples and pears should be pliable but quite dry. Remove from the oven and set aside to cool.

Allow the apricots to continue drying for about another 2 hours, or until quite dry but still pliable. Remove and allow them to cool.

Mix all of the fruits and store in an airtight container.

Makes about 2 cups.

DISTRICT 12 JERKY

SERVES 8

Venison was a rare treat in District 12, and Katniss was able to sell deer meat at a good price. Since meat was scarce and conditions were somewhat primitive, what couldn't be eaten fresh was preserved.

Drying or jerking was a popular way to preserve and serve venison in the real Appalachia, and it results in a deliciously different snack.

1 POUND BONELESS VENISON ROAST, TRIMMED OF ALL VISIBLE FAT AND CONNECTIVE TISSUE

4 TABLESPOONS SOY SAUCE

2 TABLESPOONS HONEY

2 TABLESPOONS LIQUID SMOKE FLAVORING

1 TABLESPOON KETCHUP

½ TEASPOON PEPPER

¼ TEASPOON GARLIC POWDER

¼ TEASPOON ONION SALT POWDER

½ TEASPOON SALT

Slice the venison into long strips about 1 inch wide and ⅛ inch thick.

In a large re-sealable plastic bag, combine soy sauce, honey, liquid smoke, ketchup and all of the spices and seasonings. Shake well to blend.

Place meat into the bag and close securely. Place on a plate or glass-baking dish and refrigerate overnight.

Turn the bag occasionally to evenly distribute the liquid.

Preheat oven to 150 degrees. Place a baking sheet on the bottom rack of the oven to catch drips.

Place meat strips on cake cooling racks so that they do not touch each other, and dehydrate for 6-7 hours, or until desired consistency is reached.

To store, seal in clean plastic bag.

Venison, or deer meat, is much leaner than most beef or pork, but it's wonderful in the form of steaks. The key to keeping it juicy and flavorful is to sear it well on both sides, which seals in the juices. You'll also want to be sure to let the steaks rest for about ten minutes before cutting. This allows the juices to return to the meat rather than pool on the plate.

CAMPFIRE BONY FISH ON A STICK

SERVES 4

On her own in the Arena, Katniss related that she warded off starvation in part by eating little bony fish she found in the creek. Since she knew better than to start a fire, we can assume she ate them raw. If she'd been back home, however, she and Gale may have cooked them over a fire.

We're using smelt, which is indeed a tiny (about the size of a sardine) and bony fish, but absolutely delicious. It's widely available in the freezer section of most supermarkets if you can't catch them yourself.

1 POUND SMELT, DRESSED, RINSED AND
   THOROUGHLY DRIED ON PAPER TOWELS
4 TABLESPOONS OLIVE OIL
2 TEASPOONS SALT
4 LONG BAMBOO SKEWERS, SOAKED IN WATER
   FOR 30 MINUTES

Build your fire and get it down to red coals with a thin layer of ash.

Lay the fish out on a baking sheet and pour oil over. Use your hands to coat all fish well, then sprinkle with salt and toss well again.

Thread fish onto skewers by pushing them on skewers vertically through the thickest part of the body. You should be able to fit 10–15 per skewer.

Hold skewers of fish about 3–4 inches over the coals and cook for just 2–3 minutes, turning once.

The fish are extremely delicate and will likely fall apart if you try to remove them from the skewers, so just eat them right off the stick.

GOAT TRADER'S STEW

SERVES 4

For Prim's birthday, Katniss traded the meat of a deer to purchase an ailing goat. Another potential buyer of the goat doubted she'd get much for its meat and Katniss was allowed to take it. This goat was the source of a lot of joy for Prim, and a lot of goat cheese for everyone else.

Goat can be a tough meat, so it does very well when slow-cooked in a stew. Be sure to brown the meat well on all sides to seal in the natural juices.

2 TABLESPOONS OLIVE OIL
4½ POUNDS GOAT STEW MEAT
1 TEASPOON SALT
½ TEASPOON FRESHLY GROUND BLACK PEPPER
1 LARGE WHITE ONION, SLICED
3 CLOVES OF GARLIC, CRUSHED
2 TEASPOONS CORIANDER
½ TEASPOON CARDAMOM
1 BAY LEAF
2 CARROTS, PEELED AND CUT ON A DIAGONAL
    INTO 1-INCH PIECES
1 CUP DRY WHITE WINE
2 CUPS BEEF STOCK
¼ CUP FRESH PARSLEY, CHOPPED

Preheat oven to 350 degrees.

In a large, heavy Dutch oven, heat oil on medium-high heat.

Season the meat with salt and pepper and brown well on all sides, removing batches of meat as they're done.

Remove all but about 2 tablespoons of the oil (leave the browned bits in the pot) and add the onions, garlic, coriander, cardamom and bay leaf.

Sauté just until onions are translucent and soft.

Pour in the wine and deglaze the pot, scraping loose all of the brown bits with a wooden spoon.

Add carrots to pot and stir well, then return the meat to the pot and add the beef stock.

Cover tightly and place in oven. Cook for 1½ hours.

Remove lid, skim any excess fat at the surface and replace the lid so that it's loose and will allow moisture to escape.

Cook for another 1–1½ hours, or until meat is tender.

To serve, use a spoon or ladle to place carrots and onions in deep bowls.

Place a few pieces of meat on top and then ladle juices over all. Garnish with parsley.

NOTES

SECTION TWO
CATCHING FIRE

8 RETURN TO DISTRICT 12 AND TOURING PANEM

9 THE TRAIN TO QUARTER QUELL

10 THE QUARTER QUELL FESTIVITIES AND TRAINING

11 THE 75TH GAMES

12 RECIPES INSPIRED BY CATCHING FIRE

13 AUTHENTICITY FOR THE ADVENTUROUS

IN *Catching Fire*—the second book of the *Hunger Games* trilogy—the story continues with Katniss and Peeta returning home as the victors of their Hunger Games. This part of the trilogy follows Katniss as she tries to return to a normal life and is instead thrown back into the Arena.

In Chapter 8 (Return to District 12 and Touring Panem), dishes like Hazelle's Hearty Beaver Stew represent the comfort of being home once again. Chapter 9 (The Train to Quarter Quell) includes the Soothing Honey and Spiced Milk that was meant to both calm and comfort Katniss. And in Chapter 10 (The Quarter Quell Festivities and Training), Snow's Suckling Pig is an over-the-top dish typical of President Snow's parties.

Chapter 11 (The 75th Hunger Games) returns readers to the Arena and features such dishes as Burnt "Tree Rat" and Fence-Roasted Tree Nuts. In Chapter 12 (Recipes Inspired by *Catching Fire)* you will find recipes inspired by many of the themes, characters and events of the second book of the *Hunger Games* trilogy. These include Rue's Cold Carrot and Yam Puree and Tiny Plum Tarts. Chapter 13 (Authenticity for the Adventurous) boasts dishes such as Charred Tree Rat and Hazelle's Authentic Beaver Stew.

Catching Fire and food share the same universal theme: survival. From the inspired to the authentic, the recipes of Section Two will transport you back into the world of *Catching Fire* and the 75th Hunger Games.

RETURN TO DISTRICT 12 AND TOURING PANEM

"You've got to go through it to get to the end of it."

GREASY SAE, *CATCHING FIRE* BY SUZANNE COLLINS, CHAPTER 1

WHEN PEETA AND KATNISS RETURN to District 12 as victors, they expected a better life. In some ways, they got it, but only for a very short time. Soon they had to leave again for yet another Hunger Games and District 12 wouldn't be there when they returned.

HAZELLE'S HEARTY BEAVER STEW

SERVES 4

Gale's mom whipped up a hearty beaver stew from a rare beaver that Katniss was able to trap. Gale would have appreciated this stew after a day in the mines. Beaver had once been a fairly common dish in rural Appalachia (where District 12 is located).

Not everyone traps beaver, so we've substituted it for beef in this recipe. For the authentic version, see the recipe in Chapter 13.

---

2 TABLESPOONS VEGETABLE OIL
2 POUNDS LEAN BEEF, CUT INTO 1-INCH CUBES
1 PINCH SALT
1 PINCH GROUND BLACK PEPPER
2 TABLESPOONS ALL-PURPOSE FLOUR
1 ONION, DICED
1 (8-OUNCE) CAN TOMATO SAUCE
1 BAY LEAF
3 LARGE POTATOES, CUT INTO LARGE CHUNKS
4 CARROTS, CUT INTO LARGE 1-INCH SEGMENTS
3 STALKS CELERY, THICKLY SLICED
½ CUP BEEF BROTH
1 BUNCH PARSLEY, CHOPPED (FOR GARNISH)

Heat oil in a pot over medium heat. Place the meat in a bowl, season with salt and pepper, sprinkle with flour and toss to coat.

Add meat to pot and brown meat on all sides.

Fill the pot with enough water to cover the meat and mix in onion, tomato sauce and bay leaf.

Bring to a boil, reduce heat to low, then cover and simmer for an hour, or until the meat is tender.

Stir in the potatoes, carrots and celery.

Add the beef broth for extra flavor.

Continue cooking over low heat for 45 minutes, until vegetables are fork tender.

Remove bay leaf before serving.

Garnish with a little parsley in the center of each bowl.

FINGER THAWING HERB TEA

SERVES 4

Katniss got a lot of comfort from being in Gale's home and being around Hazelle, Gale's mother. It was fitting that Hazelle gave Katniss this tea to warm her hands and insides after coming in from the cold.

This tea is also excellent for helping you through a cold or flu. Dissolve one tablet of vitamin C in the tea while it's hot. It'll add a lemon flavor to the tea and help you to feel better, too.

3 GREEN TEA BAGS
½ CUP SUGAR
1-INCH PIECE GINGER, SLICED, PLUS MORE FOR GARNISH
1 TEASPOON ORANGE ZEST

Put the green tea bags into a teapot and pour in 1 quart boiling water.

Let steep until it comes to room temperature. Remove the tea bags and discard.

Meanwhile, boil 1 cup water, the sugar, the ginger and the orange zest in a saucepan.

Stir to dissolve the sugar, then combine the mixture with the tea.

Garnish with a thin slice of ginger in each cup and serve immediately while warm.

GREASY SAE'S GOURD AND BEAN SOUP

SERVES 4

Just before leaving for her tour of the Districts, Katniss ordered a bowl of this soup from Greasy Sae's busy stall. It was one of the few dishes of Greasy Sae's that didn't have game in it. Perhaps it was a slow day for area trappers and hunters.

If you'd like you can substitute Great Northern beans or even black beans into this recipe. You might also enjoy using a combination of beans to change up the appearance and texture.

---

1 TABLESPOON OLIVE OIL
1 LARGE WHITE ONION, DICED
2 TABLESPOONS CHILI POWDER
1 TABLESPOON GROUND CINNAMON
4 CLOVES CRUSHED GARLIC
1 TEASPOON GROUND CUMIN
3 (28-OUNCE) CANS STEWED TOMATOES
1 MEDIUM ACORN SQUASH, PEELED AND DICED
1 (10-OUNCE) CAN PINTO BEANS
1 CUP WATER OR STOCK OF YOUR CHOICE
SALT AND PEPPER TO TASTE

In a large pot or Dutch oven, heat olive oil on medium-high heat and sauté the onions until soft and translucent.

Add the chili powder and cinnamon and continue to sauté for 2 minutes, stirring frequently.

Mix in the garlic and cumin and sauté for 2 minutes more before adding the tomatoes.

Stir until the tomatoes have broken down and have a smooth texture.

Stir the squash, pinto beans and water and mix well.

Season with salt and pepper to taste.

Let the stew simmer until squash is tender.

Stir occasionally and add more water if necessary. The finished stew should have a thick consistency.

HAYMITCH-STYLE BOILED CABBAGE AND BURNT MEAT

SERVES 4

Haymitch cared more about drink than he did food. Granted, he had a lot of reasons to drown his thoughts, and he was used to an abundance of food. Katniss was assaulted by the smells of cabbage and burnt meat when she visited his unkempt home. Perhaps he'd recently eaten this dish.

You can use either red or green cabbage for this recipe. It's a great use of leftover ham from another meal.

2 TABLESPOONS BUTTER
1 ONION, CHOPPED
1 SMALL HEAD CABBAGE, COARSELY CHOPPED
¼ CUP WATER
3 LARGE POTATOES, SCRUBBED AND SLICED
1 DASH SALT
2 CUPS CUBED, COOKED HAM

In a large skillet over medium-high heat, sauté onions in the butter until soft and translucent.

Add cabbage and stir. Add the water, cover and simmer on medium-low for 10 minutes, then add potatoes and salt, cover and allow to simmer for 10 minutes.

Allow to simmer, covered, for an additional 5–10 minutes, until cabbage is soft and potatoes are almost completely cooked and fork tender.

Add the ham to the cabbage and continue cooking until potatoes are done, about 10 minutes. Add more water if necessary and season to taste with salt.

LAVENDER COOKIES FIT FOR A PRESIDENT

YIELDS 24 COOKIES

When President Snow paid the Everdeen home a visit, Mrs. Everdeen brought him a plate of cookies delicately decorated with flowers. Such a pretty display for such an ominous and tense teatime!

These cookies are a little trouble to make, but they're unusually pretty. They'd make a beautiful display for a Hunger Games *party or a holiday platter.*

1 CUP BUTTER
1 CUP VEGETABLE OIL
1 CUP WHITE SUGAR
1 CUP CONFECTIONER'S SUGAR
2 EGGS
1 TEASPOON VANILLA EXTRACT
1 TABLESPOON FRESH LAVENDER FLOWERS
4 CUPS ALL-PURPOSE FLOUR
1 TEASPOON BAKING SODA
1 TEASPOON CREAM OF TARTAR
1 TEASPOON SALT
½ CUP WHITE CAKE FROSTING WITH 3-4 DROPS GREEN FOOD COLORING, MIXED WELL
24 INDIVIDUAL LAVENDER FLOWERS FOR DECORATION

Flowers are a beautiful way to decorate cakes, cookies, cupcakes and other treats, and using them isn't as difficult as you might think. There are many edible flowers that are easily accessible and very affordable. If you'd like to dress them up a bit, dip them into beaten egg white, and then gently roll in sugar. Shake off the excess and allow them to dry on a cookie sheet while you prepare the rest of your recipe.

In a large bowl, whip together the butter, oil, white sugar and confectioner's sugar until smooth.

Beat in the eggs 1 at a time, and then stir in the vanilla and the tablespoon of lavender. (It is best to chop the lavender finely before adding it to the mixture.)

Combine the flour, baking soda, cream of tartar and salt; stir into the sugar mixture until just blended.

Cover and chill dough for 3-4 hours.

Preheat oven to 350 degrees.

Grease cookie sheets. Use an ice cream scoop to scoop out balls of dough.

Roll the chilled dough into Ping-Pong-sized balls and roll them in sugar if desired.

Place the balls onto the cookie sheets, 2 inches apart. Press into each ball with the open end of a clean plastic thread spool. (Dip the spool into the sugar between each cookie to prevent sticking problems.)

Bake for 8-10 minutes in the preheated oven.

Do not over bake or your cookies will not be chewy and moist.

Allow cookies to cool for at least 30 minutes before removing them from the oven.

Load a frosting bag with the green frosting and place a dollop in the center of each cookie.

Place 1 lavender flower in the center of each dollop.

PAPRIKA DUCK AND ROSEMARY TUBERS WITH GRAVY

SERVES 8

Katniss tubers and groosling featured heavily in the Hunger Games trilogy. Both were a huge part of the survival of the characters that had the hunting and foraging skills to acquire them.

Since we've included other groosling and katniss dishes, we'll use duck and yucca here. The duck adds an interesting flavor and texture that goes very well with the starchiness of the yucca.

DUCK:
2 TEASPOONS SALT
2 TEASPOONS PAPRIKA
1 TEASPOON BLACK PEPPER
1 (5-POUND) WHOLE DUCK
1 LARGE ONION, QUARTERED
2 LARGE SPRIGS OF FRESH ROSEMARY
½ CUP MELTED BUTTER, DIVIDED

YUCCA:
1¼ POUNDS FRESH YUCCA
1 TEASPOON SALT, DIVIDED
4 TABLESPOONS SALTED BUTTER, MELTED
6–8 GARLIC CLOVES, MINCED
1 LARGE SPRIG OF FRESH ROSEMARY LEAVES
½ TEASPOON FRESHLY GROUND BLACK PEPPER
1 CUP CREAM
1 BUNCH ITALIAN PARSLEY, LEAVES CHOPPED

GRAVY:
4 TABLESPOONS FLOUR
1 CUP CHICKEN OR DUCK STOCK

DUCK:

Preheat oven to 375 degrees.

Make a dry rub of salt, paprika and pepper and generously rub into the skin and cavity.

Put the duck into a roasting pan and stuff with onion and 2 sprigs of rosemary.

Roast for 1 hour. Then baste duck with about ¼ cup of melted butter until skin is nicely coated.

Cook for another 45 minutes.

Baste again and allow 15 more minutes in the oven. Duck should be a nice golden brown.

YUCCA:

Peel and wash the yucca. Put in a small pan and fill with water, just until yucca is covered.

Add ½ teaspoon of salt to water. Bring to a boil, then reduce and simmer, covered, about 30 minutes, until a fork goes through the yucca without effort.

Drain and leave in the colander for cooling.

When it's cool enough to handle, pull the roots and veins out of the yucca.

Melt the butter and sweat the garlic and the rosemary petals on medium-low heat until tender but not brown, then add the remaining salt and pepper.

Add the cream and bring to a soft simmer, stirring frequently so the bottom doesn't burn.

Add the yucca and mash until desired consistency (a bit lumpy).

Put the mixture into a baking dish, cover and place in oven (already preheated to 375) for 8–10 minutes.

Garnish with chopped parsley.

GRAVY:

Use drippings from the duck. Measure out ½ cup of drippings, pour into a heavy pan and bring to a boil on high heat.

Reduce heat to medium, whisk in the flour and whisk constantly until it forms a thick golden paste.

Slowly pour in stock, whisking constantly to avoid lumps.

Continue to cook over medium heat until thickened.

HAYMITCH'S HANGOVER MUFFINS

YIELDS 18 MUFFINS

One morning during the tour of the districts, Katniss found Haymitch nursing a hangover and nibbling at a muffin. It's doubtful that any muffin could have cured Haymitch, but these are at least very tasty.

These muffins are especially good as a breakfast or snack in the winter months. Try them with some cream cheese or a smear of orange marmalade.

---

3 CUPS ALL-PURPOSE WHEAT FLOUR
¾ CUP BROWN SUGAR
¾ CUP WHITE SUGAR
1 TABLESPOON BAKING POWDER
2 TEASPOONS GROUND CINNAMON
1 TEASPOON GROUND GINGER
½ TEASPOON BAKING SODA
½ TEASPOON SALT
½ TEASPOON GROUND NUTMEG
1¼ CUP MILK
1 CUP BUTTER, MELTED
2 EGGS, BEATEN
1 CUP DRIED CHERRIES, CHOPPED
1 CUP APPLE, PEELED AND CHOPPED
¾ CUP TOASTED HAZELNUTS, CHOPPED
½ CUP DRIED FIGS, CHOPPED

Preheat oven to 375 degrees.

Mix together all the dry ingredients minus the fruit and nuts.

Add milk, butter and eggs to mix. (Create a well in the middle of your dry ingredients to effectively combine liquids and solids.)

When batter is smooth and without dry pockets, add the cherries, hazelnuts, apples and figs.

Grease a muffin pan well and sprinkle it lightly with flour.

Fill each muffin pan cup ¾ full.

Bake 15-20 minutes.

PEETA'S MULTIGRAIN BREAD

MAKES 2 LOAVES

Peeta brought this yeasty bread to Haymitch one morning and Haymitch had the bad grace to hand him a filthy knife to cut it. Ever respectful of the work and ingredients that go into a loaf of bread, Peeta opted to clean the knife before using it.

If you've never baked bread, this is a good recipe to use for your first time. It's a very basic recipe that yields delicious results.

1 CUP WARM WATER (110 DEGREES)
1 PACKAGE ACTIVE DRY YEAST (2¼ TEASPOONS)
1 TABLESPOON WHITE SUGAR
6 CUPS WHEAT BREAD FLOUR, DIVIDED
1 CUP MILK, ROOM TEMPERATURE
2 EGGS
2 TABLESPOONS BUTTER, SOFTENED
2 TEASPOONS SALT
¼ CUP FRESH THYME, CHOPPED
¼ CUP FRESH CHIVES, CHOPPED
1 EGG WHITE
2 TABLESPOONS WATER

In a small mixing bowl, dissolve yeast and sugar in 1 cup warm water. Let stand about 10 minutes.

In a large bowl, stir together the yeast mixture with four cups of flour, milk, eggs, butter, salt, thyme and chives. Add the remaining flour ½ cup at a time.

Turn dough out onto a lightly floured surface and knead about 8 minutes. The dough should be soft, smooth and not sticky.

Place dough in a lightly greased bowl, cover with a damp cloth and put in a warm area to rise for about an hour, or until double in size.

Grease 2 aluminum loaf pans. Punch down the dough and turn it out onto a lightly floured surface.

Knead gently for 1 minute and form into 2 ovals.

Place in loaf pans, cover with a warm cloth and let sit for another 40 minutes.

Preheat oven to 350 degrees.

Lightly beat the egg white and 2 tablespoons of water and brush over bread. Bake for 30 minutes.

SOOTHE MY SOUL TEA

MAKES 2 CUPS

Katniss recalled when Gale's little brother had nothing to eat for an entire week but corn syrup on bread, and tea flavored with corn syrup. This would have been trying for anyone, even someone as strong as Katniss.

This tea, made with honey rather than corn syrup, is more palatable. It's wonderful served hot or cold, so enjoy it over ice in the warmer months.

1 (2-INCH) PIECE LEMON PEEL, CUT INTO THIN
   SLIVERS
2 TEASPOONS BOILING WATER
¾ CUP HOT WATER
2 TEASPOONS GREEN TEA POWDER
3 TABLESPOONS FRESHLY SQUEEZED
   LEMON JUICE
1 TEASPOON HONEY

Put lemon peel into a large cup or mug.

Cover with 2 teaspoons boiling water and let steep for about 3 minutes to release the oils.

Stir in the hot water and green tea powder.

Add the lemon juice and honey.

Mix well and serve with a thick slice of bread slathered with honey.

MELLARK'S CINNAMON BREAD

MAKES 1 LOAF

As Katniss walked past the Mellark Bakery, she inhaled the scent of cinnamon bread baking. It reminded her of her hunger, but also reminded her of someone she may have lost.

This cinnamon bread is moist and flavorful, and will keep well in a sealed bag or container. It's delicious with cream cheese or even peanut butter as a topping.

3 CUPS ALL-PURPOSE WHEAT FLOUR

2 CUPS SUGAR

1 (5.1 OUNCE) PACKAGE INSTANT VANILLA PUDDING MIX

2 TEASPOONS GROUND CINNAMON

1½ TEASPOONS BAKING POWDER

½ TEASPOON BAKING SODA

½ TEASPOON SALT

1½ CUPS MILK

½ CUP CANOLA OIL

2 EGGS, BEATEN

1 TEASPOON VANILLA EXTRACT

2 TABLESPOONS CINNAMON SUGAR

Preheat oven to 325 degrees.

Spray two 5 x 9-inch loaf pans with baking spray.

In a large bowl, mix the flour, sugar, pudding mix, cinnamon, baking powder, baking soda and salt.

In a separate bowl, mix the milk, oil, eggs and vanilla.

Stir the milk mixture into the flour mixture until well mixed and all the lumps have been smoothed out.

Cover the bottoms of the loaf pans lightly with cinnamon sugar and pour the batter into each pan evenly.

Bake 1 hour, or until a toothpick inserted in the center of a loaf comes out clean.

BITTERSWEET MEMORIES DILL BREAD

MAKES 2 LOAVES

Once she truly knew Peeta and had grown to care for him, the odors of the bakery would evoke memories and fears that troubled Katniss instead of evoking an appetite.

This bread is simple to make but the flavor and texture are outstanding. Try toasting a few slices and topping with cream cheese and salmon.

3½ CUPS ALL-PURPOSE FLOUR, DIVIDED
1½ CUPS WHEAT FLOUR
½ CUP INSTANT NONFAT DRY MILK POWDER
2 (1½ TEASPOONS) PACKAGES ACTIVE
    DRY YEAST
2 TEASPOONS SUGAR
1 TEASPOON SALT
1 TEASPOON DILL SEED
1 TEASPOON DILL WEED
1¾ CUPS WATER
2 TEASPOONS SHORTENING

In a mixing bowl, combine 2 cups all-purpose flour, wheat flour, milk powder, yeast, sugar, salt and the dill.

In a pan, heat water and shortening to between 120 and 130 degrees. (You can use a candy thermometer to be more precise.) Then pour into dry ingredients. Beat until blended well and the mixture is smooth.

Stir in enough remaining all-purpose flour to form soft dough.

Turn onto a floured surface and knead until smooth and elastic, adding flour as needed.

Place in a greased bowl and flip once to coat both sides.

Cover and let rise in a warm place for about 45 minutes.

Punch dough down. Turn onto a lightly floured surface; divide in half.

Shape into 2 balls. Place on 2 greased baking sheets.

Cover and let rest in a warm place about 35 more minutes. With a sharp knife, score the bread (make several shallow slashes across the top of each loaf).

Bake at 375 degrees for 30–35 minutes, or until golden brown.

Remove from pans to cool.

PRIM'S HEARTY BEEF STEW

SERVES 4

This bowl of stew was both comforting and nourishing to Katniss as she faced the prospect of returning to the Arena. Stew wasn't often available to Katniss before her first Hunger Games, but her victory had changed her circumstances and diet considerably.

Beef stew is one of the most popular of comfort foods, and it's a great meal to have with a salad or chunk of bread on a cool evening.

½ CUP WATER

¼ CUP RED WINE VINEGAR

1 TABLESPOON SUGAR

1 POUND BONELESS BEEF CHUCK ROAST, CUT INTO 1-INCH CUBES

¼ TEASPOON PEPPER

¼ TEASPOON GROUND NUTMEG

¾ TEASPOON SALT

1 SMALL ONION, SLICED

2 STALKS CELERY, CHOPPED

1 BAY LEAF

1 PACKAGE EGG NOODLES, COOKED ACCORDING TO INSTRUCTIONS

2 TEASPOONS CORNSTARCH

2 TABLESPOONS HALF-AND-HALF OR CREAM

Combine the water, vinegar and sugar in a small pan and heat over medium heat.

Cook and stir until sugar is dissolved, then let cool.

Season beef with pepper, nutmeg, and salt and place in a large re-sealable plastic bag.

Add onion, celery and bay leaf to the cooled marinade.

Pour marinade into the re-sealable plastic bag and seal. Shake gently to coat and refrigerate overnight.

Reserve ½ cup marinade, and drain the rest. Remove the bay leaf.

Place the beef and reserved marinade in a pan and bring to a boil.

Cook noodles while meat simmers.

Turn down the heat. Cover and simmer until meat is tender, about 30 minutes.

Combine cornstarch and half-and-half and stir into beef mixture.

Bring to a boil, then cook and stir for 2 minutes, or until slightly thickened.

Serve over noodles.

MRS. EVERDEEN'S SIMPLE BROTH

Katniss shared a cup of her mother's broth with Haymitch shortly before leaving once again for the Capitol to participate in the Quarter Quell.

This traditional recipe is probably similar to what Mrs. Everdeen would have been able to make. If marrow bones aren't a regular sight in your supermarket, ask the butcher if they're available. They often are, but only if you ask.

---

3 QUARTS WATER
3 BEEF MARROW BONES
1 CARROT, COARSELY CHOPPED
½ TURNIP, PEELED AND CHOPPED
2 STALKS CELERY, CHOPPED
1 LEEK, SLICED
SEVERAL SPRIGS OF FRESH THYME
SALT AND PEPPER TO TASTE
½ CUP FRESH PARSLEY, CHOPPED

Bring the water to a boil in heavy-bottomed stockpot.

Add the marrow bone, carrot, turnip, celery and leek.

Add the thyme sprigs, salt and pepper.

Bring to a boil and then simmer gently over medium heat for 4 hours.

Remove the bones from the pot. Strain broth through fine mesh strainer.

Return to a boil and then stir in the parsley. Season broth with salt, pepper and fresh parsley.

Serve hot or freeze broth and substitute for beef stock in future recipes.

NOTES

NOTES

THE TRAIN TO QUARTER QUELL

"And I'm left standing at the window, watching District 12 disappear, with all my goodbyes still hanging on my lips."

KATNISS, *CATCHING FIRE* BY SUZANNE COLLINS, CHAPTER 13

THE FIRST TIME THAT KATNISS AND PEETA took the train to the Capitol they were overwhelmed by not only what was ahead of them, but also by the foods that were placed before them.

On this second trip, the food was no less startling, and no less needed. Unfortunately the tension between Katniss and Peeta and the knowledge of what they were returning to in the Arena distracted them from any enjoyment they might have gotten from the meals.

SILENT, COLD SOUP OF BEET PUREE

SERVES 6

When Peeta and Katniss joined Effie for dinner on the train back to the Capitol, the silence between them made for a very cold meal indeed. No one spent much time enjoying the food.

Cold soups are a traditional favorite in Scandinavian homes and are also seen in the Midwest. They're refreshing as either an entrée or a starter, especially in the summer.

---

4 MEDIUM BEETS
4 CUPS BEEF BROTH
1 ONION, CHOPPED
2 TABLESPOONS RED WINE VINEGAR
½ TEASPOON SALT
¼ TEASPOON BLACK PEPPER

Trim the beets and remove the tops, but leave the skins.

In a stockpot, cover beets with cold water and bring to a boil.

Boil about 40 minutes.

Drain beets, but reserve 2 cups of the beet liquid.

Strain the liquid and add to a large saucepan.

Remove skin from beets with a peeler or the edge of a teaspoon.

Grate beets coarsely and add to beet liquid.

Add beef broth, onion, vinegar, salt and pepper. Bring to a boil, cover and reduce heat. Simmer on low heat for 20 minutes.

Chill in refrigerator for 1 hour, or until cold.

Many people are unfamiliar with cold soups or have only heard of famous cold soups such as gazpacho or vichyssoise. There's a wide array, however, of delicious cold soups from many different cultures. Cold soups don't necessarily have to be cold; some are better at room temperature. They also don't have to be savory; there are a number of sweet cold soups that are wonderful for dessert.

FISH CAKES WITH WASABI-LIME MAYO

SERVES 6

If there had been any chance that Peeta and Katniss might have been able to enjoy their dinner on the train, this recipe would have been welcomed. As it was, food was the last thing on either of their minds.

The sauce for this fish has a bit of a kick that plays off the mildness of the dish very well. If you have leftover mayo, try it as a spread on your sandwich.

FISH CAKES:

3 CUPS WATER
2 POTATOES, PEELED
½ CUP CELERY, CHOPPED
¼ CUP MINCED ONION
¼ CUP GREEN BELL PEPPER, CHOPPED
¼ CUP RED BELL PEPPER, CHOPPED
2 TABLESPOONS BUTTER
3½ CUPS COOKED COD, BONED AND FLAKED
½ CUP MILK
4 TABLESPOONS ALL-PURPOSE FLOUR
2 TABLESPOONS GRATED PARMESAN CHEESE
¼ TEASPOON MUSTARD POWDER
½ TEASPOON SALT
GROUND BLACK PEPPER TO TASTE
½ CUP DRY BREADCRUMBS

WASABI-LIME MAYO:

2¼ TEASPOONS WASABI POWDER
1½ TEASPOONS WATER
¼ CUP AND 1 TEASPOON MAYONNAISE
1 TABLESPOON FRESH SQUEEZED LIME JUICE

FISH CAKES:

Preheat oven to 400 degrees. Spray 2 baking sheets.

Bring 3 cups of water to a boil.

Add the potatoes and cook until just about done; slightly firm in the middle, but not too soft.

Drain and mash. Reserve 1 cup mashed potatoes, discard the rest or save for later.

In a large pan, sauté the celery, onion and green and red bell peppers in butter over medium-high heat until tender.

Turn heat to low and add the cod.

Slowly mix in milk, flour, cheese, dry mustard, salt, pepper and mashed potatoes.

Mix gently but thoroughly. Take off heat and let cool enough to handle.

Coat your hands with flour and shape batter into ½-inch x 3-inch patties.

Cover with breadcrumbs.

Bake for 10 minutes, flip and bake for 15 minutes, until brown on both sides. Makes 6 patties.

WASABI-LIME MAYO:

Mix wasabi powder and water to form a paste and let sit for 1 minute.

Add mayonnaise and lime. Whisk well.

Serve with fish cakes and enjoy.

CORNISH HENS STUFFED WITH ORANGES OVER RICE

SERVES 4

This dish is reminiscent of the fowl dish that Katniss ate her first time in the Capitol, when her mouth was filled with the flavors of an orange sauce. It's ironic that she had a dish so similar on her return.

Cornish game hens are flavorful and moist, and make a very elegant presentation for a special meal. You can usually find them in the freezer section of your supermarket.

4 CORNISH GAME HENS
2 ORANGES, HALVED
2 TEASPOONS OLIVE OIL
¼ TEASPOON CHILI POWDER
¼ TEASPOON GROUND CUMIN
SEA SALT TO TASTE
GROUND BLACK PEPPER TO TASTE
4 SPRIGS FRESH ROSEMARY
2 BOXES WILD RICE
2 TABLESPOONS BUTTER
2 CUPS WATER

Preheat oven to 425 degrees.

Rub each hen with an orange half.

Coat the hens with olive oil and season with chili powder, cumin, sea salt and pepper.

Stuff the hens with the oranges and rosemary sprigs (cut the orange halves into quarters).

Place hens on a rack in a shallow roasting pan.

Roast for 15 minutes, then turn heat down to 350 degrees and cook for 30 minutes, or to an internal temperature of 165 degrees.

For rice, simply follow box instructions and serve hens over a bed of the wild rice.

Pairs well with Watercress and Almond Salad.

WATERCRESS AND ALMOND SALAD

The sight of watercress, a wild green Katniss was accustomed to foraging back home, must have made her long to be back with Prim, her mother and Gale.

If you can find watercress growing wild, by all means use it. It will lend an extra layer of authenticity to your meal. If not, you can often find it in farmer's markets or produce sections in the grocery store.

---

1 TABLESPOONS FRESH LIME JUICE
¼ TEASPOON WHITE SUGAR
¼ TEASPOON MINCED FRESH GINGER ROOT
2 TABLESPOONS OLIVE OIL
SALT AND PEPPER TO TASTE
2 BUNCHES WATERCRESS, TRIMMED AND CHOPPED
½ CUP ALMONDS, TOASTED AND SLICED

In a large bowl, whisk together lime juice, sugar and ginger. Gradually add oil and season with salt and pepper to taste.

Gently toss watercress and almonds with dressing.

CHOCOLATE COVERED CHERRY CUSTARD

Chocolate was almost unheard of in District 12 and would probably have been exciting for Katniss if she hadn't been on her way to the Quarter Quell. The symbol of luxury on her plate must have been bittersweet.

Custard is one of those deliciously rich desserts that seem like they should be a lot of trouble to make. Fortunately it's actually rather simple.

½ CUP WHITE SUGAR
¼ CUP CORNSTARCH
3 TABLESPOONS UNSWEETENED COCOA
    POWDER
DASH OF SALT
2¾ CUPS MILK
2 TABLESPOONS BUTTER
1 TEASPOON VANILLA EXTRACT
¼ POUND BING CHERRIES, PITTED, SLICED
    IN HALF

In a saucepan, mix together sugar, cornstarch, cocoa and salt.

Place over medium heat and stir in milk.

Bring to a slow boil and cook, stirring constantly, until mixture thickens like pudding.

Remove from heat and stir in butter and vanilla.

Let cool briefly and serve warm.

Garnish with cherry halves.

SOOTHING HONEY AND SPICED MILK

The night before they arrived in the Capitol, Peeta and Katniss were served a soothing drink that should have helped them sleep. Unfortunately, sleep was not easy to come by with so much awaiting them.

If you'd like a slightly richer version of this drink, substitute a cup of half-and-half for one of the cups of milk. It's a wonderful hot drink for bedtime, or for curling up with Catching Fire *on a cool night.*

4 CUPS MILK
1 TABLESPOON AND 1 TEASPOON HONEY
8 DROPS VANILLA EXTRACT
4 PINCHES OF GROUND CARDAMOM
4 PINCHES GROUND CINNAMON

Pour milk into a saucepan over medium-low heat.

Acquire a low simmer (takes about 3 minutes).

Add honey, vanilla and cardamom to milk.

Stir until honey disappears into milk.

Sprinkle each mug with a pinch of cinnamon before serving.

NOTES

10

THE QUARTER QUELL FESTIVITIES AND TRAINING

"I just want to spend every possible minute of the rest of my life with you."

PEETA, *CATCHING FIRE* BY SUZANNE COLLINS, CHAPTER 17

THE CELEBRATIONS AND BANQUETS that greeted Katniss on her first trip to the Capitol had seemed surreal because they had been so far outside her realm of experience. However, the Quarter Quell festivities must have seemed even more surreal; she had never dreamed she would have to return, and it was certainly nothing to celebrate.

HOMESICK CHEESE BUNS

MAKES TWO DOZEN MUFFINS

These cheese buns reminded Katniss of home, of family and of Peeta. When Peeta discovered they were her favorites, he made sure she got some.

For a change of flavor, you can vary the cheese you use in this recipe. Muenster, provolone and Colby all work well.

3½ CUPS ALL-PURPOSE FLOUR
¼ CUP SUGAR
2 TEASPOONS BAKING POWDER
1½ TEASPOONS SALT
1½ CUPS MILK
¾ CUP CANOLA OIL
2 EGGS
2 CUPS SHREDDED CHEESE

In a bowl, combine flour, sugar, baking powder and salt.

In another bowl, combine egg, milk and oil; mix well until mixture is smooth.

Stir wet ingredients into dry ingredients and mix just until moistened through.

Fold in 2 cups of cheese.

Fill greased muffin cups ⅔ full.

Bake at 400 degrees for 25 minutes.

SNOW'S SUCKLING PIG

SERVES 12

In Section One there's an involved recipe for the Gamemakers' Suckling Pig. Here is a less work-intensive version that tastes almost as good—perhaps even good enough for Snow.

Reserve some leftover ham to use in Greasy Sae's Gourd and Bean Soup, or cut a few slices for a delicious breakfast ham.

1 (8-POUND) BONE-IN SHANK HAM
4 CUPS WATER
½ TEASPOON SALT
½ CUP HONEY
½ CUP BROWN SUGAR
2 TABLESPOONS LIQUID SMOKE FLAVORING
2 TABLESPOONS WORCESTERSHIRE SAUCE
1 TABLESPOON WHOLE CLOVES

Preheat the oven to 275 degrees.

Put the ham in a roasting pan, skin side up.

Pour in enough water to reach a 2-inch depth.

Sprinkle with the salt and cover with a tight fitting lid or foil.

Bake for 6–7 hours, depending on size (follow directions on the wrapper).

Remove from the oven, pour off drippings and reserve for later use.

Debone ham, removing any excess fat as well and return to the roasting pan.

Skim fat from the top of the drippings and toss out.

In a bowl, mix 1 cup of the drippings with honey, brown sugar, liquid smoke and Worcestershire sauce.

Pour drippings over the top of the ham then pour the mixture over the ham.

Lightly score the ham and push the cloves into the surface of the ham, about an inch or so apart.

Cover and return to the oven. Remaining drippings may be discarded or reserved for other uses.

Bake for another 30–40 minutes in the preheated oven. Let cool for 10 minutes before serving.

CAPITOL LAMB STEW WITH PLUM DUMPLINGS

SERVES 8

Lamb stew with plums was mentioned several times throughout the trilogy. Katniss first fell in love with it in the Capitol, before the 74th Hunger Games. Later, she was relieved to have some sent in while she was in the Arena. In yet another instance, she found canned lamb stew with plums when gathering supplies.

Here's a version of the stew that's somewhat different from the one featured in Chapter 4. The plum dumplings are an unusual addition that makes a wonderful presentation and is sure to please guests.

LAMB STEW:
1 POUND LAMB STEW MEAT, CUBED
¼ TEASPOON SALT, DIVIDED
¼ TEASPOON BLACK PEPPER, DIVIDED
2 TABLESPOONS CANOLA OIL
2 CUPS BEEF BROTH
1 CUP RED WINE
2 CLOVES GARLIC, MINCED
1 TABLESPOON FRESH THYME, CHOPPED
1 BAY LEAF
2 CUPS PEELED, SEEDED AND SLICED
    BUTTERNUT SQUASH
1½ CUPS ENGLISH PEAS
1 CUP PEELED, SLICED PARSNIPS
1 CUP SWEET POTATOES, PEELED AND CHOPPED
1 CUP SLICED CARROTS
1 MEDIUM ONION, THINLY SLICED
½ CUP SOUR CREAM
3 TABLESPOONS ALL-PURPOSE FLOUR

DUMPLINGS:
4 LARGE RED POTATOES, PEELED
1 TABLESPOON BUTTER
2 CUPS ALL-PURPOSE WHEAT FLOUR
1 EGG
1 PINCH SALT
16 ITALIAN PRUNE PLUMS, PITTED AND LEFT
    WHOLE
16 TEASPOONS WHITE SUGAR, DIVIDED

LAMB STEW:

Season the lamb with salt and pepper.

Heat the oil in a Dutch oven and brown the lamb meat on both sides on high heat. Don't overcrowd the pot.

Next, drain the fat and add the broth and wine.

Add the garlic, herbs, salt and pepper.

Bring to a boil then reduce heat, cover and simmer for 20 minutes.

Add the vegetables, bring to a boil, then reduce heat again and simmer 30 minutes, or until the vegetables are tender.

In a bowl, blend the sour cream and flour and slowly add half of the stew broth, stirring constantly.

Add the sour cream blend to the pot and take out the bay leaf, then cook on medium low until desired thickness.

DUMPLINGS:

Boil the potatoes until tender, allowing ample time to cool in a strainer. The potatoes need to be dry to form a dough.

After they cool, push them through a ricer into a bowl. (If you do not have a ricer, gently break up with a fork or use a cheese grater.)

Add butter to the potatoes and let it melt. Add the flour and mix until completely blended.

Add egg and salt.

Knead until the mixture becomes a dough (use plenty of flour on your surface to prevent sticking).

Knead about 10 minutes and add flour as needed. Dough should be soft and not sticky.

Cut dough into quarters and then fourths (makes 16 pieces).

Roll each portion into a ball, then roll the ball out on your floured surface.

Make a 3½-inch circle.

Place the pitted plum in the middle, sprinkle it with a teaspoon of sugar and seal the dough around it. Repeat until you have 16 dumplings.

Lightly salt a pot of water and bring to a boil using medium heat only.

Add dumplings and stir gently to make sure none stick together. (Cook in batches of 4 if your pot is not big enough.)

After they rise to the top, allow about 5 more minutes of cooking and remove dumplings.

Serve dumplings directly on top of stew, or on the side.

PRESIDENTIAL STUFFED FOWL

SERVES 5

President Snow served a lot of elaborate and fanciful poultry dishes at his parties and dinners, using food to impress people and illustrate his status as the most powerful man in Panem. He may have had bad judgment and a real evil streak, but he knew good food. While not everything met with Katniss and Peeta's approval, they seemed to like the poultry dishes quite well.

This recipe will impress your dinner table, but it's just as much about flavor as it is about good looks. The cranberries add a wonderful tartness to the rice stuffing.

2 TABLESPOONS OLIVE OIL
2 TABLESPOONS BUTTER
½ CUP CELERY, CHOPPED
¼ CUP FRESH MUSHROOMS, SLICED
1 (6-OUNCE) PACKAGE FAST-COOKING LONG
    GRAIN AND WILD RICE MIX
1½ CUPS CHICKEN BROTH OR STOCK
¼ CUP WATER
½ CUP WATER CHESTNUTS, CHOPPED
½ CUP DRIED CRANBERRIES
½ CUP DRIED APRICOTS, CHOPPED
½ CUP GREEN ONIONS, CHOPPED
2 TABLESPOONS REDUCED-SODIUM SOY SAUCE
5 CORNISH GAME HENS

In a saucepan, melt butter with olive oil until no longer frothy.

Cook celery and mushrooms on medium-high heat in butter and olive oil until tender.

Stir in rice and cook for 1 minute.

Stir in the contents of the rice seasoning packet (if one), broth and water. Bring to a boil. Reduce heat, cover and simmer for 5–6 minutes, or until rice is tender.

Add the water chestnuts, cranberries, apricots, onions and soy sauce to rice.

Stuff the hens with rice mixture.

Place on a rack in a shallow roasting pan.

Bake at 375 degrees for 50–60 minutes, or until juices run clear and the hens register 160 degrees according to a meat thermometer inserted inside of the thigh.

OCEAN CREATURES AND COCKTAIL SAUCE

SERVES 24

It's hard for any dish to stand out on a table that's spread with twenty kinds of soup. However, a seafood dish like this would have been a true rarity in District 12, and surely got the attention of Katniss.

This is a great way to feed a crowd on a summer day, especially at the beach or during some type of outdoor party. If you'd like a little variety, you can add clams or mussels to the pot.

COCKTAIL SAUCE:
2 TABLESPOONS FINELY GRATED RAW
    HORSERADISH
1 TEASPOON DARK BROWN SUGAR
¼ TEASPOON FRESH LEMON JUICE
½ CUP KETCHUP

SEAFOOD:
4 LEMONS, HALVED
1 (2.5-OUNCE) JAR LIQUID SHELLFISH BOIL,
    SUCH AS ZATARAIN'S
1 TABLESPOON DICED GREEN CHILI PEPPER
SALT TO TASTE
10 POUNDS MEDIUM SHRIMP, PEELED AND
    DEVEINED
12 BLUE CRABS, CLEANED

COCKTAIL SAUCE:

Combine horseradish, brown sugar, lemon juice and ketchup.

SEAFOOD:

Use a very large stockpot and fill it half full with water; bring water to a full boil.

Add lemons, shellfish boil, hot peppers and salt. Bring to a boil.

When everything is tender, turn off the heat.

Mix in shrimp and crab.

Cover pot and let it sit for 10 minutes.

When shrimp are pink and the crabmeat is opaque and flaky, remove all of the shellfish from the pot and pour them over ice. Let chill, and then serve with cocktail sauce.

You can cook fresh shrimp with or without the shell, but they'll retain a lot more flavor if you wait to peel them until after they're cooked. You should, however, devein them before cooking. An easy way to do this with the shell on is to remove the head, if still attached, then use a small pair of sharp scissors to cut along the back of the shrimp. This will help you easily peel the vein from the shrimp.

SAVORY PUMPKIN SOUP WITH NUTS

SERVES 6

This creamy soup at Snow's lavish banquet enchanted Katniss. Though she tried to set a "one plate per table" rule for herself, this dish was the first of many that night.

Pumpkin soup has a rich creaminess that makes for an especially good dish. Don't worry, this soup tastes nothing like pumpkin pie. If you've never tried pumpkin soup, this is a great one for your first taste.

3½ CUPS CUBED FRESH PUMPKIN
6 CUPS CHICKEN STOCK
1 CUP ONION, CHOPPED
1½ TEASPOONS SALT
½ TEASPOON FRESH THYME, CHOPPED
1 CLOVE GARLIC, MINCED
5 WHOLE BLACK PEPPERCORNS
½ CUP HEAVY WHIPPING CREAM
SALT AND PEPPER TO TASTE
½ CUP SLIVERED ALMONDS
½ CUP BLACK SESAME SEEDS

Cut pumpkin into ½-inch cubes.

Heat stock in a large pot over medium-high heat.

Add pumpkin, onion, salt, thyme, garlic and peppercorns.

Bring to a boil; reduce heat to low and simmer uncovered for 30 minutes.

Let soup cool until safe to handle, then puree 1 cup at a time in a food processor or blender.

Pour back into the pot and bring to a boil.

Reduce heat to low and simmer for another 30 minutes, uncovered. Stir in the cream and season with salt and pepper.

Pour into soup bowls and garnish with slivered almonds and black sesame seeds.

TASTE OF SPRING SOUP

SERVES 8

At President Snow's extravagant banquet, this springtime soup was a welcome and refreshing antidote to all of the rich fare spread before the diners.

Asparagus and leeks complement each other deliciously. The overall flavor of this soup is one of springtime and freshness, so it's a terrific soup for lunch or as a starter to a rich or heavy meal.

¼ CUP BUTTER
1 POUND LEEKS, CLEANED AND CHOPPED
4 STALKS CELERY, FINELY CHOPPED
1 ONION, CHOPPED
2 QUARTS WATER OR HIGH-QUALITY VEGETABLE
   STOCK
3 LARGE RED POTATOES, CHOPPED
2 LARGE CARROTS, CHOPPED
1 BUNCH FRESH ASPARAGUS, TRIMMED AND CUT
   INTO 1-INCH PIECES
4 TEASPOONS SALT
½ POUND FRESH SPINACH LEAVES, CHOPPED
1 CUP HEAVY CREAM

Melt the butter in a very large stockpot over medium heat.

Stir in the leeks, celery and onion. Cook until tender, stirring as necessary.

Pour the water into the pot.

Add the red potatoes, carrots, asparagus and salt to taste.

Bring to a boil, reduce heat and simmer 30 minutes, until vegetables are tender.

Stir spinach and heavy cream into the soup mixture and continue cooking about 5 minutes before serving.

COLD RASPBERRY SOUP WITH FRESH BERRIES

Raspberries grew wild in the forest where Katniss hunted. They were a rare treat, and a symbol of spring. During the Quarter Quell banquets, these simple berries, all dressed up in Capitol clothes, must have seemed out of place.

If you need to use frozen raspberries for this recipe, make sure that they're completely thawed and well drained before you use them.

4 CUPS RASPBERRIES
½ CUP SUGAR
¼ CUP CRANBERRY JUICE
½ CUP SOUR CREAM
¼ CUP HEAVY CREAM OR HALF-AND-HALF
FRESH RASPBERRIES AND MINT LEAVES FOR GARNISH

Put raspberries, sugar and cranberry juice into a blender and blend until very smooth and sugar is dissolved.

Pour into a large dish and stir in first the sour cream and then the cream.

Cover and refrigerate for 2–3 hours before serving.

To serve, ladle into shallow bowls, sprinkle with fresh raspberries and place a mint sprig in the center.

NO MANNERS NEEDED CHOCOLATE CAKE

SERVES 12—15

Katniss expressed her disregard and disdain for the Capitol in slightly covert ways. Shooting an arrow into the Gamemakers' Suckling Pig was a bit less subtle than picking a chocolate flower from an elegantly decorated cake.

Feel free to pluck the flowers from this cake with no manners at all.

1 PACKAGE DEVIL'S FOOD CAKE MIX
1 PACKAGE INSTANT CHOCOLATE PUDDING MIX
1 CUP SOUR CREAM
1 CUP CANOLA OIL
4 EGGS
½ CUP WARM WATER
2 CUPS DARK CHOCOLATE CHIPS
CANDIED FLOWERS (OR CREATE FLOWERS WITH ICING)
¼ CUP POWDERED SUGAR

Preheat oven to 350 degrees.

In a large bowl, mix together the cake and pudding mixes, sour cream, oil, beaten eggs and water.

Stir in the chocolate chips and pour batter into a well-greased, 12-cup Bundt pan.

Bake until a wooden toothpick inserted comes out clean. Cool cake thoroughly.

After cake is completely cooked, flip onto a plate carefully, sprinkle with powdered sugar and decorate with candied flowers, or, if preferred, draw flower shapes with icing.

BLOOD ORANGE QUAIL

SERVES 4

Katniss takes a bite of "fowl" and finds her mouth filled with orange juice, an ingredient that she's only tasted once—when she first visited the Capitol in The Hunger Games. *The use of blood orange here seems appropriate.*

This dish is a very elegant one for dinner parties, especially a Capitol-style Hunger Games *party for adults. The combination of wine, sage and blood orange is delicious.*

4-6 SMALL QUAILS
SALT AND PEPPER TO TASTE
8 BLOOD ORANGES, DIVIDED
1 WHOLE STALK OF CELERY
1 SMALL BUNDLE FRESH THYME
1 TABLESPOON OLIVE OIL
6 TABLESPOONS BUTTER
6 CLOVES GARLIC, WHOLE AND UNPEELED
10 SAGE LEAVES
1½ CUPS SWEET WHITE WINE, DIVIDED

QUAIL:

Preheat the oven to 425 degrees.

Wash the birds thoroughly inside and out and pat dry with paper towels.

Rub them liberally with salt and pepper.

Cut off the 2 ends of 6 of the oranges (save 2 oranges for the gravy); stand them on end and slice off the skin.

Slice the oranges into 5 or 6 rounds each. Set aside.

Remove the tougher outside ribs of the celery until you reach the white, dense bulb and slice across thinly.

Put celery into a bowl and mix in the thyme and a small pinch of salt and pepper, then stuff the cavity of each quail with it. (You will only fit barely a tablespoon of the celery mixture into each bird.)

Pull the skin at the front of each quail cavity forward to cover the filling, and tightly tie up with wet twine.

Heat a thick-bottomed pan on medium-high heat

Add the olive oil and the quail.

Cook until lightly golden on all sides.

Add the butter, garlic and sage and cook for 3-4 minutes, until golden brown.

Bake for 45 minutes, checking every 10-15 minutes and adding the wine at intervals, just enough to keep the pan slightly moist at all times.

When cooked, carefully remove the quail from the oven and rest upside down on a dish, allowing all the juices and moisture to relax back into the breast meat for at least 5 minutes.

While your meat is resting, make the gravy.

GRAVY:

Remove all the fat from the roasting pan and place the pan on low heat.

In the bottom of the pan will be your cooked, soft, sweet, whole garlic cloves and bits of browning from the birds.

When this gets hot, deglaze the pan with about ⅔ cup of wine and a wooden spoon.

Squeeze the juice from the 2 remaining blood oranges into the pan and simmer gently.

Push the cooked garlic cloves out of their skins with a spoon (discard the skins).

Pour any of the juices that have drained out of the rested birds into the pan with the gravy, simmer and season to taste.

Serve with roasted vegetable of your choice.

DISAPPEARING MINTS

MAKES ABOUT 20 COOKIES

These mints melt in your mouth, just like the mints that Katniss sampled at Snow's banquet. Katniss mentioned earlier in the book that candy was incredibly rare and expensive in District 12. It must have been surreal to see it piled up for all to take.

This recipe is easily doubled or tripled to make large batches for the holidays, or as homemade gifts for friends and family. They'll keep very well in sealed bags or jars.

---

4 EGG WHITES
¼ TEASPOON SALT
¼ TEASPOON CREAM OF TARTAR
1 CUP SUGAR
4 PEPPERMINT CANDY CANES (2 GREEN, 2 RED)
   CRUSHED

In a bowl, beat egg whites with a wire whisk until foamy.

Add salt and cream of tartar; beat until soft peaks begins to form.

Beat in sugar, 1 tablespoon at a time, until stiff and glossy.

Spoon meringue into a re-sealable plastic bag. When ready to use, cut a 1-inch hole in the corner.

Squeeze 1-inch blobs of meringue onto ungreased, foil-lined baking sheets. Sprinkle half with red crushed candy canes and half with green candy canes. (You can crush the candy canes in the food processor with several quick pulses.)

Bake at 225 degrees for 1–1½ hours, or until dry but not brown. Cool and remove from foil.

Store in an airtight container.

SWEET PHEASANT WITH CRANBERRY JEWELS

SERVES 4

This lavish meal was considered to be a regular lunch in the Capitol, but the catching of a pheasant back in District 12 would have been cause for celebration.

If you can't find pheasant in your local grocery or in the wild, call around to local game meat dealers or order one online. They make a great meal for special occasions.

1 CUP OLIVE OIL
2 SPRIGS ROSEMARY, LEAVES STRIPPED AND
   CHOPPED
1 TABLESPOON FRESH THYME, CHOPPED
1 WHOLE PHEASANT, CLEANED
SALT AND GROUND BLACK PEPPER TO TASTE
1 CAN CRANBERRY SAUCE (WITHOUT THE
   BERRIES)

PHEASANT:

Preheat oven to 250 degrees.

Stir the chopped rosemary and thyme into the olive oil and set aside.

Clean the pheasant. Rub the pheasant inside and out with salt and pepper.

Place into a roasting pan then pour olive oil and herb mixture over it.

Bake for 1 hour, then cover with aluminum foil and continue baking an additional hour.

Baste the pheasant with pan juices every 30 minutes while cooking.

Remove from the oven, cover with a sheet of aluminum foil and allow to rest for 10 minutes before slicing.

CRANBERRY JEWELS:

Thickly slice the cranberry sauce and use cookie cutters or cut diamond and circle shapes with a knife. Discard the leftovers and decorate a serving dish with the jewel-shaped cutouts.

Serve with Baby Vegetables in Lemon Butter Sauce.

BABY VEGETABLES IN LEMON BUTTER SAUCE

In District 12, bigger food would have been better, as everyone was starving—especially for something as rare as fresh vegetables. In the Capitol, there was so much plenty that vegetables were eaten for their aesthetic value rather than their nutritional value.

This dish makes a wonderful side for a poultry entrée, but goes equally well with a nice fish dish. It's light, colorful and full of flavor.

½ **CUP BUTTER**
1 **MEDIUM ONION, CHOPPED**
1 **MEDIUM RED BELL PEPPER, CHOPPED**
1 **TEASPOON GARLIC SALT**
1 **TEASPOON GARLIC PEPPER**
2 **CUPS BROCCOLI, CHOPPED**
2 **CUPS CAULIFLOWER FLORETS, CHOPPED**
1 **JAR MINIATURE BABY CORN**
1 **CUP TINY BABY PEAS**
1 **TABLESPOON FRESH LEMON JUICE**

Melt butter in a skillet over medium-low heat.

Add diced onion and bell pepper and sauté 1 minute until slightly soft.

Season with garlic salt and garlic pepper.

Add the rest of the vegetables.

Cook 15 minutes, or until vegetables are tender, then drizzle with lemon juice.

PARSLEY MASHED POTATOES

SERVES 6

Potatoes were very popular in the Capitol, which might have meant they were rare in the rest of Panem. This would seem likely, since they're grown mainly in the Western United States, where the Capitol was located.

Leaving the peel on the potatoes adds flavor, texture, color and a great deal of vitamins and minerals to what would otherwise be plain old mashed potatoes.

**5 RED POTATOES, UNPEELED, CUT INTO
   BITE-SIZED PIECES
1 LARGE ONION, QUARTERED
½ CUP FRESH PARSLEY, CHOPPED
½ STICK BUTTER
SALT AND PEPPER TO TASTE**

Boil potatoes and onion until potatoes are tender and a fork slides through them easily.

Drain potatoes and put into large bowl, then mash with a potato masher.

Add parsley, butter, salt and pepper. Stir and serve.

FRUIT KEBABS AND A FOUNTAIN OF CHOCOLATE*

MAKES 4—6 KEBABS

Katniss loved melted fountain chocolate so much that she started eating it with a spoon. For this recipe, we'll go a bit fancier, in keeping with the Capitol's typical extravagance.

Experiment with many different fruits for this dish. Firm fruits work best for dipping, but you can try apricots, peaches, orange sections or bananas for variety.

1-2 POUNDS CHOCOLATE
1 PINEAPPLE, CUT INTO CHUNKS
½ POUND BING CHERRIES, PITTED
1 HALF CANTALOUPE OR OTHER MELON
    AVAILABLE, CUT INTO CHUNKS
4-6 KEBAB STICKS

*You'll need a chocolate fountain if you don't already have one. Fountains are relatively inexpensive to buy and easy to use.

Simply follow the instructions that come with the fountain for melting chocolate.

Use the best chocolate you can afford.

Skewer the fruit in an alternating pattern and dip into melted chocolate.

MASHED ON THE FLOOR PEAS

SERVES 6

The only time Katniss felt "present" at dinner is when she purposely knocked a dish of these peas onto the floor. It was another one of her small acts of rebellion that made her feel intact.

Fresh peas work best for this dish. Their sweetness and texture is far superior to frozen peas. These reheat very well, so plan for leftovers and save some cooking time at your next meal.

2 TABLESPOONS OLIVE OIL
1 POUND ENGLISH PEAS
1 BUNCH GREEN ONIONS, CHOPPED
2 TABLESPOONS BUTTER
2 TABLESPOONS BROWN SUGAR
SALT AND PEPPER

Heat the olive oil in a pan and stir in the peas and green onions.

Cook over medium heat for 7–10 minutes until slightly soft.

Pour the peas into a bowl and mash until they are thoroughly crushed but a bit chunky.

Stir in the butter, brown sugar, salt and pepper.

Mix until the sugar has melted.

Can be served warm or cold.

BREAKFAST THROUGH A MOUTHPIECE

Back home, Katniss had to work hard for even one bite of food. In the Capitol, she could order a feast over the phone. This would have seemed even more unreal if everything else hadn't been so extraordinary.

This is an especially hearty breakfast, perfect for lazy weekends and overnight guests. You can make most of it the night before and just assemble in the morning.

1 POUND BREAKFAST SAUSAGE
1 BAG COUNTRY STYLE POTATOES
8 EGGS, BEATEN
SALT AND PEPPER TO TASTE
ONE DASH PAPRIKA
4 TABLESPOONS BUTTER, DIVIDED
1 LOAF ITALIAN BREAD CUT INTO 4 SECTIONS
    (4-5 INCHES APIECE)
1 TABLESPOON MAYONNAISE
1 QUART KATNISS' FAVORITE: FRESH-SQUEEZED
    ORANGE JUICE

Heat a large skillet to medium temperature, crumble sausage into pan and cook until all the sausage is brown.

Follow oven instructions for potatoes.

Meanwhile, beat the eggs in a bowl until just combined.

Season eggs with salt, pepper and a dash of paprika. Set aside.

When potatoes and sausage have about 5 minutes left, melt 2 tablespoons of butter in a large size non-stick skillet.

When butter is melted and no longer frothy, add eggs to the skillet.

Continuously work eggs with a spatula, creating small curds and cooking to desired consistency.

Spread remaining butter over the top of the bread with a thin layer of mayonnaise on the inside, and then put under a broiler or in a toaster oven until golden brown.

Layer the bread with scrambled eggs, then sausage and finally country potatoes. Serve with orange juice.

PLUTARCH'S ROASTED TURKEY LEG

SERVES 4

During the first Hunger Games *training, Katniss shot an arrow into the Gamemakers' roast pig to get their attention. At the first training session for Quarter Quell, Katniss spotted Plutarch chewing on a turkey leg. He had been promoted to head Gamemaker, but Katniss no longer needed to work at getting his attention.*

This is a nice way to enjoy the flavors of Thanksgiving turkey without having to roast a whole bird. Kids especially love the drama of whole turkey legs, so this is a great dish for a kids' Hunger Games *party.*

4 TURKEY LEGS
4 CELERY STALKS, CUT INTO THIRDS
½ CUP BUTTER
SALT TO TASTE
½ CUP WATER, OR AS NEEDED
4 SPRIGS ROSEMARY LEAVES

Preheat the oven to 350 degrees. Rinse the turkey legs and pat dry.

Stand the turkey legs upright (as if the turkey were standing). Use a damp paper towel to stand the turkey leg to prevent slipping.

Press a knife downward into the deep tissue, creating 2 or 3 long pockets.

Push a piece of celery into each slit.

Using the slits on the turkey legs, rub with butter and season with a little salt just under the skin.

Stuff a few rosemary leaves under the skin and put the skin back into place. (Tie with butchers twine if needed.)

Rub with more butter and season lightly with salt. Lay the legs in a roasting pan.

Roast uncovered for 1½–2 hours, until the legs are golden brown.

Add more water if needed while roasting, and baste occasionally with the juices and butter.

NOTES

11

THE 75TH HUNGER GAMES

"Surely a brief time is better than no time?"

CAESAR, *CATCHING FIRE* BY SUZANNE COLLINS, CHAPTER 18

THE RETURN TO THE ARENA was a return to scrambling and fighting for enough food to eat. Once again, Katniss had to rely on sponsors and her own skills to make it through the game. These recipes reflect the ingredients and contributions that Katniss and the other tributes had to depend on for survival.

FENCE-ROASTED TREE NUTS

SERVES 4

Finding the force field was an integral part of survival and then escape for Katniss. We don't know for sure what kind of nuts "hung like grapes" from the trees in the Arena, but this recipe for roasted chestnuts could be a good stand-in for throwing mystery nuts at a force field.

Be sure to check each nut to make sure it isn't moldy or rotten before preparing it.

1 POUND FRESH CHESTNUTS
SALT TO TASTE

Preheat oven to 425 degrees.

On the flat side of each chestnut, use a small paring knife to cut a large X all the way through the skin.

Place the chestnuts on a baking sheet and roast in the oven for about 30–40 minutes, depending on the size of the nuts.

Shake pan several times while roasting, so they cook evenly.

If you'd like them warm but not thoroughly roasted, roast for 10–15 minutes only.

Peel all the roasted chestnuts when they are cool enough to handle.

CHESTNUT AND APPLE SALAD WITH TOASTED BREAD CROUTONS

SERVES 4

In the Arena, the tributes were happy just to have apples, "tree nuts" and a bit of bread. Food was so scarce that anything edible was met with gratitude.

This recipe combines all of the ingredients of the tributes' feast into one delicious salad. The sweetness of the apples and dressing makes this salad deliciously different from run-of-the-mill greens.

4 (½-INCH) SLICES OF STALE FRENCH BREAD
8 PINK LADY APPLES, PEELED AND CUT INTO
    CHUNKS
½ CUP CHESTNUTS, CHOPPED AND ROASTED
2 CUPS FRESH SPINACH LEAVES
½ CUP RED ONION, CHOPPED
½ CUP POPPY SEED DRESSING

Preheat oven to 300 degrees and toast bread directly on rack, turning once until golden.

Cut into 1-inch chunks and set aside.

Combine apples, chestnuts, spinach and onion in a large bowl and toss well.

Pour dressing over salad and toss well to coat.

Spoon into bowls and top each salad with the French bread croutons.

BURNT "TREE RAT" FOR THE TIMID

SERVES 4

The tributes were thrilled when Katniss caught and killed a "tree rat," which Peeta cooked by skewering it and pointing it into the force field.

This recipe is easy and doesn't require "tree rats." The teriyaki sauce will give it a dark, almost burnt appearance for some added authenticity. Kids will especially love serving this to their friends.

---

8 BONELESS, SKINLESS CHICKEN THIGHS
SALT AND PEPPER TO TASTE
1 TEASPOON OLIVE OIL
1 CLOVE GARLIC, CRUSHED
½ CUP TERIYAKI SAUCE
¼ CUP BROWN SUGAR
½ TEASPOON DIJON MUSTARD
6 BAMBOO SKEWERS, SOAKED FOR 30 MINUTES
**   IN WATER**

Season the chicken with salt and pepper.

In a small saucepan, heat the olive oil over medium heat.

Sauté the garlic for 2 minutes until slightly brown.

Add the teriyaki, brown sugar and mustard and cook until sugar is melted.

Cool to room temperature and pour marinade into a baking pan.

Lay the thighs into the pan in a single layer and let marinate in the refrigerator for at least 2 hours, turning occasionally.

Preheat oven to 400 degrees.

Skewer 2 thighs onto each bamboo skewer

Reserve the leftover marinade for basting.

Place chicken skewers in 1 layer onto a baking sheet and bake for 20 minutes, basting often with the remaining marinade.

Serve with roasted vegetables.

NOTES

NOTES

12

RECIPES INSPIRED BY CATCHING FIRE

"I open my eyes and find someone I cannot block out looking down at me. Gale."

KATNISS, *CATCHING FIRE* BY SUZANNE COLLINS, CHAPTER 27

CATCHING FIRE **NOT ONLY REVISITED** many of the foods that were introduced in *The Hunger Games*, but also introduced new foods to both the readers and the characters. Between the new foods and an abundance of symbolism, there's plenty of inspiration for food in this second volume of the trilogy.

PEPPERMINT ICE CREAM

SERVES 8

Peppermints that melted in her mouth made a big impression on Katniss. Here's another peppermint recipe that will melt in your mouth—this one's an ice cream.

The half-and-half and the egg yolks make this ice cream decadently rich and creamy. There's no comparison between this recipe and commercially-made ice cream.

1 ICE CREAM MAKER
1½ CUPS HALF-AND-HALF
¾ CUP SUGAR
4 EGG YOLKS
¼ TEASPOON SALT
2 CUPS WHIPPING CREAM
4½ TEASPOONS VANILLA EXTRACT
1 TEASPOON PEPPERMINT EXTRACT
½ CUP CRUSHED PEPPERMINTS

In a large saucepan, whisk half-and-half, sugar, egg yolks and salt.

Cook and stir over low heat until mixture reaches a thickness that coats the back of a metal spoon.

Remove from the heat. Place pan in a bowl of ice water and stir for 2 minutes.

Stir in whipping cream, vanilla and peppermint extracts.

Press plastic wrap onto surface of custard. Refrigerate overnight.

Fill cylinder of ice cream freezer ⅔ full. (Refrigerate any remaining mixture until ready to freeze.)

Freeze according to the manufacturer's directions.

Allow to firm in freezer.

Garnish servings with crushed peppermint.

LAMB CHOPS WITH A BALSAMIC PLUM REDUCTION

SERVES 4

Here's another variant of Katniss' beloved lamb and plums. She loved her lamb stew with plums dearly, despite her hatred for the Capitol.

This version of her favorite recipe uses a balsamic reduction that includes plum jam. The hint of sweetness goes very well with the rich lamb.

2 TABLESPOONS OLIVE OIL, DIVIDED
¼ TEASPOON SALT
PINCH FRESHLY GROUND PEPPER
4 LAMB CHOPS (¾-INCH THICK)
¼ CUP ONIONS, MINCED
½ CUP AGED BALSAMIC VINEGAR
¾ CUP CHICKEN BROTH
½ CUP PLUM JAM
1 TABLESPOON BUTTER

Rub the lamb chops with one tablespoon of olive oil, salt and pepper.

Heat the remaining tablespoon of olive oil in a large skillet over medium-high heat.

Place lamb chops in the skillet and cook for about 3 minutes per side for rare, or as desired.

Remove from the skillet and keep warm on a serving platter in the oven on the lowest setting.

Add onions and cook until browned.

Pour in vinegar and deglaze, scraping any bits of lamb from the bottom.

Stir in the chicken broth and plum jam. Continue to cook and stir over medium-high heat until the sauce has reduced by half.

Remove from heat and stir in the butter. Taste for seasonings. Serve sauce with lamb.

Balsamic vinegar has been produced in Italy since at least the Middle Ages, but the balsamic vinegar you buy at the store is not true, traditional balsamic vinegar. Traditional balsamic is a reduction made from fresh grapes and aged for at least 12 years, whereas supermarket balsamic vinegar is made from wine, usually without aging. While you can buy good balsamic vinegar in the store for less than $10, traditional balsamic can cost as much as $400.

LAMB'S NECK WITH SWEET ROOTS AND GREENS

SERVES 6

Katniss loved her lamb dishes and the use of lamb neck here pays homage to the characters' "snout to tail" use of any available meat. Served up with some sweet roots to honor Rue, and a batch of the greens that Katniss and Gale often relied on, this delicious recipe combines several of the most prominent foods in the Hunger Games *trilogy.*

Lamb neck isn't seen very often in recipes, but the meat is extremely flavorful and juicy, and the cut is less expensive than many other parts of the animal.

---

3 TABLESPOONS OLIVE OIL, DIVIDED
2 LARGE CARROTS, DICED
2 CELERY RIBS, DICED
1 LARGE ONION, DICED
2 CLOVES GARLIC, MINCED
1½ POUNDS LAMB NECK, TRIMMED OF MOST
    VISIBLE FAT
1 TEASPOON SALT
½ TEASPOON FRESHLY GROUND PEPPER
2 CUPS RED WINE
4 CUPS BEEF OR LAMB STOCK
3 CUPS SWEET POTATOES, PEELED AND
    QUARTERED
3 CUPS DANDELION GREENS, STEMS REMOVED
3 CUPS WATERCRESS, STEMS REMOVED

Preheat oven to 250 degrees with rack in middle.

In a large skillet, heat 1 tablespoon olive oil on medium heat and add carrots, celery, onion and garlic.

Cook for 5–7 minutes or until onions are translucent.

Remove from heat and pour the mixture into a roasting pan.

Add 1 tablespoon olive oil to skillet and turn heat to medium-high.

Brown lamb neck well on all sides, season with salt and pepper, then place on top of vegetable mixture in pan.

Do not wash skillet; set aside for later use.

Roast lamb and vegetables uncovered for 5 hours.

Return skillet to burner and heat on medium-high heat.

Once hot, pour in red wine and use a wooden spoon to deglaze the pan, being sure to loosen all of the browned bits on the bottom of the pan.

Add stock, turn heat to high and bring to a boil.

Reduce heat to medium-high and allow to simmer uncovered until reduced by about half. Set aside.

When lamb has roasted for 5 hours, pour hot stock over all, cover tightly with foil or lid and return to oven for 4 hours.

After 4 hours, arrange sweet potatoes around lamb, then cover again and return pan to oven for 1 more hour.

Remove pan from oven. Remove potatoes from pan and cover to keep warm. Allow lamb to cool enough to be handled.

Use a fork to scrape the meat from the bone, removing any connective tissue or excess fat as you go. Return the meat to the roasting pan and toss well.

Add 1 tablespoon oil to a large skillet and heat over high heat. Add dandelion greens and watercress, season with salt and pepper to taste, and cook just until wilted, about 1–2 minutes.

To serve, place greens on plate and ladle lamb and sauce mixture on top. Arrange potatoes around all and serve.

FRUIT-AND-HERB-STUFFED PORTOBELLO CAPS

SERVES 8 AS AN APPETIZER OR SIDE

Mushrooms and herbs were staples for the Everdeens and the Hawthornes, who relied on forest foods for both food and medicines. With the addition of dried fruits from the Cornucopia and some of Prim's goat cheese, these mushroom caps would have been a full meal for the characters.

Portobello mushrooms have a texture and flavor that almost mimic steak. This dish makes a great appetizer or even a nice entrée for a vegetarian meal.

8 LARGE PORTOBELLO MUSHROOMS, STEMS INTACT
1 TABLESPOON PLUS 1 TEASPOON OLIVE OIL, DIVIDED
1 CUP SWEET ONION, FINELY CHOPPED
2 CLOVES GARLIC, MINCED
¼ CUP DRIED CRANBERRIES, CHOPPED
¼ CUP DRIED APRICOTS, CHOPPED
2 TEASPOONS FRESH TARRAGON, CHOPPED
1 TEASPOON FRESH THYME, CHOPPED
2 TEASPOONS SALT, DIVIDED IN HALF
½ TEASPOON FRESHLY GROUND BLACK PEPPER
½ CUP BREADCRUMBS FROM STALE BREAD (NOT CANNED)
8 (1-INCH SQUARE) SLICES GOAT CHEESE
PAPRIKA TO GARNISH

Preheat oven to 400 degrees and line a baking dish with foil.

Rinse the mushrooms under cold water, removing dirt or grit, and pat dry.

Remove stems from the caps and chop the stems.

Heat 1 tablespoon of olive oil in a skillet on medium heat.

Add onion and garlic and cook for 2 minutes, stirring occasionally.

Add the cranberries and apricots and cook for 2 more minutes.

Stir in herbs and mushroom stems and season with salt and pepper.

Remove from heat and mix in the breadcrumbs.

Using up to 1 teaspoon of olive oil, brush the outside of each mushroom cap with oil.

Season the outside of each cap lightly with salt.

Fill caps with the vegetable mixture; top each with 1 piece of goat cheese and a sprinkle of paprika.

Bake for 10 minutes, or until cheese is bubbly.

ORANGE AND SWEET BERRY COOLERS

Katniss loved the flavor of orange juice, something she had only tasted once before going to the Capitol for her first Hunger Games. *This recipe combines fresh orange juice with Deceptively Sweet Berry Syrup for a refreshing and very pretty drink.*

This drink makes a great presentation to guests at a Hunger Games-*themed dinner or party.*

CRUSHED ICE
4 CUPS FRESH ORANGE JUICE
2 CUPS SODA WATER
1 FRESH LIME, HALVED
**8 TEASPOONS DECEPTIVELY SWEET BERRY
    SYRUP (REFER TO INDEX)**
8 LEAVES FRESH MINT

Fill 8 (12-ounce) glasses ¾ full with crushed ice.

To each glass, add ½ cup orange juice, then ¼ cup soda water.

Give each glass a squeeze of lime juice, and then top with 1 teaspoon of Deceptively Sweet Berry Syrup.

Do not stir. Garnish each glass with a mint leaf and serve.

FRESH ORANGE VANILLA RICE PUDDING

On her first visit to the Capitol, Katniss tasted orange juice for only the second time. This is another recipe that uses one of her favorite drinks.

The use of orange in this pudding makes it a very nice change from ordinary rice pudding. It's a pleasant combination of creamy and fresh.

---

5 CUPS WHOLE MILK
⅔ CUP SHORT-GRAIN WHITE RICE
2 TEASPOONS VANILLA EXTRACT
½ CUP SUGAR
1 TEASPOON GRATED ORANGE PEEL
ORANGE SEGMENTS

Combine the milk and rice in a medium saucepan.

Before heating, add the vanilla extract and stir well.

Bring the milk to a boil.

Reduce the heat to medium-low and simmer, stirring often, for about 25 minutes.

Mix in the sugar and orange peel.

Cook until the mixture thickens.

Divide the rice pudding into bowls.

Cover and refrigerate for 5 hours.

Serve with orange segments.

RUE'S COLD CARROT AND YAM PUREE

SERVES 4

In Catching Fire, *Rue was remembered not only for her character and heart, but also for her knack for finding useful and edible sweet roots. This dish pays homage to her special talents.*

This dish combines the sweetness of carrots and yams with just a hint of fire from the seasonings. It's a wonderful side dish for turkey or other poultry.

2 TABLESPOONS BUTTER
1 ONION, DICED
¼ TEASPOON GROUND GINGER
¼ TEASPOON RED PEPPER FLAKES
¼ TEASPOON GROUND CINNAMON
1 PINCH CAYENNE PEPPER
2 LARGE YAMS, PEELED AND DICED
3 CARROTS, PEELED AND CHOPPED
2 CUPS WATER
1 CAN CHICKEN BROTH
SALT AND PEPPER TO TASTE

Melt the butter in a large saucepan over medium-high heat. Add the onions and cook until golden brown.

Season with ginger, pepper flakes, cinnamon and cayenne and cook about 1 minute, until fragrant.

Add the yams and carrots, then add the water and broth.

Bring to a boil then reduce heat to medium-low, cover.

Simmer until the vegetables are tender, about 25–30 minutes.

Remove from heat and puree in batches in food processor or blender until smooth. Season to taste with salt and pepper.

EASY APPLE TART

MAKES 16 BARS

Apples were a happy find throughout the trilogy. This recipe celebrates the discovery of apples while paying homage to the tarts Mr. Mellark made in his bakery.

This tart looks impressively rustic and artisanal, but it's very quick and simple to make. Firm, slightly tart apples such as Fiji, Braeburn and Granny Smith work best.

2 CUPS ALL-PURPOSE FLOUR
½ CUP SUGAR, DIVIDED
¾ CUP BUTTER, CUBED
1 EGG YOLK, LIGHTLY BEATEN
3 TABLESPOONS COLD WATER
6 MEDIUM BAKING APPLES, PEELED, CORED AND
    CHOPPED
1½ CUPS GRANOLA WITH DRIED CHERRIES
½ CUP SLIVERED ALMONDS

In a bowl, combine flour and ¼ cup of sugar.

Work in butter with a wooden spoon until mixture resembles large crumbs.

Combine egg yolk and water.

Stir egg mixture into flour mixture and mix lightly.

Knead dough into a ball, adding flour as needed.

Press dough into bottom and sides of a 15 x 10 x 1-inch baking pan.

Bake at 350 degrees for 15 minutes.

Sprinkle the apples evenly over crust.

Combine granola, almonds and remaining sugar; sprinkle over apples.

Bake at 350 degrees for 50 minutes. Let cool, and then slice into 2 x 5-inch bars.

MELLARK'S WHOLE WHEAT CINNAMON RAISIN BREAD

Katniss and her family could never have afforded this bread from Mellark's Bakery. In fact, the Mellarks couldn't have afforded it themselves. When Peeta revealed that his family only ate the stale breads, Katniss further understood that they weren't as different as she had believed.

This moist, dense bread is delicious toasted for breakfast. If you like, you can drizzle a simple white icing over the top, but it's perfectly sweet as is.

1½ CUPS MILK
1 CUP WARM WATER
2 (.25 OUNCE) PACKAGES ACTIVE DRY YEAST
1 CUP RAISINS
1¼ CUP SUGAR, DIVIDED
½ CUP BUTTER, SOFTENED
3 EGGS
1 TEASPOON SALT
8 CUPS ALL-PURPOSE FLOUR
2 TABLESPOONS MILK
2 TABLESPOONS CINNAMON
2 TABLESPOONS BUTTER, MELTED

Scald the milk in a small pan, and when it begins to bubble, remove from heat. Let cool.

Dissolve yeast in warm water (110 degrees) in a large mixing bowl. When it is foamy, add the raisins, ½ cup sugar, butter, eggs and salt. Stir in the milk. Add the flour gradually to make a dough.

Knead dough on a lightly floured surface for 5 minutes. Put dough in a large, greased mixing bowl and cover with a damp cloth. Allow to rise in a warm place, until doubled in size.

Roll out on a lightly floured surface into a large rectangle, ½-inch deep.

Moisten dough with 2 tablespoons milk.

Stir together ¾ cup sugar and 2 tablespoons cinnamon and sprinkle mixture on top of the moistened dough.

Roll up tightly; the roll should be about 3 inches in diameter.

Cut into thirds and tuck under ends.

Place loaves into greased 9 x 5-inch pans.

Lightly grease tops of loaves with butter or vegetable oil.

Let rest for 1 hour.

Bake at 350 degrees for about 45 minutes.

Let cool before slicing.

PUMPKIN PIE WITH SLIVERED NUTS

SERVES 8

Katniss enjoyed the Capitol's pumpkin soup with slivered nuts. Pumpkin was apparently rare—if not non-existent—in District 12.

In this recipe, we combine the flavors of the Capitol's pumpkin soup into a delicious dessert. The graham cracker crust is a departure from traditional pumpkin pie and gives it a delicious flavor.

PIE:
1 (20-OUNCE) CAN PLAIN PUMPKIN
1 (10-OUNCE) CAN SWEETENED CONDENSED
   MILK
2 EGGS
½ TEASPOON GROUND CINNAMON
½ TEASPOON SALT
¼ TEASPOON GINGER
¼ TEASPOON NUTMEG
1 (9-INCH) GRAHAM CRACKER PIE CRUST

TOPPING:
½ CUP FIRMLY PACKED LIGHT BROWN SUGAR
½ CUP ALL-PURPOSE FLOUR
½ TEASPOON GROUND CINNAMON
3 TABLESPOONS BUTTER
½ CUP SLIVERED WALNUTS

PIE:

Preheat oven to 425 degrees.

In a mixing bowl, combine pumpkin, sweetened condensed milk, eggs, cinnamon, salt, ginger and nutmeg; mix well with wooden spoon.

Place mixed ingredients in pie crust and bake for 15 minutes. Reduce oven to 350 degrees and bake 30 minutes.

TOPPING:

In another mixing bowl, combine light brown sugar, flour and cinnamon; mix in butter until crumbly. Stir in slivered nuts.

Take pie from oven and top evenly with crumb mixture. Place back into the oven for 10 minutes.

Cool. Garnish as desired.

POTATO LEEK SOUP

SERVES 8

Potatoes were widely available in the Capitol, but not back home in District 12. Katniss might have made this with katniss roots instead of potatoes, and wild onions instead of leeks.

Potato leek soup is considered a gourmet delight, even though it's quite simple to make. The potatoes and leeks naturally enhance each other's flavors.

1 ONION, CHOPPED
4 TABLESPOONS OF BUTTER
8 POTATOES, PEELED AND CUBED
6 CUPS WATER
1 HAM BONE
1 CUP LEEKS, CHOPPED
½ TEASPOON FRESH THYME
1 CUP HEAVY CREAM
SALT AND PEPPER TO TASTE
½ TEASPOON PAPRIKA

In a large pot over medium heat, cook onions in butter until soft and translucent.

Stir in potatoes, water, ham bone, leeks and the thyme.

Bring to a boil, and then reduce heat and cover.

Simmer until potatoes are tender, roughly 20–30 minutes.

Take out the ham bone and puree soup with your food processor in batches, or with a hand blender.

Return to pot and slowly fold in cream, salt, pepper and paprika. Heat on medium-low and serve.

HAYMITCH-INSPIRED CABBAGE CASSEROLE

SERVES 8

Katniss couldn't stand the way Haymitch's home smelled of meat and cabbage. Perhaps he often cooked something like this recipe.

This casserole is a great dish to whip up on nights when you don't have much time to fuss. It also freezes well, so make an extra pan of it to save for another day.

5 CABBAGE LEAVES
1 TABLESPOON VEGETABLE OR OLIVE OIL
1 POUND CUBED, COOKED HAM
1 ONION, CHOPPED
1 PARSNIP, SHREDDED
1 CARROT, SHREDDED
1 STALK CELERY, THINLY SLICED
1 TABLESPOON TOMATO PASTE
1 CUP INSTANT RICE, UNCOOKED
4 CUPS TOMATO SAUCE, DIVIDED
1 CUP SHREDDED CHEESE SUCH AS CHEDDAR OR
    MONTEREY JACK, DIVIDED

Preheat oven to 375 degrees.

Heat a large stock pot with water. When the water boils, add the cabbage leaves and cook until they are pliable, about 5 minutes.

Meanwhile, heat a large skillet over medium-high heat. Add the oil and cook the onions.

Add parsnips, carrot and celery; cook 3 minutes, stirring occasionally.

Remove the pan from the heat and stir in tomato paste, rice, 3 cups tomato sauce and ¾ cup cheese mixture.

Drain cabbage and dry well. Remove the vein from the middle of each leaf.

Pour ½ cup of the remaining tomato sauce into a 3-liter round casserole dish sprayed with cooking spray or greased with olive oil.

Layer with 1 cabbage leaf and 2 cups rice mixture; repeat layers 3 times.

Top with remaining cabbage leaf, remaining sauce and cheese, then cover.

Bake 1 hour 10 minutes, uncovering after 1 hour to let cheese lightly brown.

Let stand 5 minutes before serving.

SWEET ASIAN WATERCRESS SALAD

Watercress was one of the many wild greens that Katniss was able to find at home. It would have been one of the first fresh vegetables she could eat in the spring, which would likely make it a traditional favorite for rural Appalachians.

The addition of Asian flavors makes this watercress salad unique and a nice change from typical mixed spring greens.

½ CUP OLIVE OIL
¼ CUP CIDER VINEGAR
½ CUP WHITE SUGAR, DIVIDED
2 TEASPOONS FRESH PARSLEY, CHOPPED
1 TEASPOON SALT
1 PINCH GROUND BLACK PEPPER
½ CUP SLICED ALMONDS
3 HANDFULS WATERCRESS, WELL RINSED
½ HEAD RED LETTUCE
1 RED ONION, CHOPPED
1 CUP CELERY, CHOPPED
12 OUNCES MANDARIN ORANGE SEGMENTS,
    DRAINED

In a container with a tight fitting lid, combine the oil, vinegar, ¼ cup sugar, parsley, salt and pepper.

Cover and shake. Refrigerate until use.

In a pan over medium-low heat, stir the almonds and ¼ cup sugar until the almonds are coated.

Remove from heat, cool and break apart. Store at room temperature.

In a large bowl, toss together the almonds, watercress, lettuce, onion, celery, oranges and dressing until evenly coated.

STEWED YAMS AND PLUMS WITH ORANGE JUICE

SERVES 6

This recipe incorporates the plums featured in Katniss' favorite lamb stew with the sweet roots so prized by her and Rue. It's a tribute of sorts to the unlikely, but meaningful, pairing of Rue and Katniss.

This dish makes a great side for a meat entrée at dinner, but it's also delicious at breakfast time. Try topping it with a dollop of vanilla ice cream for dessert.

6 LARGE YAMS, PEELED AND CUT INTO LARGE CHUNKS
1 CUP PRUNES
2 CUPS ORANGE JUICE
¼ CUP WHITE SUGAR
4 TABLESPOONS BUTTER, MELTED
1 TEASPOON GRATED ORANGE ZEST
½ TEASPOON GRATED FRESH GINGER ROOT

Place yams and prunes in a pot and cover with the orange juice.

Bring the mixture to a boil for 10 minutes.

Add the sugar and butter.

Simmer gently for 1 hour, or until the liquid is almost absorbed.

Sprinkle with orange zest and ginger and let simmer 5 minutes.

JUICY CHOCOLATE CITRUS CAKE

SERVES 12

This cake combines Katniss' fondness for orange juice and her taste for chocolate. It would have been a nice gift from her favorite baker.

This is an excellent cake to make with kids, or as an easy, yet delicious, dessert for unexpected company. It's very moist and will keep well for several days if covered.

1 (18.25-OUNCE) PACKAGE CHOCOLATE CAKE MIX
1 (3.5-OUNCE) PACKAGE INSTANT CHOCOLATE PUDDING MIX
1 CUP COLD WATER
½ CUP CANOLA OIL
4 EGGS
½ CUP BUTTER
¾ CUP WHITE SUGAR
¾ CUP ORANGE JUICE

Preheat oven to 350 degrees. Spray a large Bundt pan with cooking oil.

Combine the cake mix, pudding mix, water, oil and eggs.

Mix with an electric mixer on medium for 2 minutes until batter is smooth and well combined.

Pour batter into Bundt pan. Transfer to the oven and bake for 30 minutes or until a fork or toothpick inserted into the middle of the cake comes out clean.

Meanwhile, combine the butter, sugar and orange juice in a saucepan. Boil for about 2 minutes.

When the cake is removed from the oven, poke holes in the top of it with a fork then pour the orange juice mixture over it.

Place cake on a plate and dust top with confectioner's sugar if desired.

CHICKEN WITH ORANGE SAUCE

SERVES 4—6, DEPENDING ON SIZE OF THIGHS

Apparently the chefs in the Capitol were rather enamored by fowl paired with orange flavorings. Here's yet another recipe along that theme.

This recipe uses chicken thighs, which are wonderfully moist and flavorful, and also take a lot less time to cook than a whole roasted bird.

6 BONELESS, SKINLESS CHICKEN THIGHS
3 TABLESPOONS DIJON-STYLE MUSTARD
½ CUP ONION, CHOPPED
¼ CUP PACKED BROWN SUGAR
2 CUPS ORANGE JUICE, DIVIDED
2 TABLESPOONS WHEAT FLOUR

Preheat oven to 375 degrees.

Place chicken in a baking dish. Spread mustard evenly over the chicken and place chopped onion on top of chicken.

Coat lightly with ¼ cup of brown sugar and pour in just enough orange juice to cover chicken.

Bake for 45 minutes, then remove leftover sauce from baking dish and pour into a saucepan.

Whisk flour into sauce in saucepan.

Add enough orange juice to make a sauce, and heat on high until the sauce thickens.

Place chicken on a serving dish; pour sauce over the chicken.

TINY PLUM TARTS

Plums and tarts were both mentioned so frequently in the Hunger Games *trilogy that this cookbook would be incomplete without a recipe that combines the two.*

For this recipe, use red plums that are just shy of perfect ripeness. They'll hold their shape better than ripe fruit, and the cooking will bring out their flavor.

TART:
1 CUP BAKING WHEAT FLOUR
¼ CUP SUGAR
¼ TEASPOON SALT
¼ CUP BUTTER-FLAVORED SHORTENING
2 TABLESPOONS COLD WATER

FILLING:
2 CUPS SLICED PLUMS
3 TABLESPOONS SUGAR
1 TABLESPOON WHEAT FLOUR
1 EGG, LIGHTLY BEATEN PLUS 1 TABLESPOON
    WATER

Tarts were featured often in the *Hunger Games* trilogy. Perhaps this is because fruit was a rare treat in District 12. It could also be that a tart would be considered somewhat fancy and frivolous in a world where you eat food to survive, not to enjoy it. Interestingly, you don't need a tart pan to make a tart. For a more rustic look, lay the dough on a baking sheet and curl the sides up towards the center.

Preheat oven to 375 degrees.

TART:

Combine the flour, sugar and salt; cut in the shortening until crumbly.

Gradually add water, kneading with a fork until a ball forms.

Cover and refrigerate for at least 1½ hours.

On a lightly floured surface, roll pastry into a 9-inch circle.

Transfer to a foil-lined 15 x 10 x 1-inch baking pan.

FILLING:

Combine the plums, 3 tablespoons sugar and flour until well mixed.

Place mixture on the center of pastry.

Bring edges of pastry over filling, leaving a 3½ inch hole in the center uncovered.

Brush crust with egg wash, then sprinkle with remaining sugar.

Bake for 40 minutes, or until bubbly and crust is golden brown.

SAUTÉED APPLES WITH BROWN SUGAR AND CINNAMON

SERVES 4

Throughout the trilogy, it seems as though Peeta was always pulling an apple or some bread out of his bag. A few slices of one of his breads would go beautifully with this comforting fruit dessert.

Granny Smith apples are best for this recipe, but you can use Braeburn, Fiji or Gala apples if Granny Smiths are not available. They're all tart enough, and will hold their shape well during cooking.

¼ CUP BUTTER
4-5 GRANNY SMITH APPLES, PEELED, CORED AND SLICED ¼-INCH THICK
½ CUP COLD WATER
2 TEASPOONS CORNSTARCH
½ CUP BROWN SUGAR
½ TEASPOON GROUND CINNAMON
½ TEASPOON CARDAMOM

In a skillet or saucepan, melt butter over medium heat until no longer frothy.

Add sliced apples to the pan.

Cook, stirring nonstop until apples are slightly softened.

Dissolve cornstarch in water and pour into skillet or pan.

Add brown sugar, cinnamon and cardamom and mix well.

Boil for 2 minutes, stirring occasionally.

Remove from heat and serve alone, over ice cream or with pancakes.

CATCHING FIRE LAMB PUFFS

MAKES 18 PUFFS

This recipe is a play on Katniss' beloved lamb and the puffy bread she so enjoyed during her first visit to the Capitol. However, this recipe adds just a bit of spice as a tribute to Catching Fire.

The cardamom, cinnamon and chili give this dish its slightly spicy flavor, but it's not too spicy for kids or those who don't care for fire on their plate.

---

1 POUND GROUND LAMB

3 ONIONS, PEELED AND CHOPPED

5 GREEN CHILI PEPPERS, DICED

1 TABLESPOON DARK SOY SAUCE

1 TABLESPOON WORCESTERSHIRE SAUCE

2 TABLESPOONS GARLIC PASTE OR MINCED GARLIC

½ TEASPOON GROUND WHITE PEPPER

½ TEASPOON GROUND CINNAMON

½ TEASPOON GROUND CARDAMOM

½ TEASPOON GROUND CLOVES

1 (17.5-OUNCE) PACKAGE PUFF PASTRY SHEETS, THAWED

1 EGG, BEATEN

Combine the ground lamb, onion, chilies, soy sauce and Worcestershire sauce in a large pot.

Season with garlic paste, white pepper, cinnamon, cardamom and cloves.

Cook over medium heat, stirring occasionally, until the meat is evenly browned and the onions are tender, about 15 minutes. Cover and set aside.

Preheat the oven to 375 degrees.

Lay sheets of puff pastry out on a lightly floured surface. Cut each pastry into 9 squares and roll out to ¼-inch thickness.

Spoon about 1½ tablespoons of the meat mixture into the center of each square.

Brush the edge with water, fold corner over to form a triangle and press to seal. Do not overstuff the triangles or they will open in the oven.

Place the patties onto a foil-lined baking sheet with at least an inch between each. Brush the tops lightly with the beaten egg.

Bake for 12–15 minutes, or until golden brown all over. Serve hot.

JEWEL-COLORED MOSAIC GELATIN

This recipe may remind you of the jewel-colored jellies that were served with pheasant, vegetables and potatoes at the Capitol. It was a typically showy spread that was meant to impress the guests, especially the tributes.

These are extremely easy to make and kids love preparing this recipe, so it's a great project to do with your children. Kids also love eating these and they look great on a buffet table, so keep them in mind for your next Hunger Games *party.*

4 3-OUNCE PACKAGES OF FLAVORED GELATIN, SUCH AS LIME, RASPBERRY, ORANGE, ETC.
5½ CUPS BOILING WATER, DIVIDED
2 ENVELOPES UNFLAVORED GELATIN
½ CUP COLD WATER
1 (14-OUNCE) CAN SWEETENED CONDENSED MILK

Add each flavor powder to a separate bowl. Add 1 cup boiling water to each flavor.

Mix each for 2 minutes, until completely dissolved.

Pour each flavor of gelatin into separate small shallow containers sprayed with cooking spray. Refrigerate until firm.

Sprinkle unflavored gelatin over cold water; let stand 1 min. Stir in 1½ cups boiling water. Add condensed milk and mix well. Cool slightly.

When the flavored gelatin is firm, cut into cubes. Place the cubes of gelatin in a greased 13 x 9-inch pan. Pour milk gelatin mixture over cubes. Stir gently if necessary to distribute gelatin cubes.

Refrigerate 2 hours or until firm and cut into squares to serve.

PEPPER JACK AND CHIVE MUFFINS

MAKES 12 MUFFINS

This recipe is inspired by Katniss' love for Peeta's cheddar muffins. Delicious alone, these muffins will also go wonderfully with any of the Hunger Games soups.

These muffins make a delightfully different foundation for a sandwich and pack very well in a brown bag lunch. Fill them with ham, roasted turkey and veggies for a slightly Southwestern sandwich.

---

2 CUPS WHEAT FLOUR
1 CUP SHREDDED PEPPER JACK CHEESE
¼ CUP SHREDDED SHARP CHEDDAR CHEESE
1½ TABLESPOONS SUGAR
4 TEASPOONS DRIED CHIVES
2 TEASPOONS BAKING POWDER
1½ TEASPOONS GARLIC POWDER
¼ TEASPOON SALT
1 EGG, BEATEN
½ CUP MILK
½ CUP CONDENSED CREAM OF MUSHROOM SOUP
½ CUP CANOLA OIL

Preheat oven to 400 degrees.

Lightly spray 12 muffin cups or use paper liners.

In a large bowl, combine flour, Pepper Jack cheese, Cheddar cheese, sugar, chives, baking powder, garlic powder and salt.

In another bowl, combine egg, milk, cream of mushroom soup and canola oil and combine well.

Stir wet ingredients into dry ingredients until moistened through and spoon batter into the muffin pans.

Bake for 20 minutes, or until a toothpick inserted into a muffin comes out clean (it's ok if there's a little cheese stuck to the toothpick).

SKEWERED BIRD

MAKES 8 KEBABS

The game birds mentioned throughout the books inspired this simple take on meat-on-a-stick. The characters in the Hunger Games *trilogy frequently ate game birds, often roasted on a stick over open fire.*

Try this entree at your next barbecue or dinner on the deck. If you like, you can marinate the chicken overnight in the rub.

8 WOODEN SKEWERS
PAPRIKA
CHICKEN RUB FOR THE GRILL
4 SKINLESS, BONELESS CHICKEN BREASTS,
    CUT INTO CUBES
2 CUPS CAULIFLOWER FLORETS
1 ONION, QUARTERED
1 GREEN BELL PEPPER, CUT INTO
    BITE-SIZE SQUARES
1 RED BELL PEPPER, CUT INTO BITE-SIZE
    SQUARES
1 SWEET ORANGE PEPPER, CUT INTO BITE-SIZE
    SQUARES

Soak skewers in water for about 20 minutes or until saturated.

Preheat grill to medium temperature.

Season chicken with paprika and chicken rub, rubbing into meat gently.

Arrange chicken and vegetables on skewers.

Cook until chicken is done and opaque all the way through and vegetables are charred slightly. Be careful not overcook the chicken as it will dry out.

NOTES

13

AUTHENTICITY FOR THE ADVENTUROUS

"This is no place for a girl on fire."

KATNISS, *CATCHING FIRE* BY SUSANNE COLLINS, CHAPTER 18

IN *CATCHING FIRE,* the main characters were not only forced to find enough food to survive in the real world, they were also required to find enough food to live on in within the confines of the Arena. These recipes reflect some of the ingredients that were common in the Districts, but also those that were found in the Arena.

CHARRED TREE RAT

SERVES 6

The tree rat that Katniss caught, and Peeta charred on the force field was described as something not known in nature. However, it's a safe bet that squirrel is pretty close to a tree rat.

Catching your your own squirrels might pose a problem, but you can often find them at game meat butchers or online for a fairly reasonable price. You can also try asking around among your hunting neighbors.

---

3 LARGE SQUIRRELS, SKINNED AND GUTTED
SALT AND PEPPER TO TASTE
½ CUP BUTTER
8 GARLIC CLOVES
3 SPRIGS FRESH ROSEMARY LEAVES
CREOLE SEASONING
2 ONIONS, QUARTERED

Clean squirrels thoroughly.

Burn away any fur that clings to the meat.

Rinse the meat thoroughly using several changes of water and pat dry.

Salt and pepper the squirrels liberally.

Cut squirrels into serving pieces or leave whole.

Preheat oven to 350 degrees.

Line a 9 x 13-inch baking pan with foil. Make the foil big enough so you can fold over the top and seal.

Place the meat on the foil; rub down with butter and season with garlic, rosemary, salt, pepper and Creole seasoning.

Place onion around the squirrel on the foil.

Wrap the foil over the top and seal. Bake for 2 hours or until done.

While squirrel is cooking, pre-heat your grill.

When squirrel is done, remove it from foil and place on grill.

Grill over medium heat until the meat has grill marks. Rotate the squirrel ¼ turn and repeat.

Flip squirrel over and add grill marks to the other side.

SWEET RAW SHELLFISH

SERVES 9

Many people enjoy raw shellfish. Katniss, Peeta and the others certainly appreciated it when they were hungry. However, they only ate it raw because they were unable to safely build a fire.

This dish is extremely light and refreshing, and it makes a great appetizer for a summer barbecue or an outdoor party. If you can, enjoy it on the beach.

2 LARGE ONIONS, SLICED
1 CAN STEWED TOMATOES
¾ CUP FRESH LEMON JUICE
½ CUP OLIVE OIL
45 RAW, SHUCKED OYSTERS
1 CAN DICED TOMATOES
¼ CUP KETCHUP
3 GREEN ONIONS, CHOPPED
½ TEASPOON SOY SAUCE
2 TABLESPOONS FRESH PARSLEY, CHOPPED
½ TEASPOON GRANULATED SUGAR
SALT TO TASTE
HORSERADISH TO TASTE

In a saucepan over medium heat, add the sliced onions and just enough water to cover.

Bring to a simmer and cook just enough to soften about 5 minutes.

Remove from heat and drain. Rinse with cold water and drain again.

Place stewed tomatoes in a blender and puree.

In a large glass dish or bowl, combine the onions, lemon juice and olive oil.

Stir in the oysters, pureed tomato, diced tomato, ketchup, green onions and soy sauce.

Season with parsley, sugar and salt to taste.

Garnish with a dollop of horseradish.

AUTHENTIC ARENA CLAMBAKE

SERVES 4

This recipe combines the best of a traditional clambake with the foods that the tributes feasted on in the Arena. If you prefer your shellfish cooked rather than raw, this is a great way to have it.

Get the freshest seafood that you can find and be sure to check over the clams and oysters to be certain none have opened (this indicates that they're dead and possibly bad).

---

8 MEDIUM RED POTATOES, SCRUBBED
1 POUND CLAMS IN SHELL, SCRUBBED
½ POUND DEBONED COD
2 POUNDS FRESH OYSTERS, SCRUBBED AND SHUCKED
3 CUPS CHICKEN BROTH OR STOCK
¼ CUP DRY WHITE WINE (SAUVIGNON BLANC WORKS WELL)
½ CUP BUTTER
1 LOAF FRENCH BREAD

It's important to make sure you scrub the shellfish thoroughly to remove any sand or grit that will otherwise wind up in your food. Use a stiff brush and cold water when you scrub.

To shuck the oysters use an oyster knife or a butter knife.

Place the potatoes at the bottom of a large stockpot.

Cover with a layer of clams, then cod and finally the oysters.

Pour in the wine and enough chicken broth to fill the pot halfway.

You may not need all of the broth, depending on the size of your pot.

Cut the butter into cubes and place on top of the seafood.

Cover well by sealing the lid with aluminum foil.

Bring to a boil, then lower heat and simmer over medium-low heat for 45 minutes.

Remove from the heat and carefully remove the foil and lid.

Serve with French bread.

DISTRICT 4 SHELLFISH IN A SPICY CHILE SAUCE

SERVES 8

Shellfish was a rare treat for Katniss and her friends, but it was the specialty of District 4, which was in a coastal area.

This recipe is quite spicy, but delicious. It may not be exactly how they served it in District 4, but if you enjoy fire in your food, you'll like this dish. The Creole flavors give this dish a bit of a unique flair that will appeal to anyone who enjoys Cajun food.

3 TABLESPOONS OLIVE OIL
1 TABLESPOON BUTTER
3 (10-OUNCE) CANS CHOPPED CLAMS, DRAINED, WITH JUICES RESERVED
2 TABLESPOONS MINCED GARLIC
GROUND BLACK PEPPER TO TASTE
1 TEASPOON RED PEPPER FLAKES, OR TO TASTE
1 POUND PACKAGE LINGUINE
3 TABLESPOONS FRESH PARSLEY, CHOPPED

Heat the olive oil and melt butter in a large skillet over medium-high heat.

Add the drained clams and garlic; cook and stir for about 3–5 minutes.

Season with black pepper and red pepper flakes to taste.

Pour in the reserved clam juice. Reduce heat to low and simmer for about 10 minutes.

Meanwhile bring a large pot of salted water to boil.

Cook linguine according to directions. Drain pasta and toss with the clam sauce. Garnish with parsley.

HAZELLE'S AUTHENTIC BEAVER STEW

SERVES 4—6

Hazelle, a widow and the mother of Gale, Rory, Vick and Posy, was devoted to her family, and did everything she could to help them survive. This recipe is the authentic version of her beaver stew. Beaver was a rare find in District 12 and was treated with appreciation. It wouldn't have been unusual to make several meals out of one large beaver.

You can find beaver from specialty game purveyors online or go trap your own. It has a slightly gamey, but not unpleasant, flavor and is very tender when prepared correctly.

---

1 SMALL OR MEDIUM-SIZED BEAVER
BAKING SODA
1 QUART WATER
SALT AND PEPPER TO TASTE
1 CUP WHOLE WHEAT FLOUR
3 TABLESPOONS BUTTER
2 MEDIUM ONIONS, CHOPPED
3 CUPS OF BEEF BROTH (MAY NEED MORE
    DEPENDING ON SIZE OF POT)
2 CARROTS, CHOPPED
2 RED POTATOES, CHOPPED
2 STALKS CELERY, SLICED THIN
4 GARLIC CLOVES, PEELED, LEFT WHOLE
4 SPRIGS FRESH THYME
2 CLOVES
1 BAY LEAF

Remove all surface fat from beaver.

Cover meat with a weak solution of baking soda and water (1 teaspoon baking soda to 1 quart water).

Boil 10 minutes and drain.

Cut beaver meat into chunks, season with salt and pepper and toss in a large re-sealable plastic bag with whole wheat flour.

Heat a heavy pot with 3 tablespoons of butter at medium heat until the butter is no longer frothy.

Brown meat until all sides are golden brown. Do not overcrowd pot.

When golden brown, add onion and stir.

Add broth until pot is half full.

Stir well with a wooden spoon, scraping bits off bottom of pan for flavoring.

Cover and simmer for 30 minutes, stirring occasionally and making sure liquid stays above meat.

Add the rest of the veggies, thyme, cloves, bay leaf and salt to taste. Stir well and cover.

Cook 1 hour, keeping it at a simmer and stirring occasionally. Season with salt and pepper as needed.

Check regularly and make sure broth stays above all ingredients. Add more broth as needed.

When meat is tender and veggies are done, serve with bread.

Homemade stock or broth is much more flavorful than canned and will really add flavor to your soups and stews. Besides, it isn't difficult to make. Simply roast some marrow bones or soup bones in the oven for an hour, and then add to a pot with water, salt, pepper and the trimmings from celery, carrots, onions and other veggies. Simmer for a few hours, skimming the fat, then strain and cool.

SPIT-ROASTED GOAT

SERVES 32—40

Katniss remarked on the whole cows, goats and turkeys being spit-roasted in the Capitol. Such a feast of meat, which was so rare in District 12, must have been eye opening.

This is a very old recipe for roasting goat on a spit. It's long and involved, but if authenticity is what you seek, this is a great recipe to try. This method of cooking renders the goat moist and beautifully tender.

---

12 SPRIGS FRESH ROSEMARY
3 HEADS GARLIC, SEPARATED INTO CLOVES AND PEELED
1 WHOLE GOAT, ABOUT 25 POUNDS
2 LEMONS, HALVED
¼ CUP OLIVE OIL, DIVIDED, MORE AS NEEDED
3 TABLESPOONS SEA SALT, DIVIDED
1½ TABLESPOONS GROUND BLACK PEPPER, DIVIDED
3 LARGE ONIONS, QUARTERED
STAINLESS STEEL OR COPPER WIRE
1 LARGE FIREBOX
ABOUT 30 POUNDS OF CHARCOAL

Pull the leaves from 8 of the rosemary sprigs and put them in a food processor, along with the peeled cloves from the heads of garlic.

Finely chop. Refrigerate for 2 days! (It is worth the time.)

Put the goat on a large work surface with the chest cavity up.

Squeeze the juice from the lemons into a bowl, discarding the seeds but saving the rinds.

Rub the entire goat inside and out with the lemon juice.

Rub the entire cavity of the goat with ¼ cup of the olive oil and season the goat with salt and pepper.

Put the onions, remaining rosemary and lemon rinds into the cavity.

Push the spit rod through the goat, parallel to the backbone, and out through the neck or upper chest.

Lay the goat on its side with the cavity towards you so that you can wire the backbone to the spit rod.

Secure the goat to the spit rod using wire.

Slide the spit rod's skewers over the front and rear ends of the rod. Push the skewers firmly into the shoulders and thighs or hips of the goat, then tighten the skewers onto the rod.

Attach the hind legs and forelegs to the rod with wire, twisting the ends of the wire until secured. Afterward, attach the neck the same way.

Wire the goat cavity shut by sewing from one end to the other with 1 long piece of wire. Twist each end of the wire with pliers to secure it.

Rub the goat all over with the remainder of the olive oil, then sprinkle with 2 tablespoons salt and 2½ teaspoons pepper.

Roast over indirect heat for 4½–5½ hours, turning slowly but constantly.

When done, the meat should be well browned on the outside and tender on the inside, with some pink meat only near the bones. An instant-read thermometer inserted into the thickest parts of the thighs and shoulders should register 155 degrees.

Move the goat to a large, clean work surface and let rest for 20 minutes. Pull meat off bone and serve.

NOTES

NOTES

SECTION THREE
MOCKINGJAY

14 ESCAPE TO DISTRICT 13

15 HUNTING ONCE MORE WITH GALE

16 THE MISSIONS AND VICTORS' VILLAGE

17 RECIPES INSPIRED BY MOCKINGJAY

18 AUTHENTICITY FOR THE ADVENTUROUS

THE focus of *Mockingjay,* the third book of the trilogy, was the rebellion of the Districts against the Capitol, and Katniss' vital role as the face and symbol of freedom.

In *Mockingjay,* food was not featured as prominently as it was in *The Hunger Games* and *Catching Fire*. Katniss and the others were on the run or in battle for much of the book, thus most foods were only mentioned as memories of better times and better places.

Chapter 14 (Escape to District 13) features foods that nursed Katniss back to wellness, such as "Wish There Was Meat" Bean and Onion Stew. In Chapter 15 (Hunting Once More With Gale), recipes such as Wind in Your Hare Pie use the ingredients Katniss and Gale hunted in their brief trips above ground. Chapter 16 (The Missions and Victors' Village) offers more recipes from the pragmatic and industrious Greasy Sae, such as Greasy Sae's Chicken Fried Slop.

In Chapter 17 (Recipes Inspired by *Mockingjay),* you'll find recipes that recall the many characters and events of *Mockingjay,* including Panem Biscuits and Prim's Blackberry Cobbler. Chapter 18 (Authenticity for the Adventurous) is all about the adventure of eating foods that might be odd in the real world, but would have been gladly received in the districts of Panem. These include such unusual dishes as Greasy Sae's Holiday Stuffed Possum and Gale's Rat on a Stick.

No matter which dishes you choose to cook, eating them will deliver you back to District 13, back to the Victors' Village and back to the story that you hoped would never end.

14

ESCAPE TO DISTRICT 13

"Katniss Everdeen, the girl who was on fire, you have provided a spark that, left unattended, may grow to an inferno that destroys Panem."

PRESIDENT SNOW, *MOCKINGJAY* BY SUZANNE COLLINS, CHAPTER 1

KATNISS AND PEETA'S ESCAPE from the Arena at the end of *Catching Fire* was the beginning of a journey that would take them from tribute to revolutionary, and from closeness to fear, and eventually mistrust. In the first chapters of *Mockingjay,* the food was all about comfort, healing, sustenance, and nutrition.

GET YOU THROUGH 'TIL LUNCH HOT BREAKFAST GRAIN

SERVES 4

District 13 had nutrition down to a science and took an extremely utilitarian view of food. Food was strictly a tool for energy and survival, thus it was closely monitored and controlled. This is similar to how Katniss was viewed by President Coin—just a means to an end, with no extraneous facets other than the ones directly necessary to achieve her goals.

No particular grain was named in this recipe, but it's entirely possible that barley was used, as it was readily available in District 13. Thus, that's the one that we will go with.

**3 CUPS WATER
1 CUP HULLED BARLEY
¼ CUP HONEY
½ CUP DRIED CHERRIES
½ CUP GOAT'S MILK
1 TEASPOON CINNAMON
¼ TEASPOON SALT**

In a 2-quart saucepan, bring the water to a boil.

Reduce heat to medium and add the barley.

Cover and cook at a simmer for 30–40 minutes, or until about 20 percent of the barley has split open and most of the water is absorbed. The barley will be tender but still a little chewy.

Remove from heat and add the honey, cherries, goat's milk, cinnamon and salt and stir until incorporated.

With the exception of the salt, these last ingredients would probably have been considered frivolous in District 13 and wouldn't have been served. They would have been ingredients used regularly in District 12, however.

To reduce cook time to about 15 minutes, soak the barley overnight and drain before adding the water. The amount of cooking water remains the same regardless of whether you soak the barley or not.

DISTRICT 13'S MASHED BREAKFAST TURNIPS

SERVES 4

When Katniss was eating breakfast with Gale before her meeting with President Coin, he shared his turnips with her. Just minutes later, she made his company one of her contingencies to accepting the position of Mockingjay.

These turnips are sweet and subtle in flavor and unexpectedly good for breakfast, or as a side dish at dinner.

4 LARGE TURNIPS
1 TEASPOON SALT, PLUS EXTRA SALT TO TASTE
PEPPER TO TASTE
2 TABLESPOONS BUTTER
¼ CUP MILK OR CREAM

Peel and cube the turnips and put them into a 2-quart saucepan.

Cover with water and add 1 teaspoon of salt.

Bring to a boil and continue to cook until the turnips are tender, 15–20 minutes.

Remove from heat and drain. Transfer turnips to a medium-sized mixing bowl and season with salt and pepper.

Add the butter and mash until most of the big lumps are gone, then add the milk and use a hand mixer to mix until smooth.

If your turnips are a bit too thick, add a little bit more milk and a touch of butter until they reach a nice smooth consistency.

"WISH THERE WAS MEAT" BEAN AND ONION STEW

SERVES 4

One of Katniss' biggest pleasures was hunting with Gale, which is why she bargained daily hunting into her deal when she agreed to be the Mockingjay. Not only did she enjoy the simple pleasure of being outdoors and the freedom that being above ground represented, but District 13 was also in need of the meat.

Beans have long been used to add protein to a meal when meat is unavailable. This dish is so good that you won't miss the meat at all.

---

1 CUP PINTO BEANS
1 CUP BLACK-EYED PEAS
1½ TEASPOONS SALT
1½ TEASPOONS BLACK PEPPER
2 LARGE ONIONS, QUARTERED, WITH THE LAYERS SEPARATED

Sort the beans and black-eyed peas to make sure that there are no stones in them, and rinse.

Soak peas and beans overnight in enough cold water to cover them by 2 inches.

Drain beans and black-eyed peas, put them into a 4-quart stockpot and add 2 quarts of water and the salt.

Bring to a boil and reduce heat to medium.

Gently boil for 1¼ hours, or until beans are nearly tender, adding 2 cups of water as necessary to keep them from boiling dry.

When the beans are almost tender, add the pepper and onions, and cook for another 15–20 minutes.

Let the water reduce so that the broth thickens into a nice, hearty stew. Serve with District 13's Bread.

DISTRICT 13'S BREAD
MAKES 2 LOAVES

This is the type of bread that was served with the "Wish There Was Meat" Bean and Onion Stew. Remember, each district had its own bread, and it was a source of pride to them—it represented who they were.

Since District 13's tools tended to be rudimentary and their view of food was utilitarian, the bread was more like local artisan whole grain bread that we can buy in the markets. This recipe requires whole grain buckwheat flour, which was particularly indigenous to District 13.

---

4 CUPS WARM WATER (110 DEGREES)
3 PACKETS ACTIVE DRY YEAST
2 TABLESPOONS MOLASSES
2 TABLESPOONS HONEY
1 CUP MILLED FLAX SEED
½ CUP SUNFLOWER SEEDS
½ CUP TOASTED PUMPKIN SEEDS
5 CUPS WHOLE GRAIN WHEAT FLOUR
1 CUP WHOLE GRAIN BUCKWHEAT FLOUR
½ CUP WHOLE GRAIN BARLEY FLOUR
½ CUP WHOLE GRAIN RYE FLOUR
½ CUP BARLEY
1 CUP ROLLED OATS
1 TEASPOON SALT

Preheat oven to 375 degrees.

Dissolve the yeast in the water and let it stand for a few minutes to activate and get foamy.

Add the molasses, honey and seeds.

Combine the flours, barley, oats, salt, and mix well, reserving a cup or so.

Add to the foamy water and seed mixture 1 cup at a time until the dough starts to form.

Mix with your hands or a wooden spoon until dough comes together.

Flour a clean surface or cutting board with leftover flour.

Turn out dough onto floured surface.

Knead the dough by folding it in half, smashing it together with the heel of your hand, turning a quarter turn and repeating until the bread is nice and elastic.

Add flour in from the surface as needed to eliminate stickiness and make it smooth. If it's still sticky, just add a little more of your favorite flour until it's the right texture.

Once it's smooth and elastic, place the dough in a greased bowl (use vegetable or canola oil) and roll to lightly coat the loaf in oil.

Cover with a damp dishtowel, place in a warm, draft-free area and let rise until double in size, about 30 minutes to an hour.

Punch down the dough and separate into 2 separate loaves.

Cover and let rise again until double in size. Preheat oven to 300 degrees.

When dough is double in size, shape dough into 2 loafs or rounds.

Place loafs in the oven on the middle rack.

Bake 45–60 minutes, or until top of loaf is browned.

Remove from oven and turn the bread out onto a rack to cool. Allow to cool before slicing.

SLIGHTLY SLIMY BUT DELICIOUS GRAY FISH AND OKRA STEW

SERVES 6

This dish was served the first time that Katniss brought her preps into the dining room. Amid stares, pointing and explanations, the group gathered their meal and sat to eat. Perhaps this meal symbolically represented how Katniss felt about her recent deal with Coin and the resulting public announcement regarding her assignment as the Mockingjay.

The soup was described as tasting better than it looked, but with a slightly slimy texture that was hard to get down. Despite its texture, many people love the flavor of okra.

3 WHOLE LARGE TROUT
6 CUPS COLD WATER
1 CUP CELERY, CHOPPED
1 CUP ONION, CHOPPED
1 LARGE CARROT, PEELED AND CHOPPED
2 BAY LEAVES
2 CUPS SLICED OKRA
1 JALAPEÑO PEPPER, SLICED
1 GREEN BELL PEPPER, CHOPPED
2 CLOVES GARLIC, MINCED
2 TABLESPOONS OLIVE OIL
2 TEASPOONS SALT
2 TEASPOONS PEPPER
½ CUP GREEN ONIONS, CHOPPED

Clean and filet the fish. Cut the filets into chunks and set aside.

Take remaining fish bones and add them to a medium stockpot with 6 cups of water, celery, onion, carrot and bay leaves.

Bring to a boil, then simmer for 2 hours or until you have about 3–4 cups of stock.

Strain finished stock through a fine mesh strainer and reserve stock.

Add okra, jalapeño, bell pepper, garlic and olive oil to cleaned medium stock pot and sauté on medium-high heat for 5 minutes, or until vegetables are tender.

Add strained fish stock to vegetable mixture and bring to boil.

Add reserved fish filets and reduce to a simmer for 10 minutes, or until fish is cooked through.

Season with salt and pepper and garnish with finely chopped scallions.

FEEL BETTER FAST BREAD SOAKED IN WARM MILK

SERVES 4

Katniss awoke feeling like she'd let everyone down. The small amount of milk and bread that she had for breakfast reflected Katniss' belief that she had come up short.

For best results, use day old bread—it'll hold up better when soaking in warm milk. This is a great dish for cold mornings or a late night snack.

4 SLICES BRIOCHE BREAD (OR ANY KIND OF
   RUSTIC, HEARTY BREAD)
2 TABLESPOONS BUTTER, SOFTENED
2 TEASPOONS HONEY
2 TEASPOONS CINNAMON
1 CUP MILK (COW'S OR ALMOND WILL WORK
   WONDERFULLY)

Butter the bread, then drizzle with honey and sprinkle with cinnamon.

Cut into bite-sized pieces and spread onto an ungreased cookie sheet.

Bake in the oven at 400 degrees until toasted, about 10 minutes.

While the bread is baking, warm the milk up in a small saucepan and divide into 4 warm bowls or mugs.

Remove the bread from the oven and add the equivalent of 1 slice to each mug or bowl of milk.

SAY IT ISN'T SO BREAD AND CABBAGE

SERVES 6

After Katniss saw Peeta address her on TV, she was extremely upset. Once again, bread came to her rescue by simply filling her mouth up so that she could act normally in front of the others.

This dish is hearty enough to serve alone, but it goes very well alongside lamb or pork entrées. It has a simple, yet comfortably rich flavor.

1 MEDIUM HEAD OF CABBAGE
1 MEDIUM ONION
1 TABLESPOON SALT
1 TEASPOON PEPPER
2 CUPS WATER
1 TABLESPOON BUTTER
6 SLICES OF DISTRICT 13'S BREAD

Rough chop the cabbage and onion into medium-sized chunks.

Place the cabbage, onion, salt and pepper into a large skillet or wok and add the water.

Bring to a boil, then reduce heat and simmer until cabbage is tender, about 15 minutes, stirring occasionally.

Drain liquid and reserve cabbage.

Add the butter to skillet and increase the heat to medium-high.

Lightly brown the cabbage and onions.

Season with salt and pepper.

Remove from heat. Serve with a slice of District 13's Bread.

PEETA'S MINCED VENISON STEW

Katniss was so upset with Peeta when she went hunting with Finnick that she had a rare inattentive moment while stalking game—she almost missed a buck passing by. Fortunately, everyone still ate meat with dinner that night.

Venison is a fairly lean meat that dries quickly if not cooked carefully. This roast makes great use of a cut that can be tougher than others.

2 TABLESPOONS BUTTER
1 POUND VENISON ROAST, MINCED OR GROUND
2 TABLESPOONS FLOUR
3 CUPS WATER
1 CUP CARROTS, CHOPPED
1 CUP POTATOES, CHOPPED
½ CUP ONIONS, CHOPPED
2 TABLESPOONS SALT
1 TABLESPOON BLACK PEPPER
1 SPRIG ROSEMARY
½ TEASPOON THYME
1 CUP CELERY, CHOPPED

In a medium stockpot, melt the butter and lightly sauté the venison.

When brown, remove venison to a plate with a slotted spoon and set aside.

Add the flour and a little more butter as needed to make a roux.

Cook while stirring constantly until the flour is nicely browned. Be careful not to burn the roux.

Slowly whisk in 3 cups of water a ladle full at a time, whisking aggressively so that you don't get any lumps.

Add the carrots, potatoes, onions, salt and pepper, fresh herbs and venison to the pot and bring to a simmer.

Add more water if necessary to keep the vegetables well covered.

Cover and cook for about 15 minutes, or until the carrots start to get soft.

Add the celery and cook until the veggies are tender, about 1 hour.

HOT UNDER THE COLLAR GRAIN AND MILK

SERVES 2

Katniss ate breakfast after a long night spent thinking about Peeta's propo. This cereal may have reminded her somewhat of the hot grain that her mother often made at home.

This dish is very versatile. The addition of currents, nuts or bananas makes it an especially filling meal. You can substitute honey for the molasses to get a very different flavor.

---

1 CUP WATER
½ TEASPOON SALT
1 CUP QUICK OATS
½ CUP MILK
1 TABLESPOON MOLASSES
¼ CUP RAISINS

Bring the water and salt to a boil in a small saucepan.

Reduce the heat and add the quick oats, cooking for 1 minute while stirring.

Remove from heat and stir in the milk, molasses and raisins.

Divide into 2 bowls.

Though Katniss had mushy beets with hers, a toasted slice of District 13's Bread might go nicely with this rich, creamy dish.

MUSHIER THAN MUD BEETS

SERVES 4

Mushy beets accompanied Katniss' breakfast of hot grains and milk. Her entire meal that dreary morning seemed to reflect her feelings that everything was going badly, or turning to a bitter mush.

Beets have a wonderful natural sweetness brought to life during cooking. This dish would be delicious with a fish or lamb entrée.

4 WHOLE MEDIUM BEETS
SEASON TO TASTE WITH SALT AND PEPPER
2 TABLESPOONS BUTTER
1 TABLESPOON CINNAMON

The sweetest beets are usually the smaller ones, since larger beets typically have less sugar in them. To get beets with the most sugar content, choose smaller beets that have a moist, rather than woody, appearance. Beets with the greens still attached also have an added value: those greens are wonderful when sautéed with some bacon or oil and garlic.

Clean, peel and quarter the beets, then put them in a steamer.

Steam until a fork can be easily inserted into the beets, about 15 minutes.

Remove from the steamer and separate into 4 dishes.

Season with salt and pepper, then add a dollop of butter and a sprinkle of cinnamon to each beet and serve.

GOOD FOR YOUR SOUL PEA SOUP

After a hard day of production, Katniss was feeling the pressure. A hot bowl of this soup gave her a bit of comfort and some hope that she was not fighting in vain.

Split pea soup is one of the all-time great comfort foods. If you happen to have some leftover ham, add it to the soup for extra flavor and heartiness.

---

4 CUPS WATER

4 CUPS CHICKEN STOCK

1 POUND DRIED SPLIT PEAS

2 MEDIUM POTATOES, CUBED

2 MEDIUM CARROTS, PEELED AND CUBED

1½ CUPS CRUMBLED BACON OR CUBED HAM

1 CUP CELERY, CHUNKED INTO BITE-SIZED PIECES

2 MEDIUM ONIONS, CHOPPED

2 CLOVES OF GARLIC

1 TABLESPOON SALT

6 MEDIUM BASIL LEAVES, SHREDDED

1 TEASPOON RUBBED SAGE

1 TEASPOON BLACK PEPPER

In a Dutch oven or large stockpot, combine all ingredients and bring to a boil.

Reduce heat and simmer for 1–1½ hours, until the peas and veggies are tender.

Serve with some crusty bread.

NOTES

NOTES

15

HUNTING ONCE MORE WITH GALE

"While I was waiting, I ate your lunch."

HAYMITCH, *MOCKINGJAY* BY SUZANNE COLLINS, CHAPTER 8

IN *MOCKINGJAY* KATNISS AND GALE WERE hunting together again, but everything had changed. They had both been changed by the events that had taken place, and Katniss was conflicted about her feelings for both Gale and Peeta. In *The Hunger Games* and *Catching Fire,* Katniss longed to be back in the woods with Gale. When her wish finally came true, nothing was as it used to be.

WIND IN YOUR HARE PIE

SERVES 8

The first time that Katniss had the opportunity to go hunting with Gale above ground is a small dose of what it was like when she was free, before the Hunger Games.

If you're unable to hunt your own rabbit, check with online retailers or local game butchers. Get the rabbit fresh if at all possible in order to have the most flavorful meat.

RABBIT:
1 RABBIT
4 CUPS WATER
1 TEASPOON SALT

CRUST:
2 CUPS FLOUR
⅓ CUP MILK OR CREAM
¼ CUP BUTTER
4 TEASPOONS BAKING POWDER
2 TEASPOONS THYME
1 TEASPOON SAGE
¼ TEASPOON SALT

FILLING:
1 CUP SLICED CARROTS
½ CUP CELERY, CHOPPED
½ CUP ONION, CHOPPED
1 CUP RABBIT BROTH
1 CUP CREAM
2 TABLESPOONS FLOUR
1½ CUPS COOKED RABBIT
1 CUP GREEN BEANS, EITHER FRESH OR CANNED
2 CLOVES CRUSHED GARLIC
1 TEASPOON SALT
1 TEASPOON BLACK PEPPER

RABBIT:

Clean and debone rabbit and rinse and pat dry.

Place the cooked rabbit meat in about 4 cups of water and 1 teaspoon salt.

Bring to a boil and cook until meat is done, about 20 minutes. Rabbit has a texture similar to chicken, so when the meat "flakes," it's done. Cut rabbit into bite-sized pieces.

Continue to cook the broth until it has reduced by half. Use this as the rabbit broth called for in the recipe.

CRUST:

Preheat oven to 350 degrees. In a large mixing bowl, combine all of the ingredients well.

Form mixture into a ball and roll it out into a big circle on a lightly floured clean surface.

FILLING:

To make the filling, add the carrots, celery and onion to a pan.

Add enough broth to cover them and bring to a boil. Cook until the vegetables are tender but still firm in the middle, 10–15 minutes.

In the same bowl that you made the crust in, add the flour and cream, mixing until there are no lumps.

Add green beans and garlic, using only enough broth to make it "soupy."

Center the crust in a 9 x 9-inch pie plate with the edges hanging over.

Add the filling, then fold the crust over the top and pinch around the edges.

Brush with egg white or butter. Bake for 30–35 minutes, or until crust is brown and filling is bubbly.

Cool 15 minutes and serve.

CRISPY JUICY ROASTED TURKEY

SERVES 10

Turkeys were used in a variety of ways throughout the books, but there's no doubt that they were a prized food. Filling and nutritious, the meat is delicious with very little seasoning. It's a good analogy for the way in which District 13 lived: simple, utilitarian and efficient.

A small turkey such as this one will be especially tender and juicy. It would be delicious served with some of Rue's Cold Carrot and Yam Puree.

1 (8-POUND) WHOLE TURKEY
1 STICK BUTTER, ROOM TEMPERATURE
1 CUP MIXED FRESH GREEN HERBS, YOUR CHOICE (BASIL, PARSLEY, ROSEMARY AND THYME ARE GREAT)
2 TABLESPOONS SALT
1 APPLE

Preheat oven to 425 degrees.

Remove the neck and giblet pouch from the insides of the turkey.

Rinse the bird and make sure that all of the feather quills are out. Pat dry with paper towels.

Put the bird in a roasting pan.

Mix the stick of butter with the herbs.

Rub the salt on the entire bird along the outside of the skin, as well as inside the cavity.

Slide your hand between the skin and the meat of the breast.

Put about half of the herb butter between the skin and the meat.

Smear the rest of the herb butter inside the turkey and put the apple inside.

If you cover your bird with foil, make sure that the shiny side is toward the bird.

Put the turkey in the oven and allow to cook at 425 degrees for 20 minutes.

Reduce heat to 250 degrees and cook for 20 minutes per pound.

Start timing as soon as you reduce the heat. Leave the door shut as much as possible.

Remove the foil about 40 minutes prior to the bird being finished so that the skin can brown.

IT'S NOT REALLY DOG AND RHUBARB STEW

SERVES 8

In order to feed the people of District 12, Greasy Sae had to be extremely creative with her use of available ingredients. Many times she had to be creative about what constituted edible ingredients! Katniss told us that Greasy Sae's winter specialty included pig entrails, mice, meat, wild dog and tree bark. Needless to say, Greasy Sae's transition to the no-frills District 13 was a bit of a change, and not, according to her, for the better.

The sweetness of the turnips and tartness of the rhubarb give this stew a unique and complex flavor. It's a great way to use up leftover roasted venison, too.

2 TABLESPOONS BUTTER
2 POUNDS VENISON ROAST, CHUNKED INTO BITE-SIZED PIECES
1 LARGE ONION, CHOPPED
2 CLOVES GARLIC, MINCED
1 TABLESPOON SALT
1 TEASPOON BLACK PEPPER
2 ROSEMARY SPRIGS
1 POUND FRESH RHUBARB, CUBED
2 LARGE TURNIPS, CUBED
2 TABLESPOONS FLOUR
ABOUT 4 CUPS WATER, WARMED

Heat butter over medium heat in a medium-sized skillet.

Add the venison and brown well on all sides.

Add onion, garlic, salt, pepper, and rosemary.

Simmer, covered, for 1½ hours, or until meat is tender.

Add the rhubarb and turnips. If they aren't covered with water, add more water until they are.

Combine flour and water and stir into the stew.

Bring to a simmer and cook until the veggies are tender and the water is reduced to a nice rich broth, about 25 minutes.

DELICIOUSLY SIMPLE GRILLED GROOSLING KEBABS

Groosling is an important food throughout the Hunger Games trilogy. It's not only necessary to sustain Katniss, but it often brought her warm memories of times with Gale and Rue.

These goose kebabs are tender, delicious and filling—in other words, the perfect comfort food. They're also a great way to use the breast of the bird without it getting too dry.

---

6 SKEWERS, METAL OR BAMBOO

3 GOOSE OR DUCK BREASTS, CUT INTO
   BITE-SIZED CUBES

1 TABLESPOON KOSHER SALT

6 SLICES OF BACON, QUARTERED

2 GREEN PEPPERS, CUT IN EIGHTHS

12 MEDIUM BABY BELLA MUSHROOMS

If you're using bamboo skewers, soak them well in cold water for half an hour or so before using.

Sprinkle the kosher salt over the goose cubes and wrap each one in bacon.

Starting with the meat, alternately skewer the goose, peppers and mushrooms evenly onto the skewers.

Place skewers on grill or over fire and rotate as necessary until the meat is done and the veggies are tender, about 15 minutes.

NOTES

16

THE MISSIONS AND VICTORS' VILLAGE

"What do you think, Peeta?"

"I think you still have no idea the effect you can have."

KATNISS & PEETA, *MOCKINGJAY* BY SUZANNE COLLINS, CHAPTER 25

WHILE PREPARING FOR and eventually going on their missions, Katniss and the others were concerned only with eating enough to live so that they could fight for everyone else to survive. The foods in this chapter are filling, basic and inventive.

GREASY SAE'S CHICKEN FRIED SLOP

SERVES 4

Although Katniss, Gale and Peeta may have questioned what was in Greasy Sae's "slop," they were always grateful to have it. It may not have been lamb stew, but it was hot and it was filling.

This recipe has just enough spice to appeal to those who like a kick to their meal, but it's not overly spicy. Pair with a green salad for a delicious yet light meal.

CHICKEN:
½ CUP FLOUR
1 TEASPOON SALT
1 TEASPOON BLACK PEPPER
1 TEASPOON CAYENNE PEPPER
¼ CUP MILK
4 CHICKEN CUTLETS
3 TABLESPOONS PEANUT OIL

GRAVY:
4 TABLESPOONS PAN DRIPPINGS
2 TABLESPOONS FLOUR
½ CUP CHICKEN BROTH
½ CUP MILK
½ TABLESPOON SALT
½ TABLESPOON BLACK PEPPER

CHICKEN:

Mix the salt, black pepper and cayenne pepper into the flour.

Put the milk in a flat bowl and the flour on a plate.

Lightly coat the first cutlet in flour, and then dredge in the milk.

Coat it with the flour again and add it to the hot peanut oil in your skillet. Repeat with the other 3 cutlets.

Fry one side of cutlet on medium heat until it is golden brown, then flip it.

Once the other side is golden brown remove from skillet. Place on a paper towel to drain.

GRAVY:

Combine pan drippings and flour in saucepan and heat over medium flame.

Continuously stir with a whisk until the flour is smooth.

Brown the flour then slowly add the chicken broth, followed by the milk.

Add salt and pepper.

Continue to cook for about 5 minutes, until gravy thickens.

Plate the chicken cutlets and drizzle the gravy over them.

GREASY SAE'S SERIOUSLY BEEF STEW

SERVES 8

This is a big, hearty stew that has a tomato base. It's really a stick-to-your-ribs type of meal, and that's exactly what was needed in Mockingjay. *A full belly is a wonderful thing and is to be appreciated for what it is—good fortune.*

The longer this stew sits, the better it will taste. Make it a day or two ahead or make an extra pot for eating later. The flavors intensify over time.

2 TABLESPOONS PEANUT OIL
2 POUNDS BEEF TIPS, CUBED
2 CUPS WATER
4 POTATOES, WASHED AND CUBED
4 STALKS OF CELERY, CHOPPED
4 CARROTS, PEELED AND CHOPPED
4 TOMATOES, CHOPPED
1 CAN TOMATO PASTE
2 TABLESPOONS SALT
2 TABLESPOONS DRIED BASIL
1 TABLESPOON BLACK PEPPER
2 SPRIGS ROSEMARY

Heat oil in a large stockpot on high heat.

Brown the meat, turning to make sure all sides are evenly browned.

Add 2 cups of water to deglaze the pot and use a wooden spoon to scrape up the brown bits.

Combine the rest of the ingredients in the stockpot and add enough water to cover the vegetables and meat, plus a few inches.

Bring to a boil and simmer for 1½–2 hours, or until the meat and veggies are tender.

NOT FROM A CAN COD CHOWDER

SERVES 4

When Katniss was digging through an empty apartment looking for something to eat, she took a can of generic cod chowder, but Peeta gave her a can of lamb stew. That was her favorite meal at the Capitol and it takes them back to shared memories, as food often does.

If you're not able to get cod, use another firm-fleshed fish such as haddock. These fish will hold together better than the flakier types, which tend to fall apart in soup or a stew.

3 SLICES BACON, FINELY CHOPPED
1 ONION, DICED
2 RIBS CELERY, DICED
1 MEDIUM CARROT, PEELED AND CHOPPED
1½ TEASPOONS FRESH THYME LEAVES, CHOPPED
1 BAY LEAF
1 POUND RED POTATOES, CUT INTO ⅓-INCH DICE
2 (8-OUNCE) BOTTLES CLAM JUICE
2 CUPS CHICKEN BROTH
1 POUND COD FILETS, CUT INTO ¾-INCH PIECES
½ CUP CORN
SALT AND PEPPER TO TASTE
2 TABLESPOONS FLOUR
1 CUP HALF-AND-HALF, HEATED

In a heavy stockpot, fry the bacon and remove, leaving the grease in the bottom.

Add the onion, celery, carrot, thyme and bay leaf to the bacon grease and cook for 10 minutes, or until tender.

Toss in the potatoes, clam juice and broth and bring to a boil.

Cook 5 minutes, or until potatoes are almost tender but still have resistance in the center when poked with a fork.

Add the cod and the corn, and season with salt and pepper.

In a separate bowl add flour to the cream and whisk until smooth and there are no lumps.

Remove stockpot from heat and add the bacon bits and cream.

Return to heat just long enough to get it hot again.

Taste and add more salt and pepper as necessary.

FANCY CAPITOL CREAM-FILLED COOKIES

MAKES 2 DOZEN

Katniss was eating from a box of cookies while watching her eulogy by President Coin. Like Coin's words, these cookies are light and fluffy, with no real substance or nutritional value. They do taste excellent though.

These cookies take a bit of time to make, but if you enlist the help of children or friends, the project can be fun. The results are certainly worthwhile.

COOKIES:
2 CUPS SUGAR
1 CUP BUTTER (NO SUBSTITUTES), SOFTENED
2 EGGS
1 TEASPOON VANILLA
3 CUPS ALL-PURPOSE FLOUR
⅔ CUP BAKER'S COCOA
1 TEASPOON BAKING SODA
1 TEASPOON SALT
½ CUP MILK

CREAM FILLING:
½ CUP BUTTER, SOFTENED
1½ CUPS POWDERED SUGAR
1 CUP MARSHMALLOW FLUFF
1 TEASPOON VANILLA

COOKIES:

Cream together the sugar and butter, making sure that it's nice and fluffy.

Add the eggs to the creamed mixture, beating well between each, then add the vanilla.

Combine the dry ingredients in a separate bowl, and add to the creamed mixture a little at a time, alternating with adding the milk.

Refrigerate overnight, or at least a couple of hours.

Preheat oven to 375 degrees.

Drop by rounded teaspoonful onto a greased cookie sheet, making sure to leave 2 inches between each. Bake for 10–12 minutes until edges are firm. Remove from oven and cool completely.

CREAM FILLING:

Combine the butter, powdered sugar, marshmallow fluff and vanilla. Blend well.

Spread filling on one side of half of the cookies.

Put the other half of the cookies on top to create a sandwich.

Store for up to a week in the fridge.

Butter makes much better cookies than margarine, which is why most recipes call for real butter. Margarine is made from oil, not milk, and most butter substitutes have a great deal of water in them. This greatly affects the texture and flavor of homemade cookies. If a recipe calls for unsalted butter and all you have is salted butter, just omit half the added salt called for in the recipe.

GREASY SAE'S PLUM LAMB STEW

SERVES 10

In this version, the sweetness of the plums plays beautifully with the savory tones of the meat and veggies. Just like when Peeta and Katniss shared memories of the lamb stew at the Capitol, the feelings were bittersweet.

Lamb shoulder tends to be tough, so it's one of the less expensive cuts of lamb. This recipe makes the most of the shoulder's flavor while keeping it tender and moist.

1½ POUNDS BACON, DICED
6 POUNDS BONELESS LAMB SHOULDER, CUT
    INTO 2-INCH PIECES
½ CUP ALL-PURPOSE FLOUR
½ TEASPOON SALT
½ TEASPOON GROUND BLACK PEPPER
1 LARGE ONION, CHOPPED
3 CLOVES GARLIC, MINCED
½ CUP WATER
4 CUPS BEEF STOCK
1 CUP PLUMS, CHOPPED
4 CUPS DICED CARROTS
2 LARGE ONIONS, CUT INTO BITE-SIZE PIECES
3 POTATOES
1 CUP BEEF STOCK
1 TEASPOON DRIED THYME
2 BAY LEAVES

Fry the bacon in a large, heavy stockpot and drain on paper towels, leaving all but one tablespoon of bacon grease in the pot.

Toss the lamb, flour, salt and pepper in a mixing bowl to coat.

Add meat to the pot and brown on all sides, then remove and set aside on a plate.

Add the onion and garlic to the pot and cook until starting to brown. Add ½ cup of water to the pan to deglaze it.

Add the reserved bacon, plums, carrots, onions, potatoes, stock, thyme, bay leaves and lamb. Bring to a boil. Reduce heat and simmer for about 1½ hours or until tender.

BETTER THAN NOTHING BREAD WITH MOLDY CHEESE AND MUSTARD SAUCE

SERVES 8 AS AN APPETIZER

Seeing this dish on a shelf reminded Katniss that some people in the Capitol don't have full bellies and would be grateful to have anything to eat. We've made it much tastier for you, so enjoy!

The addition of honey to this dish may seem odd, but it works beautifully with the blue cheese. You can also use Roquefort in this recipe if you don't have blue on hand.

1 LOAF DISTRICT 13'S BREAD, CUT INTO
   BITE-SIZED CUBES
1 POUND BLUE CHEESE, CRUMBLED
¼ CUP DIJON MUSTARD
¼ TABLESPOON HONEY
1 TABLESPOON MAYONNAISE
2 TEASPOONS LEMON JUICE

Preheat oven to 350 degrees.

Spread bread cubes out in a layer and sprinkle the blue cheese crumbles over them.

Bake for 15 minutes, or until cheese is melting and bread is toasted.

Set aside to cool.

In a small bowl, combine the mustard, honey, mayo and lemon juice. Mix well and place in a dip bowl.

Arrange the breadcrumbs on a serving plate around the dip.

CAPITOL LIVING LIVER PATE

SERVES 4

Liver pate has been a staple for both the rich and poor for centuries, though the ingredients differ vastly between the two. When back at the Capitol, one of Katniss' biggest advantages was that she once again had access to unlimited food. Here's an example of the pate that she may have eaten for breakfast.

Have your supermarket butcher grind the pork shoulder for you if it isn't available packaged. Most supermarkets offer this service for free.

1 TABLESPOON COGNAC OR BRANDY
1 CLOVE GARLIC
1 SPRIG PARSLEY
½ SMALL WHITE ONION
½ TEASPOON ALLSPICE
½ TEASPOON SALT
¼ TEASPOON FRESHLY GROUND PEPPER
DASH OF CAYENNE
½ POUND FINELY GROUND PORK SHOULDER
½ POUND CLEANED, FINELY GROUND LIVER—
    CHICKEN, CALF OR PIG
SLICED BACON—ABOUT ¼ POUND

Preheat oven to 350 degrees.

Mix the alcohol, garlic, parsley, onion, allspice, salt, pepper and cayenne in a blender or food processor and pulse until finely chopped.

Add the ground meat in a little at a time and continue to pulse until a fine paste is achieved.

Line a terrine with bacon and add the meat mixture.

Top with bacon and place in a larger baking dish in a water bath. This is important because it keeps your pate moist and gives it a smoother texture.

Bake for about 1½ hours.

Cool under a weighted plate or cutting board so that it will set firm with a smooth texture.

Chill for several hours or overnight.

Serve with pieces of District 13's Bread.

CAPITOL FIG COOKIES
MAKES ABOUT 2 DOZEN COOKIES

Katniss would never have eaten these if she had not been the "guest" of the Capitol, because sugar and sweet treats were enormously expensive. It's a great representation of the difference between the Capitol—which had so much—and the districts—which had so little.

The taste of these cookies is similar to Fig Newtons, but don't be deceived, the flavor and texture of these homemade treats are far superior to what you can get at the store.

DOUGH:
2 CUPS SHORTENING OR BUTTER
1½ CUPS SUGAR
3 MEDIUM EGGS
1 TABLESPOON VANILLA EXTRACT
¼ TEASPOON SALT
4 CUPS ALL-PURPOSE FLOUR
4 TEASPOONS BAKING POWDER
1 CUP WHOLE MILK

FILLING:
2 POUNDS DRIED FIGS
½ FRESH ORANGE, WITH PEEL
1 SMALL APPLE
½ CUP WATER (OPTIONAL)
¾ CUP PECANS, CHOPPED
1 TEASPOON GROUND CINNAMON
1 CUP RAISINS
¼ CUP SUGAR

Preheat oven to 375 degrees.

DOUGH:

Cream the shortening/butter and sugar together with an electric mixer until fluffy.

Slowly add the eggs, vanilla and salt and continue to mix on medium.

Add the flour and baking powder a little bit at a time then knead the dough until smooth.

Add just enough of the milk to make it workable but not sticky. If it gets sticky, just add a little more flour.

FILLING:

Dice figs, orange and apple, then grind the mix in a food processor or blender.

If it's too dry, add some of the water, but usually the juice from the orange and apple is sufficient.

Add the nuts, cinnamon, raisins and sugar, and either stir or knead by hand.

Roll dough out into a strip about 6 inches wide. Put the fig mixture down the center (the long way), then wrap the dough over it to seal (think Fig Newton while you're doing this).

Slice cookies every 2 inches or so and place on an ungreased cookie sheet, leaving a bit of room between them.

Bake 10-15 minutes, or until cookies start to brown.

TIGRIS' HAM AND POTATO HASH

SERVES 4

This was the first hot meal that Katniss had eaten in days. When she smelled it while Tigris was cooking, she actually drooled, and you will too. This is probably a close rendition of what they ate.

This is a great way to use leftover ham and makes a very hearty dish for either breakfast or dinner. Serve with a vegetable or some fresh fruit and you will have a complete meal.

Heat the oil in a large skillet or wok on high heat.

Add all ingredients.

Cook on medium heat, stirring frequently, until the potatoes are tender.

Serve immediately.

2 TABLESPOONS OIL, YOUR CHOICE
1 POUND SMOKED HAM, CHOPPED
4 MEDIUM POTATOES, CUBED SMALL
1 TEASPOON DRY ROSEMARY
1 TEASPOON SALT
½ TEASPOON BLACK PEPPER

GREASY SAE'S EGGS AND TOAST

SERVES 2

Everybody has a way in which they express love, concern or the desire to help. Greasy Sae's method was always through food. When Katniss returned to District 12, she awakens on her first morning to Greasy Sae banging in the kitchen, making her eggs and toast. Katniss didn't know her motive, but from Sae's position throughout the books, it's pretty safe to assume that it was love and concern.

Simple yet sustaining, this meal is a good representation of Greasy Sae herself. It's also easy to make and very comforting.

2 SLICES RUSTIC WHITE BREAD
1 TABLESPOON OIL
2 EGGS
¼ TEASPOON SALT
¼ TEASPOON BLACK PEPPER
2 TABLESPOONS BUTTER
4 TEASPOONS BUTTER
1 TEASPOON CINNAMON
1 TEASPOON SUGAR

Put the slices of bread in the toaster.

Heat the oil in the skillet and carefully crack both eggs in. Salt and pepper to taste.

Cook for 2 minutes on the first side, then carefully loosen the edges of the eggs and turn them with a spatula. Be sure to keep the yolks intact.

Cook another 2 minutes and remove carefully from the skillet to a plate.

Remove the toast from the toaster and butter each slice.

Lightly sprinkle the cinnamon and sugar over the slices, and then cut each slice in half, diagonally.

Place 2 pieces on either side of the eggs.

BUTTERCUP'S BACON AND FRENCH TOAST

SERVES 4

Near the end of the book, Prim's cat Buttercup arrived home beaten and battered but alive, much like Katniss. When Peeta shows up with a loaf of warm bread and Greasy Sae makes breakfast, Katniss gave Buttercup all of her bacon. They had both lost Prim, and now Katniss would care for Buttercup as Buttercup had cared for Prim.

For the best results, use day old bread for this recipe. It soaks up the flavors of the egg mixture without getting soggy.

---

1 POUND HICKORY SMOKED BACON
1 CUP MILK
2 EGGS
1 TEASPOON VANILLA
1 TEASPOON CINNAMON
¼ TEASPOON NUTMEG
1 TABLESPOON OIL
8 SLICES RUSTIC WHITE BREAD
1 STICK BUTTER, DIVIDED
3 TABLESPOONS CONFECTIONER'S SUGAR

Fry the bacon in a skillet until crispy and set aside in a warm place.

Add the milk, eggs, vanilla, cinnamon and nutmeg to a medium-sized bowl and mix well.

Heat the oil in a skillet or griddle.

Dredge a slice of bread through the milk and egg mixture and place in the hot skillet.

Repeat for 2 more slices, or until the skillet or griddle is full.

Fry on medium heat for 3 minutes on the first side, checking after 2 minutes to make sure it doesn't burn.

Flip and fry on the other side for 2 minutes.

Place 2 slices on each plate and add 1 tablespoon of butter.

Lightly sprinkle with powdered sugar. Serve with maple syrup or strawberries, and of course the bacon.

FINNICK AND ANNIE'S WEDDING CIDER

YIELDS 1 GALLON OR 16 SERVINGS

Apples have long been a sign of health and happiness. Cider is usually shared at times of great happiness and is often part of the memories that are created. The fact that Finnick and Annie's wedding toast was made with cider represented the richness and pleasure shared by two people for whom the occasion was only a distant dream at one point.

If the apple juice is fermented, cider has an alcoholic content similar to ale. This is the non-alcoholic version.

8 CUPS WATER
8 CUPS APPLE JUICE
2 (12-OUNCE) CANS OF FROZEN APPLE JUICE
   CONCENTRATE
2 MEDIUM APPLES, PEELED, CORED AND DICED
2 CUPS CRANBERRIES
2 MEDIUM ORANGES, PEELED AND SECTIONED
2 CINNAMON STICKS

In a stockpot, combine all ingredients.

Cover and cook on low for about 2 hours, or until all the flavors have melded.

Remove fruit and cinnamon sticks with a slotted spoon or strain. Serve immediately or chill if you prefer it cold.

FINNICK AND ANNIE'S WEDDING CAKE

Though there wasn't a clear description about the flavor or size of Finnick and Annie's wedding cake, there was the impression that it was grand, because it took Peeta days to decorate. The decorations are up to your imagination, but here's a good, rustic cake recipe that may very well have been used as the foundation for this gorgeous, decadent creation.

Use cake flour for best results with this recipe. It's available in the same section as regular flour, but yields a more tender crumb.

BUTTER
2½ CUPS SIFTED CAKE FLOUR
1¾ CUPS SUGAR
3 TABLESPOONS DRY MILK
3 TEASPOONS BAKING POWDER
1 TEASPOON SALT
1 CUP WATER
⅔ CUP WHITE SHORTENING
1 TEASPOON WHITE VANILLA
¼ TEASPOON ALMOND EXTRACT
5 EGG WHITES, UNBEATEN

Preheat oven to 350 degrees. Butter and flour a 9 x 12-inch rectangle or 10 x 10-inch round pan.

In a large bowl, combine the flour, sugar, dry milk, baking powder and salt.

Add in the water, shortening, vanilla and almond extract.

Beat at medium speed for 2 minutes then add the egg whites and beat for another minute.

Pour into prepared pan.

Bake for about 30 minutes, or until sides and center of the cake spring back when touched.

NOTES

NOTES

17
RECIPES INSPIRED BY MOCKINGJAY

"My name is Katniss Everdeen. I am seventeen years old. I am from District 12. There is no District 12. I am the Mockingjay."

KATNISS, *MOCKINGJAY* BY SUZANNE COLLINS, CHAPTER 25

THERE WERE FAR FEWER references to food in *Mockingjay* than in the other books of the trilogy. This is partly due to the fact that there was less food available to the characters as they took refuge in District 13 and went into battle. In an effort to survive, times of scarcity often lead cooks to get very creative with what they have. According to Greasy Sae cooks in District 13 lacked imagination, however, there's plenty of inspiration in *Mockingjay,* if creativity is given free rein.

PANEM BISCUITS
MAKES 1 DOZEN BISCUITS

Throughout the districts, bread was used to sustain life, but it was also symbolic throughout the trilogy.

This recipe for biscuits is simple and common to the area. It's highly probable that they were a staple among all classes.

---

2 CUPS ALL-PURPOSE FLOUR
4 TEASPOONS BAKING POWDER
3 TEASPOONS SUGAR
½ TEASPOON SALT
1 STICK BUTTER
1 EGG
⅔ CUP MILK

Preheat oven to 450 degrees.

In a medium bowl, mix the dry ingredients well.

Cut the butter into the flour mixture until it's distributed throughout in pea-sized balls.

Add the egg, and then stir in the milk just until well mixed. Do not over mix or the biscuits will be tough.

Using an ice cream scoop, drop biscuit dough onto a greased pan and pat down so that the dough is about an inch thick.

Arrange so that the biscuits are just touching.

Bake for 8–10 minutes, or until browned.

It's very easy to make your own biscuit mix, and it's convenient to have it on hand. Simply mix all of the dry ingredients and sift well, then divide into zippered bags. It's a good idea to fill each bag with enough to make one batch, and then put them into a large jar or container with the recipe taped on the outside. All you'll need to do is grab a bag, add milk and eggs and you'll have homemade biscuits in minutes.

DISTRICT 13'S SAUSAGE GRAVY

SERVES 4

Sausage gravy is a dish indigenous to the areas where District 12 and 13 were located. Rich and hearty but extremely simple, it's similar to hot grain in that it's very utilitarian. It's meant to fill you up for very little money, with very little meat.

Serve this dish over Panem Biscuits, for a tasty meal of biscuits and gravy. It also works over sliced bread or even cooked rice for a filling and simple meal.

1 POUND PORK SAUSAGE
¼ CUP FLOUR
1 CUP WATER
2 CUPS WHOLE OR 2 PERCENT MILK
1 TEASPOON SALT
1 TEASPOON BLACK PEPPER

Crumble the sausage in a skillet and brown it.

Add the flour into the mixture and stir it as it browns.

Slowly add in the water, using a spatula to smooth the lumps out.

Add the milk, salt and pepper slowly and bring to a boil.

Allow to cool and thicken, then spoon over Panem Biscuits.

STICK TO YOUR RIBS

Whether you choose to use cow, pork or venison, these ribs will fall off the bone, leaving you full and ready to face any battlefield. In the Hunger Games *trilogy, food didn't come at regular intervals, so meals that filled you up and stayed with you awhile were best.*

This is a great recipe for an outdoor Hunger Games *party, or your next barbecue. Make the sauce a day or two ahead to allow the flavors to develop.*

4 POUNDS BABY BACK OR SPARE RIBS
½ CUP FIRMLY PACKED BROWN SUGAR
3 TABLESPOONS DIJON MUSTARD
1 TABLESPOON PAPRIKA
1 TABLESPOON GARLIC POWDER
1 TEASPOON ONION POWDER
1 TEASPOON BLACK PEPPER
1 TEASPOON LIQUID SMOKE
½ TEASPOON GROUND CUMIN

Preheat your grill to medium, or your oven to 300 degrees.

Set up 2 sheets of aluminum foil about 2½ feet long and divide your ribs on them.

Combine all other ingredients, rub generously on all of the ribs and refrigerate for at least 2 hours.

Fold the extra foil around the ribs so that they are completely sealed and enclosed, with room in the foil for the air and steam to circulate.

Put the packets on the grill or in the oven and cook until the ribs are tender, about 45 minutes, and a meat thermometer reads at least 160 degrees.

Remove from foil and put them on the grill.

Grill for 10 minutes or so, or until you get a nice char.

GALE'S VENISON POT ROAST

SERVES 4

Common throughout the entire Appalachian region, venison is a delicious, nutritious meat that has very little fat and a ton of protein. It was a staple of locals for years and was frequently mentioned throughout Mockingjay as a rare treat.

This is a very traditional recipe for venison roast that is similar to beef pot roast, but with a slightly different flavor.

3 TABLESPOONS VEGETABLE OIL
2 POUNDS VENISON ROAST
2 CUPS WATER
6 LARGE CARROTS, CHUNKED
1 LARGE ONION, CUT INTO CHUNKS AND
    SEPARATED BY LAYER
2 CLOVES GARLIC, CHOPPED
1 TABLESPOON SALT
½ TABLESPOON BLACK PEPPER
6 MEDIUM POTATOES, CUT INTO SPEARS

Preheat oven to 350 degrees

Heat a large Dutch oven on stove top with vegetable oil.

Brown roast on all sides.

When well browned, put the roast in a 9 x 12-inch baking dish and add the water.

Place the carrots and onions around the roast and sprinkle the garlic, salt and pepper over the meat and veggies. Cover with foil and bake for an hour, or until the carrots start to get tender.

Add the potatoes and bake for another hour, or until the veggies are tender and the roast is cooked through.

Roast should be between 145–160 degrees, depending on desired doneness.

Slice the roast and serve with the vegetables.

GREASY SAE'S BLACK WALNUT COOKIES

MAKES 3 DOZEN COOKIES

Sweets are a rarity in the districts, as illustrated throughout the Hunger Games trilogy. But if Greasy Sae had the time and desire to make a sweet treat, she would have found black walnuts plentiful in the region. These cookies are easy to make and all of the ingredients could have been found in District 13.

These keep very well for several days in a tightly covered container. You can also freeze them for up to six months if you'd like to make an extra batch for later.

2 CUPS LIGHT BROWN SUGAR
4 EGGS
½ CUP FLOUR
½ TEASPOON SALT
½ TEASPOON BAKING POWDER
2 CUPS WALNUTS, CHOPPED

Preheat oven to 325 degrees.

Cream the brown sugar and eggs.

Add the flour, salt and baking powder and mix well into a dough.

Stir in the walnuts.

Drop by teaspoonful onto a greased baking sheet, leaving about 2 inches between the cookies.

Bake 12 minutes, or until edges start to brown.

DISTRICT 13'S HOE CAKES

SERVES 4

The hallmark of District 13 was that the food there was simple and useful. No frills. Though it wasn't fancy it was nutritious and was intended to get you from one meal to the next.

These hoe cakes did the same for the Appalachian soldiers of the Civil War. They were as simple as food gets, but did the job of filling stomachs. Now they're considered a sentimental favorite, prized by older folks who grew up on such simple fare.

**2 CUPS CORNMEAL
1 TEASPOON SALT
1 CUP BOILING WATER**

Mix cornmeal and salt. Add the boiling water slowly until you have a stiff dough.

When cool enough to handle, form into a brick, wrap in plastic and set aside for an hour.

Refrigerate for another hour.

Grease a griddle and heat on high.

Slice brick into ½-inch cakes and fry on the griddle until each side is browned.

Remove from heat and serve with syrup of your choice.

APPALACHIAN HOMESTEAD CORNBREAD

SERVES 8

In the Appalachian communities of the real United States, corn is the cheap grain that's relied on. If the tesserae had been made up of corn meal, Mrs. Everdeen probably would have used it this way.

This is a slightly sweet cornbread that is especially good with butter and honey. You can also serve it as a nice contrast to a spicy stew or chili.

1 CUP ALL-PURPOSE FLOUR
1 CUP CORNMEAL
½ TEASPOON SALT
½ TEASPOON BAKING SODA
⅔ CUP SUGAR
1 STICK MELTED BUTTER
2 EGGS
1 CUP MILK OR BUTTERMILK

Preheat oven to 350 degrees and grease an 8 x 8-inch pan.

In a medium bowl, mix the flour, cornmeal, salt and baking soda together.

Combine the sugar and butter, and then add the eggs and milk.

Beat well and add to the dry mixture.

Mix until all ingredients are combined.

Pour into the pan and bake for 30–40 minutes, or until the top is browned and a toothpick inserted into the center comes out clean.

GREASY SAE'S FRIED HAM AND RED-EYE GRAVY

SERVES 4

This simple country meal is great for breakfast or dinner. It's relatively fast and easy, so it would have made a great meal for Greasy Sae to feed her army.

Country ham is much saltier and a good deal drier than smoked ham, but it's preferable for true red-eye gravy. You can usually find it in the unrefrigerated section of cured meats in your grocery store.

**2 TABLESPOONS BACON GREASE
1 POUND SMOKED OR COUNTRY HAM,
    THICK SLICED
½ CUP WATER
½ CUP COFFEE**

Melt the bacon grease in a skillet then fry the ham on both sides just until hot.

Add the water and coffee to the pan drippings and bring to a full boil.

Serve over Panem Biscuits.

GREASY SAE'S PICKLED CRAB APPLES

YIELDS ABOUT 5 QUARTS, DEPENDING UPON THE SIZE OF THE APPLES

This pickle recipe is one that Mrs. Everdeen might have used if her daughters had brought some of this fruit home. Though they're not great for eating right off of the ground, crab apples do have nutritional value and can be tasty if prepared correctly.

8 CUPS BROWN SUGAR
6 CUPS WHITE VINEGAR
2 TEASPOONS CLOVES
2 CINNAMON STICKS
7 POUNDS CRAB APPLES, RINSED

Mix all ingredients except for the crab apples and bring to a boil.

Add apples and boil until the fruit is tender.

Pack the apples into canning jars (pint or quart, whichever you prefer) and add syrup. Fill jars just to 1½ or 2 inches below rim. Use a butter knife or spatula to remove any air bubbles. Wipe the rims with a clean cloth.

Place lids and rims onto jars and seal securely. Place onto rack in pot and add water to 2 inches above the tops of the jars. Boil for 12 minutes. Allow the jars to sit in the pot for at least 5 minutes to allow them to cool a bit before being exposed to the cool air of the room.

Use tongs to lift out the jars and set them on a folded towel in a secure area where they won't be bumped.

Leave for 24 hours. Check lids to make sure that each jar has sealed properly. You should not be able to peel off the lid with your fingers.

KATNISS' FAVORITE FRIED OKRA

SERVES 6

Okra is mentioned several times throughout the book and was a favorite of Greasy Sae. It's nutritious and tasty if prepared right, but if undercooked it can be slimy.

Make sure that you get it crispy by heating the grease well before adding the okra and not adding too much to the skillet at once. If the skillet is overcrowded, it won't brown well.

---

2 POUNDS RAW OKRA, SLICED INTO ¼-INCH RINGS
1 CUP CORNMEAL
1 TEASPOON SALT
½ TEASPOON BLACK PEPPER
¼ CUP BACON GREASE

Moisten the okra slightly with water.

Add the cornmeal, salt and pepper to a large plastic re-sealable plastic bag and shake well to mix.

Put the okra rings in and shake to coat.

Heat bacon grease in a medium cast iron skillet.

Fry okra in the bacon grease on medium-high heat until crispy and golden brown.

PRIM'S BLACKBERRY COBBLER

SERVES 6

A favorite foraging find in the summertime, blackberries would have been a real treat in the Everdeen home. Sweets weren't available very often, but the family always made good use of wild strawberries and blackberries.

This cobbler is simple, and not overly sweet. It makes a great breakfast as well as a dessert. You can top it with a dollop of whipped cream or vanilla ice cream, but it's also wonderful as it is.

5 CUPS FRESH BLACKBERRIES
1¼ CUP PLUS 2 TABLESPOONS SUGAR, DIVIDED
2 CUPS PLUS 4 TABLESPOONS ALL-PURPOSE FLOUR, DIVIDED
1½ STICKS BUTTER, DIVIDED
4 TEASPOONS BAKING POWDER
½ TEASPOON SALT
½ TEASPOON CREAM OF TARTAR
½ CUP MILK
1 EGG WHITE

Preheat oven to 400 degrees.

Put the blackberries into a bowl with 1¼ cups sugar and 4 tablespoons sifted flour.

Toss together and crumb ½ stick of butter over them.

Put them into a buttered 2-quart baking dish.

In a medium bowl, mix all remaining ingredients except the milk and egg white until they form a crumbly mixture.

Add the milk and mix with a fork.

Roll the dough out into a ¼-inch sheet and drape over the berries.

Brush with egg white and sprinkle with sugar.

Bake for 40 minutes, or until the crust is nicely browned.

COLE SLAW SALAD FOR HAYMITCH

SERVES 6

This slaw-like salad might have been a good cabbage dish for Haymitch. Katniss, on the other hand, would probably have appreciated not having to smell cooked cabbage.

Cole slaw's flavor and texture improves as it sits, so make this dish a day or two ahead if you can. You can combine red cabbage and green for an especially pretty slaw.

¼ CUP MAYONNAISE

2 TEASPOONS SUGAR

1 TEASPOON SALT

1 TEASPOON CIDER VINEGAR

1 TEASPOON MUSTARD

½ TEASPOON GROUND BLACK PEPPER

1 MEDIUM HEAD CABBAGE, CHOPPED THIN

2 TOMATOES, CHOPPED

2 CUCUMBERS, CUBED

½ CUP ONION, CHOPPED

With a fork or a whisk mix together the mayonnaise, sugar, salt, vinegar, mustard and pepper to make the dressing.

In a large bowl, toss together the vegetables.

Pour the dressing over the veggies and lightly toss to coat.

Cole slaw is one of the tastiest and most versatile side dishes you can make. Vary the colors and textures by adding things like slivered or diced red peppers, finely diced jalapeño peppers, shredded carrots or even chopped apples. You can also play with flavors by adding balsamic vinegar, hot sauce, cayenne pepper or poppy seeds.

EAT IT ON THE GO DEER JERKY

YIELDS ABOUT 1 POUND JERKY

Katniss, Peeta and Gale did a lot of eating on the run, whether they were hunting, in the Arena or out on a mission. Jerky has always been a favorite of hunters and soldiers as it provides nourishment that requires no cooking and almost no space.

Since the Appalachian area was settled, venison has been a huge part of the local diet. This jerky is great for traveling since it doesn't need refrigeration.

½ CUP WORCESTERSHIRE SAUCE
½ CUP SOY SAUCE
2 TEASPOONS GARLIC POWDER
2 TEASPOONS ONION POWDER
2 TEASPOONS SEASONED SALT
2 TEASPOONS BLACK PEPPER
2 POUNDS EXTREMELY LEAN (TRIMMED OF FAT
    OR CONNECTIVE TISSUE) VENISON, THINLY
    SLICED WITH THE GRAIN OF THE MEAT

Combine all ingredients except the meat in a large bowl.

Add the venison, make sure that it's covered, and set in the refrigerator to marinate.

Stir every few hours to evenly marinate. Leave in the marinade 24 hours, or at least overnight.

Layer the meat on a dehydrator and dry for 5-7 hours, or until there is no moisture when you tear the meat.

If you don't have a dehydrator, you can use your oven. Just bake at 200 degrees with the door cracked a bit open for the same amount of time, checking every hour after 3 hours.

GREASY SAE'S 5-BEAN SOUP

Greasy Sae always made the most of the ingredients she had. Very often, scrap meats were the only ones on hand, and soups and stews stretched them as much as possible.

This hearty bean soup is amazing with cornbread and, in the tradition of District 13, is extremely simple, nutritious and utilitarian.

¼ **CUP DRIED NAVY BEANS**
¼ **CUP DRIED PINTO BEANS**
¼ **CUP DRIED GREEN SPLIT PEAS**
¼ **CUP DRIED NORTHERN BEANS**
¼ **CUP GREEN LENTILS**
1 **HAM BONE OR 2-3 HAM HOCKS (DON'T USE NECK BONES)**
1 **TEASPOON SALT AND PEPPER**

Sort the beans and lentils to make sure that there are no stones in them, then rinse them and soak them overnight.

Drain beans and put them in a medium saucepan with the ham bone.

Fill the pan ⅔ of the way with water and add the salt.

Bring to a boil and cook for 1½ hours, or until beans are cooked, adding water as needed.

Start checking them at about 45 minutes, and when they're nearly done, let the water reduce to a nice broth.

Taste after the beans start to get soft, and add salt and pepper to taste.

Tastes great when served with Appalachian Homestead Cornbread.

PRIM'S PICKLED BEETS

YIELDS ABOUT 8—10 PINTS

Pickling is a great, time-honored way of preserving food because it not only keeps your hard work from rotting so quickly, but also tastes good. Often pickled food needs no refrigeration, so it's a great snack to carry with you, or to have if you're living off the grid, as Katniss often had to do.

Small to medium-sized beets are sweeter and less woody, so try to steer clear of the larger roots. Don't throw away the greens—they're wonderful sautéed with a little bacon.

---

2 CUPS VINEGAR

2 CUPS WATER

2 CUPS SUGAR

2 TABLESPOONS PICKLING SPICES

ABOUT 20 MEDIUM BEETS, PEELED
      AND WEDGED

Mix all ingredients except beets together in a large saucepan and bring to a boil.

Add beets and cook until hot. Stuff beets in pint jars and top with liquid.

Place lids and rims onto jars and seal securely. Place onto rack in pot and add water to 2 inches above the tops of the jars. Boil for 12 minutes. Allow the jars to sit in the pot for at least 5 minutes to allow them to cool a bit before being exposed to the cool air of the room.

Use tongs to lift out the jars and set them on a folded towel in a secure area where they won't be bumped.

Leave for 24 hours. Check lids to make sure that each jar has sealed properly. You should not be able to peel off the lid with your fingers.

DRY LAND FISH FRY

Known as "dry land fish," morel mushrooms are a tasty, nutritious food that's native to the area that some of the districts were located in. Found in the mountains, it takes a bag full of them to make a meal but they're well worth the hunt. Katniss might have hunted for them while she was keeping an eye out for game.

If you're going to hunt your own mushrooms, be sure you know what you're doing first. Take a mushrooming class or use a reliable guide with excellent photos. Better yet, take along a more experienced friend.

2 POUNDS MOREL MUSHROOMS
1 CUP MILK
3 EGGS
1 CUP FLOUR OR CORNMEAL
1 TEASPOON SALT
1 TEASPOON BLACK PEPPER
½ CUP PEANUT OIL OR BACON GREASE

Wash the mushrooms and soak them in salt water for 2 hours. This kills any bugs or other unwanted ingredients. Dry with a paper towel.

Make an egg wash by combining the milk and eggs.

Combine the flour with the salt and pepper in a bowl.

Cut the mushrooms lengthwise and place in the egg wash.

Heat a cast iron skillet with about an inch of oil or bacon grease on medium-high heat.

Dip the egg-washed morels in the dry mix and add to the hot grease 3–4 at a time, depending on size.

Fry until golden brown and drain on a paper towel.

DISTRICT DUMPLINGS

MAKES ABOUT 10 DUMPLINGS

Dumplings would have been a staple food in District 13 because of their simplicity and ability to get a person from one meal to the next as they have a filling effect.

Dumplings are very simple to make and take very little time. They're a great way to add some heartiness to a soup or stew. You can vary the flavor a great deal by adding fresh chopped herbs such as parsley or dill.

2 CUPS SELF-RISING FLOUR
½ CUP MILK
3 TABLESPOONS OIL OR BACON GREASE
1 EGG
1 TEASPOON SALT
CHICKEN STOCK OR SOUP

Mix all ingredients together, except stock or soup, in a large mixing bowl.

Spoon the dumpling batter into boiling chicken stock or soup 1 tablespoon at a time.

Cook 10–14 minutes, or until they're somewhat flakey inside when you cut in half.

POTATO BISCUITS
MAKES ABOUT 9 BIG BISCUITS

In addition to being a staple, bread is used throughout the series for different things: to trade, to show off cooking skills, and to reveal district pride. This potato biscuit beautifully reflects District 13's "waste not, want not" attitude.

Potato biscuits are moist and flavorful, with a very fine texture. They're so good that you'll want to plan for leftovers every time you make mashed potatoes.

---

1 CUP LEFTOVER MASHED POTATOES
2 CUPS ALL-PURPOSE FLOUR
1 CUP MILK OR BUTTERMILK
2 TABLESPOONS BUTTER, SOFTENED
2 TEASPOONS BAKING POWDER
1 TEASPOON SALT

Preheat oven to 400 degrees.

In a medium bowl, combine all ingredients.

Using an ice cream scoop or large spoon, drop mixture into a greased 9 x 9-inch baking pan, leaving enough space so they don't stick together.

Pat flat until biscuit is about 1 inch thick.

Bake 10–12 minutes, or until golden brown on top.

GREASY SAE'S ZUCCHINI AND CORN MEDLEY

Fresh vegetables were rare in District 12, and Greasy Sae did her best to make them delicious as well as nutritious when they were available. These veggies and herbs may very well have been enjoyed by Katniss, Prim and family.

For this recipe, use smaller zucchini, as they are more tender and flavorful. Very large zucchini tend to get a bit tough. If you have a garden, this is a great way to use up such a prolific vegetable.

1½ CUPS FRESH CORN
4 CUPS SLICED ZUCCHINI
½ CUP ONION, CHOPPED
2 CLOVES GARLIC
2 TABLESPOONS VEGETABLE OIL
2 TABLESPOONS BUTTER
1 TEASPOON FRESH OREGANO, CHOPPED
5-7 FRESH BASIL LEAVES, CHOPPED
SALT AND PEPPER TO TASTE

Chop all the vegetables either into slices or bite-sized chunks.

Heat the oil and butter on medium-high heat in a heavy skillet until the butter is melted.

Add the veggies and stir occasionally to prevent burning.

Sprinkle with the seasonings and stir.

Sauté until the vegetables are tender and lightly browned.

Garnish with a few whole basil leaves. Salt and pepper to taste.

NOTES

NOTES

18

AUTHENTICITY FOR THE ADVENTUROUS

"Closing my eyes doesn't help.
Fire burns brighter in the darkness."

KATNISS, *MOCKINGJAY* BY SUZANNE COLLINS, CHAPTER 25

TIMES WERE PARTICULARLY TOUGH in the final book of the trilogy. Since there was a real scarcity in *Mockingjay,* the recipes in this chapter are far more adventurous than in the previous sections.

These are the foods people might eat when they're waging a revolution or training in the woods. They're definitely for the most adventurous fans of the *Hunger Games* trilogy!

GREASY SAE'S HOLIDAY STUFFED POSSUM

SERVES 4—6

Possum isn't something that many people today have tried, but it's entirely probable that Katniss made a meal or two out of the marsupial.

If you don't hunt, ask around your community to find someone who does. You may be able to find an inexpensive source for possum locally. If not, you can order it from online retailers specializing in game.

1 MEDIUM DRESSED POSSUM
1 TABLESPOON BUTTER
1 LARGE ONION, CHOPPED
1 CUP BREADCRUMBS
1 MEDIUM RED PEPPER, DICED
1 TEASPOON WORCESTERSHIRE SAUCE
1 CUP SALT
1 HARDBOILED EGG, CHOPPED

To begin, you need to dress the possum. To do this, remove the entrails, head and tail.

Set aside the entrails to be used in the stew further along in this chapter.

Soak dressed possum in iced salt water overnight to get rid of the wild taste.

Separate the liver and set aside.

Remove from salt water and rinse well.

Combine butter and onion in a skillet on medium-high heat. Cook until soft and translucent.

Chop the liver and add to the skillet when the onions start to brown.

Cook until liver is well done, about 5 minutes.

Add breadcrumbs, red pepper and Worcestershire sauce and stir until incorporated.

Mix in salt and boiled egg and add enough water to moisten.

Stuff the mix into the possum cavity and sew shut with kitchen twine.

Roast possum at 350 degrees until tender, basting with the drippings from roasting pan.

PEETA'S POSITIVELY AWESOME ROASTED RACCOON

SERVES 4

Katniss and her family relied on game meats to get by and escape starvation. None of the animals in the nearby woods would have been passed up as a source of meat.

Raccoons have a lot of meat, though they tend to be a bit greasy, much the way bear is. The meat can also be a bit tough; so don't skip the meat tenderizer.

5-POUND RACCOON, DRESSED AND BUTCHERED
½ CUP BARBEQUE SAUCE
3 TABLESPOONS MEAT TENDERIZER
2 CUPS DIET COLA
1 GALLON WATER
1 STICK BUTTER
3 GARLIC CLOVES, CHOPPED
1 TABLESPOON SALT
10 SLICES BACON
1 SMALL ONION

Put the raccoon in a baking bag and add the barbeque sauce, meat tenderizer and diet cola.

Marinate for 8 hours.

Transfer the raccoon to stockpot, add the water, butter, garlic and salt, bring to a boil then reduce heat and simmer.

Cook 1–1½ hours. Remove raccoon from stockpot and debone.

Chop up the bacon and onion. Fry them in a large skillet until almost done and add the raccoon meat.

Cook an additional 15 minutes and serve.

CAPITOL FRIED SQUIRREL WINGS

Squirrel was a welcome source of meat in Katniss' hunting days with Gale, and is mentioned several times throughout the trilogy.

Fried squirrel tastes similar to fried chicken, though it may be a bit greasier. The legs even look like small chicken wing drums. Breaded and tossed in buffalo sauce, they're absolutely delicious. It does take several squirrels to make these though.

½ CUP PEANUT OIL
¼ CUP FLOUR
½ TEASPOON PEPPER
1 TEASPOON SALT
10 SQUIRREL LEGS
¼ CUP HOT SAUCE
¼ CUP MELTED BUTTER
1 STALK CELERY
1 CUP BLUE CHEESE DRESSING

Preheat a cast iron skillet with ½ cup oil until hot.

Combine the flour, pepper and salt.

Rinse the squirrel legs and dust in the flour mixture.

Fry the legs for 5–10 minutes, or until golden brown.

In a medium bowl, combine the hot sauce and butter.

When the legs are done, put them in the bowl and toss in the sauce.

Serve with blue cheese dressing and celery.

Many people love the taste of squirrel and include squirrel meat in their diets fairly regularly. People who hunt and eat squirrels insist that those fattened on chestnuts or other fall nuts taste best. This makes sense, since gourmet hogs are "finished," or fattened, on nuts to improve the flavor of their meat. To get this tastier squirrel meat, find a hunter who's willing to share or sell his autumn catch with you.

GREASY SAE'S BAKED GROUNDHOG

It's not easy to come up with dishes that are both nutritious and palatable, but Greasy Sae was at the top of her class when it came to this exercise. This baked groundhog tops the charts in both flavor and creativity.

Look online for a reputable game meats retailer if you don't hunt yourself or know a local hunter. Groundhog has a slightly gamey taste, but is quite nutritious and most people enjoy the flavor.

---

1 LARGE GROUNDHOG
1 TABLESPOON APPLE CIDER VINEGAR
½ CUP CORNMEAL
½ CUP FLOUR
2 TEASPOONS SALT
1 TEASPOON PAPRIKA
1 TEASPOON BLACK PEPPER

Butcher the groundhog like you would a chicken, breaking down the legs, thighs and breasts.

Soak the meat in apple cider vinegar and one quart of water overnight.

Preheat oven to 350 degrees.

Mix the cornmeal, flour, paprika, salt and pepper together.

Roll the pieces of groundhog in the mixture and place on a baking sheet.

Bake 35–40 minutes, or until tender.

GALE'S RAT ON A STICK

SERVES 1—2, DEPENDING UPON THE SIZE OF THE RAT

When you're hungry and food is scarce, you eat what you can catch and hope that it's safe to build a fire without being caught by the Careers.

This recipe is strictly for the truly adventurous, but if it's authenticity you seek, this is where you'll find it. It's up to you to find your own rat; even game retailers don't sell it.

1 LARGE RAT, SKINNED AND DRESSED
1 TABLESPOON SALT
1 SKEWER, EITHER METAL OR WOODEN

Sprinkle the salt over the rat. Skewer the rat on a stick and roast over an open fire or on the grill.

Cook for 20 minutes, or until meat is cooked through and pulls away from the bone.

KEEP YOU GOING POSSUM ENTRAILS STEW

SERVES 1

It may not sound like the most appetizing dish, but if possum entrails are all you have, they sure are better than nothing. It's still protein, and it'll keep you fighting one more day. This is the sensibility that dictated the diets of the trilogy's main characters.

If you're going to prepare one of the other possum dishes in this book, freeze the entrails to use for this recipe.

2 CUPS BOILING WATER
1 TABLESPOON SALT
ENTRAILS FROM 1 POSSUM, INCLUDING STOMACH, LIVER, LUNGS, KIDNEYS, HEART AND INTESTINES
1 TOMATO, CHOPPED IN HALF
1 POTATO, QUARTERED
1 ONION, QUARTERED
FRESH GROUND PEPPER

Bring the water and salt to a boil in a medium saucepan.

Add the entrails and veggies to the 2 cups of water.

Boil for about 30 minutes, or until the meat is semi-tender.

Add pepper. If you have fresh herbs such as basil or oregano, that would be great as well.

If not, enjoy!

FRIED SNAKE STEAK

SERVES 1—3, DEPENDING UPON THE SIZE OF THE SNAKE

Snake is actually a delicacy in many parts of the world and, when cooked properly, is delicious. Katniss would have surely eaten it, as her views on food were very pragmatic.

Snake can be purchased at many game butchers or ordered online. Alternatively, you could go out and find your own. Don't forget to proceed with caution, as some snakes are poisonous.

¼ CUP FLOUR
1 TEASPOON CRUSHED RED PEPPER
1 TABLESPOON SALT
½ TEASPOON BLACK PEPPER
1 SNAKE, SKINNED, CLEANED AND SLICED
    INTO 1-INCH STEAKS
2 TABLESPOONS OLIVE OIL

Combine the flour, crushed red pepper, salt and black pepper.

Heat the oil in a medium-to-large skillet on high heat.

Roll the snake steaks in the flour mixture and add to the hot oil.

Fry 3–4 minutes on each side, until brown and done through the middle. The meat should be white and opaque.

KATNISS' BAKED PIGEON

Pigeons may seem like dirty birds, but when your stomach's growling and you're getting lightheaded from hunger, it's likely that they're extremely tasty.

There may not be any salt or herbs if you're out hunting, but this recipe adds seasoning for a better taste. Pigeons are small birds once dressed, but the meat is tender and juicy.

1½ TABLESPOON BUTTER, SOFTENED
1 TEASPOON SALT
2 BASIL LEAVES, CHOPPED
2 SPRIGS OF PARSLEY, CHOPPED
1 PIGEON, PLUCKED AND GUTTED

Preheat oven to 350 degrees.

Combine the butter, salt, basil and parsley to make herb butter.

Thoroughly rinse the pigeon with cold water. Trim away the excess fat.

Rub the herb butter on the pigeon and inside the cavity. Get it between the skin and the meat if you can do so.

Place on a baking sheet and bake for 30 minutes, or until meat easily pulls away from the bone.

GREASY SAE'S BADGER STEW

SERVES 4

Greasy Sae cooked whatever meat she was lucky enough to be given. This was true in the Hub and remained true after she was relocated to District 13.

If you can manage to find a badger and kill it, it's delicious meat. This wonderful stew is rich with broth and extremely nutritious.

---

1 MEDIUM BADGER, CLEANED, DEBONED AND
    BUTCHERED
2 TABLESPOONS SALT
1 TABLESPOON FRESH GROUND PEPPER
½ CUP FLOUR
¼ CUP VEGETABLE OIL
1 ONION, CHOPPED
1 POUND OF CARROTS, PEELED AND CHUNKED
1 CUP CELERY, CHOPPED
3 CLOVES GARLIC, CHOPPED
4 SPRIGS ROSEMARY
1 TABLESPOON THYME
2 CUPS WATER, APPROXIMATE
4 POTATOES, CUBED
2 ACORN SQUASH, PEELED AND CUBED

Trim fat from badger and cut into bite-sized pieces.

Salt and pepper the badger liberally, then toss in flour.

In a large stockpot, heat the oil on medium-heat.

Add the badger and onions to the stockpot. Sauté until the badger is browned on all sides, stirring frequently.

Add the carrots, celery, onion, garlic and herbs. Add water until the meat is covered.

Bring to a boil and cook until the carrots begin to get tender.

Add the rest of the vegetables.

Reduce heat, cover and simmer for about 1 hour, or until the meat and vegetables are fully cooked and fork tender.

Add water as needed to keep the stew from boiling dry.

GRILLED MINNOW HASH

SERVES 2

In Catching Fire, *Katniss discovered little minnows in the Arena that may be similar to the ones used in this recipe. If she came across them in* Mockingjay *she would have likely indulged. Fish is extremely nutritious, but the big ones aren't always readily available. All you need is a net or cloth and you can scoop the small ones right up.*

If you can't find minnows then substitute smelt, which are commonly found in most seafood sections at the supermarket. You can also purchase them frozen if nothing else is available.

1 TABLESPOON OLIVE OIL
10 MINNOWS
1 SMALL ONION, SLICED
1 TEASPOON SALT
1 TEASPOON LEMON JUICE
1 TEASPOON BLACK PEPPER
2 MEDIUM POTATOES, CUBED SMALL

Heat the oil in a large skillet and add all of the ingredients except the potatoes.

Cook over medium heat. Place a lid on the skillet so that the fish can steam and the bones can soften.

About 5 minutes before the fish is done, add the potatoes and cook covered for 10 minutes.

Uncover and cook until the entire dish begins to brown and crisp.

FRIED SNAIL SCAMPI

SERVES 2

Deliciously decadent, when snails are prepared properly, you'll never know that you're eating snails. All of the ingredients in this recipe are local to the Appalachian region, so this dish is something that may have been served in any of the Appalachian-area districts.

You can find fresh snails wild in many parts of the country, but they're also commonly sold at many seafood and gourmet markets.

4 CUPS SALTED WATER
10 LARGE SNAILS
2 TABLESPOONS BUTTER
½ CUP DANDELION WINE
½ SMALL ONION, CHOPPED
2 CLOVES GARLIC, CHOPPED
4 SLICES RUSTIC BREAD, TOASTED

Bring 4 cups water to boil in a medium-size pot.

Blanch the snails in the boiling salt water for a few minutes.

Drain the snails and set aside.

Melt the butter in a skillet on medium-high heat.

When the butter is no longer frothy, add the wine, onions and garlic.

When the onions begin to become translucent, add the snails.

Once the snails are cooked through, remove from the fire and serve with a side of bread.

NOTES

CELEBRATING THE HUNGER GAMES

19 LET THE GAMES BEGIN

19

LET THE GAMES BEGIN

HUNGER GAMES-THEMED PARTIES are a great way to transport you and your friends back into the post-apocalyptic world known as Panem. Parties also provide an excellent excuse to prepare an assortment of the recipes offered in this cookbook.

This section offers party menus that allow you and your guests the opportunity to inhabit District 12 and devour the more rustic and unusual foods of the series. Or better yet, take a trip to the Capitol and treat your guests to a table filled with opulence and delicacies.

No matter what type of *Hunger Games* party you decide to host, this section offers plenty of ideas to get you started. The menus for kids offer dishes that youngsters will love, such as All for Rue Groosling Legs and Pale Purple Melon. Adventurous teens can experiment with the rustic menu, while a more mature audience will find pleasure engaging in conversation over an elegant dinner party at the Capitol.

From President Snow's Snowy Rose Cupcakes to Capitol Lamb Stew with Plums, there's a dish for everyone and every type of party.

Like the books themselves, *Hunger Games*-themed celebrations provide entertainment for all ages.

DECEPTIVELY SWEET PARTY FOR KIDS

SNACKS

Fence-Roasted Tree Nuts

Backpack Treasure Dried Fruits

Arena Beef Strips

Orange and Sweet Berry Coolers

ENTREES AND SIDES

All For Rue Groosling Legs

Burnt "Tree Rat" For the Timid

Goat Cheese Toasts With Fresh Apple

Homesick Cheese Buns

Pale Purple Melon

Deceptively Sweet Berry Syrup Soda

DESSERTS

Cake on Fire

No Manners Needed Chocolate Cake

This section includes menu plans for kids, but don't forget the activities. Set up your own "Hunger Games" by creating an obstacle course where kids can compete as individuals or as boy/girl tribute teams. Turn up the heat and hold a reaping to draw teams for paired competitions like a balloon toss or three-legged races. When it comes time to serve the snacks, hide them in a bag and have the kids "hunt" for their food.

Menu

CHILDREN AT THE CAPITOL

SNACKS

Disappearing Mints

Catching Fire Lamb Puffs

Fancy Capitol Cream-Filled Cookies

ENTREES AND SIDES

Flower-Shaped Rolls

Noodles in Green Sauce

Deliciously Simple Grilled Groosling Kebabs

Chestnut and Apple Salad With Toasted Bread Croutons

DESSERTS

President Snow's Snowy Rose Cupcakes

Peppermint Ice Cream

Menu

CORNUCOPIA BUFFET FOR KIDS

SNACKS AND TREATS

Jewel-Colored Mosaic Gelatin

Cold Raspberry Soup With Fresh Berries

District 11's Seeded Crescent Loaf

ENTREES AND SIDES

Real Bakery Loaf Bread

Creamy Mashed Potatoes

Prim's Hearty Beef Stew

Baby Vegetables in Lemon Butter Sauce

DESSERTS

Cake on Fire

Juicy Chocolate Citrus Cake

Menu

A RUSTIC MENU FOR ADVENTUROUS TEENS

SNACKS AND TREATS

Better Than Nothing Bread With Moldy Cheese and Mustard Sauce

Pepper Jack and Chive Muffins

Mellark Bakery's Goat Cheese and Apple Tarts

Finnick and Annie's Wedding Cider

ENTRÉES AND SIDES

Charred Tree Rat

Peeta's Multigrain Bread

Goat Trader's Stew

Campfire Bony Fish on a Stick

DESSERTS

Tiny Plum Tarts

Peeta's Sweet Breakfast Rolls

Irresistible Hot Chocolate

Teens and young adults are probably the most intense *Hunger Games* fans there are.
And since nobody knows *Hunger Games* trivia like this age group, trilogy trivia
could be a great group activity. For the more adventurous teens, stage a pre-meal
"Hunger Games" with a lively scavenger hunt.

Menu

TEENS PARTYING AT THE CAPITOL

SNACKS AND TREATS

Goose Liver and Puffy Bread

Fruit-and-Herb-Stuffed Portobello Caps

District 12 Jerky

ENTREES AND SIDES

Beloved Lamb Stew With Dried Plums

Flower-Shaped Rolls

Sweet Peas With Tiny Onions

Taste of Spring Soup

Orange Chicken in Cream Sauce

DESSERTS

Cake on Fire

Chocolate Covered Cherry Custard

CORNUCOPIA BUFFET FOR ADULTS

SNACKS AND TREATS

Prim's Goat Cheese Gifts

Real Bakery Loaf Bread

Thick and Creamy Carrot Soup

Backpack Treasure Dried Fruits

ENTREES AND SIDES

Noodles in Green Sauce

Fish Cakes With Wasabi-Lime Mayo

Homesick Cheese Buns

Watercress and Almond Salad

DESSERTS

Golden Cornucopia Cake

Lavender Cookies Fit for a President

Costumes add an extra flavor of festivity to any party, and even more so when it comes to showcasing the exotic garb worn by the characters in the *Hunger Games* trilogy. From the drab apparel in District 12 to the over-the-top flamboyancy at the Capitol, invite your guests to use their creativity to bring the characters of *The Hunger Games* to life.

Menu

DINING WITH PRESIDENT SNOW

APPETIZERS
Sweet Raw Shellfish

Creamy Mixed Mushroom Soup

ENTREES AND SIDES
District 4's Loaves and Fishes

Sweet Peas With Tiny Onions

Bitter Greens With Pea-Sized Tomatoes

Beloved Lamb Stew With Dried Plums

DESSERTS
Fiery Spirits Banana Rum Cake

Golden Honey Custard

CONCLUSION

Creative edibles combined with a passion for the *Hunger Games* is a recipe for adventure. The *Hunger Games* trilogy has become a phenomenon, not only because it's wonderfully crafted, but also because the story and the characters are so compelling. Food is practically its own character in the *Hunger Games* trilogy; it was scarce and precious to Panem's poor, and a status symbol to the rich. The lack of food in the Districts and the abundance of it in the Capitol was at the foundation of Katniss' adventure.

The ability to cook the foods that feature so prominently in the trilogy is another way to relive the captivating story. Like the trilogy, *The Unofficial Recipes of The Hunger Games* will whisk you away and deliver your senses to the land of the *Hunger Games.*

INDEX

A

Acorn Squash
in Badger Stew, Greasy Sae's, 238
in Gourd and Bean Soup, Greasy
Sae's, 86
All for Rue Groosling Legs, 47
Almond(s)
Pumpkin Soup, Savory, with Nuts, 114
and Watercress Salad, 103
Appalachian Homestead Cornbread, 214
Appetizers
Beef Strips, Arena, 49
Bread with Moldy Cheese and
Mustard Sauce, Better Than
Nothing, 197
Goat Cheese Gifts, Prim's, 4
Liver Pate, Capitol Living, 198
Portobello Caps, Fruit-and-Herb-
Stuffed, 139
Apple(s)
and Chestnut Salad with Toasted
Bread Croutons, 131
Crab Apples, Pickled, Greasy Sae's,
216
Dried Fruit, Backpack Treasure, 75
Goat Cheese Toasts with Fresh
Apple, 54
Muffins, Haymitch's Hangover, 90
Sautéed, with Brown Sugar and
Cinnamon, 153
Tart, Easy, 143
Tarts, and Goat Cheese, Mellark
Bakery's, 55
Apple Cider, Finnick and Annie's
Wedding, 203
Apricots
Dried Fruits, Backpack Treasure, 75
Stuffed Fowl, Presidential, 112
Stuffed Portobello Caps, Fruit-and-
Herb-, 139
Arena Beef Strips, 49
Asian Watercress Salad, Sweet, 148
Asparagus, in Taste of Spring Soup, 115

B

Baby Vegetables in Lemon Butter
Sauce, 122
Backpack Treasure Dried Fruits, 75
Bacon
in Dandelion Salad, Hope Springs
Eternal, 8
Dressing, Warm, 8
and French Toast, Buttercup's, 202
in Lamb Stew, Plum Good, Greasy
Sae's, 196
Badger Stew, Greasy Sae's, 238
Bakery Loaf Bread, Real, 12
Balsamic Plum Reduction, Lamb Chops
with a, 137
Banana Rum Cake, Fiery Spirits, 38
Barley
Beef Soup, Greasy Sal's Call It, 13
Bread, District 13's, 175
Bread, Real Bakery Loaf, 12
Bread, Tesserae Hearth, 5
Cereal, Tesserae, with Mixed Berries,
60
Hot Breakfast Grain, Get You
Through 'Til Lunch, 172
iron in, 71
Mush, Mom Everdeen's Breakfast
of, 71
Basil
in Goat Cheese Gifts, Prim's, 4
Green Sauce (Pesto), Noodles in, 37
Batter Cakes with Thick Orange
Preserves, 39
Bean
and Gourd Soup, Greasy Sae's, 86
Soup, 5-Bean, Greasy Sae's, 221
Stew, and Onion, "Wish There Was
Meat," 174
Beaver (Beef) Stew, Hazelle's Hearty, 84
Beaver Stew, Hazelle's Authentic, 164
Beef
Broth, Mrs. Everdeen's Simple, 96
Ribs, Stick to Your, 210

Soup, Greasy Sae's Call It, 13
Stew (Beaver), Hazelle's Hearty, 84
Stew, Greasy Sae's Seriously, 193
Stew, Prim's Hearty, 95
Strips, Arena, 49
Beet(s)
Mushier Than Mud, 181
Pickled, Prim's, 222
Puree, Silent, Cold Soup of, 100
Beet greens, 181
Beloved Lamb Stew with Dried Plums,
42
Berry(ies). See also specific berries
Cereal, Tesserae, with Mixed Berries,
60
Coolers, Orange and Sweet Berry,
140
Jam, Sugar Berry, Mrs. Everdeen's,
58
Soda, Deceptively Sweet Berry
Syrup, 53
Better Than Nothing Bread with Moldy
Cheese and Mustard Sauce, 197
Beverages. See also Tea
Cider, Finnick and Annie's Wedding,
203
Coolers, Orange and Sweet Berry,
140
Hot Chocolate, Irresistible, 25
Milk, Soothing Honey and Spiced,
105
Soda, Deceptively Sweet Berry
Syrup, 53
Biscuits
mix for, 208
Panem, 208
Potato, 225
Bitter Greens with Pea-Sized
Tomatoes, 36
Bittersweet Memories Dill Bread, 94
Blackberry(ies)
Cereal, Tesserae, with Mixed Berries,
60

Cobbler, Prim's, 218
Jam, Mrs. Everdeen's Sugar Berry, 58
Blood Orange Quail, 118–119
Blue Cheese, Mustard Sauce and Moldy Cheese, Better Than Nothing Bread with, 197
Bread(s). *See also* Toast(s)
    Bakery Loaf, Real, 12
    Biscuits, Panem, 208
    Biscuits, Potato, 225
    Buns, Cheese, Homesick, 108
    and Cabbage, Say It Isn't So, 178
    Cinnamon, Mellark's, 93
    Cornbread, Appalachian Homestead, 214
    Dill, Bittersweet Memories, 94
    District 13's, 175
    kneading, 46
    Loaves and Fishes, District 4's, 46
    with Moldy Cheese and Mustard Sauce, Better Than Nothing, 197
    Muffins, Haymitch's Hangover, 90
    Muffins, Pepper Jack and Chive, 156
    Multigrain, Peeta's, 91
    Puffy, and Goose (Chicken) Liver, 34
    Raisin Nut, Peeta's Burnt, 14
    Rolls, Flower-Shaped, 31
    Rolls, Sweet Breakfast, Peeta's, 26
    Seeded Crescent Loaf, District 11's, 48
    Soaked in Warm Milk, Feel Better Fast, 177
    Tesserae Hearth, 5
    Whole Wheat Cinnamon Raisin, Mellark's, 144
Breakfast dishes. *See also* Cereal
    Bacon and French Toast, Buttercup's, 202
    Beets, Mushier Than Mud, 181
    Bread Soaked in Warm Milk, Feel Better Fast, 177
    Eggs, Coddled, Glazed Ham Steaks with, New Day Dawning, 23
    Eggs and Toast, Greasy Sae's, 201
    French Toast and Bacon, Buttercup's, 202
    Grain, Hot, Get You Through 'Til Lunch, 172
    Ham, Fried, and Red-Eye Gravy, Greasy Sae's, 215
    Ham and Potato Hash, Tigris', 200
    Mush, Mom Everdeen's Breakfast of, 71
    Rolls, Peeta's Sweet Breakfast, 26
    Through a Mouthpiece, 126

Turnips, Mashed, District 13's, 173
Broccoli, Baby Vegetables in Lemon Butter Sauce, 122
Broth
    homemade, 164
    Mrs. Everdeen's Simple, 96
Buns, Cheese, Homesick, 108
Burnt Meat and Boiled Cabbage, Haymitch-Style, 87
Burnt Raisin Nut Bread, Peeta's, 14
Burnt "Tree Rat" for the Timid, 132
Butternut Squash, in Capitol Lamb Stew with Plum Dumplings, 110–111

C
Cabbage
    Boiled, and Burnt Meat, Haymitch-Style, 87
    Bread and, Say It Isn't So, 178
    Casserole, Haymitch Inspired, 147
    Cole Slaw Salad for Haymitch, 219
Cakes
    Banana Rum, Fiery Spirits, 38
    Cake on Fire, 62
    Chocolate Citrus, Juicy, 150
    Chocolate, Finger Licking, 22
    Chocolate, No Manners Needed, 117
    Cornucopia, Golden, 61
    Cupcakes, President Snow's Snowy Rose, 63
    flowers, edible, for decoration, 88
    Wedding, Finnick and Annie's, 204
Campfire Bony Fish on a Stick, 77
Capitol Fig Cookies, 199
Capitol Fried Squirrel Wings, 232
Capitol Lamb Stew with Plum Dumplings, 110–111
Capitol Living Liver Pate, 198
Carrot(s)
    in Groosling Soup with Sweet Root Vegetables, Peeta's Healing, 51
    Soup, Thick and Creamy, 18
    in Venison Pot Roast, Gale's, 211
    in Venison Stew with Sweet Roots for Rue, 64
    and Yam Puree, Cold, Rue's, 142
Cassava, Roasted Katniss Tubers and Fried Catfish, 9
Catching Fire Lamb Puffs, 154
Catfish
    Fried, Roasted Katniss Tubers and, 9
    Stew with Greens, 6
Cauliflower, Baby Vegetables in Lemon Butter Sauce, 122

Cereal
    Grain and Milk, Hot Under the Collar, 180
    Hot Breakfast Grain, Get You Through 'Til Lunch, 172
    Tesserae, with Mixed Berries, 60
Chard, Bitter Greens with Pea-Sized Tomatoes, 36
Charred Tree Rat, 160
Cheese. *See also* Goat Cheese
    Buns, Homesick, 108
    in Cabbage Casserole, Haymitch Inspired, 147
    Moldy, and Mustard Sauce, Better Than Nothing Bread with, 197
    Pepper Jack and Chive Muffins, 156
Cherry(ies)
    Custard, Chocolate-Covered, 104
    Fruit Kebabs and a Fountain of Chocolate, 124
    Muffins, Haymitch's Hangover, 90
Chestnut(s)
    and Apple Salad with Toasted Bread Croutons, 131
    Fence-Roasted Tree Nuts, 130
Chicken
    Burnt "Tree Rat" for the Timid, 132
    Fried Slop, Greasy Sae's, 192
    Orange, in Cream Sauce, 30
    with Orange Sauce, 151
    Skewered Bird, 157
Chicken Liver
    Pate, Capitol Living, 198
    and Puffy Bread, 34
Chile Sauce, Spicy, Shellfish in a, District 4, 163
Chitterlings, in Greasy Sae's Special Winter Soup, 70
Chocolate
    Cake, Finger Licking, 22
    Cake, Juicy Citrus, 150
    Cake, No Manners Needed, 117
    Cherry Custard, -Covered, 104
    a Fountain of, and Fruit Kebabs, 124
    Glaze, 22
    Hot Chocolate, Irresistible, 25
    Hot Chocolate Pudding, Peeta's, 65
Chowder, Cod, Not From a Can, 194
Cider, Finnick and Annie's Wedding, 203
Cinnamon
    Apples, Sautéed, with Brown Sugar and, 153
    Bread, Mellark's, 93

Cinnamon (*continued*)
    Raisin Whole Wheat Bread,
        Mellark's, 144
Clambake, Authentic Arena, 162
Cobbler, Blackberry, Prim's, 218
Cocktail Sauce, 113
Coconut Frosting, 63
Cod
    Chowder, Not From a Can, 194
    Clambake, Authentic Arena, 162
    Fish Cakes with Wasabi-Lime Mayo,
        101
    Fish Soup, Salty Tears, 41
Cole Slaw Salad for Haymitch, 219
Cold Raspberry Soup with Fresh
    Berries, 116
Cookies
    Black Walnut, Greasy Sae's, 212
    butter *vs* margarine, 195
    Cream-Filled, Fancy Capitol, 195
    Fig, Capitol, 199
    flowers, edible, for decoration, 88
    Lavender, Fit for a President, 88
    Mints, Disappearing, 120
    Mr. Mellark s Farewell, 15
Coolers, Orange and Sweet Berry, 140
Corn, and Zucchini Medley, Greasy
    Sae's, 226
Cornbread, Appalachian Homestead,
    214
Cornish Hens
    Stuffed Fowl, Presidential, 112
    Stuffed with Oranges over Rice,
        102
Cornmeal
    Catfish, Fried, Roasted Katniss
        Tubers and, 9
    Cornbread, Appalachian Homestead,
        214
    Dry Land Fish Fry, 223
    Hoe Cakes, District 13's, 213
    Okra, Fried, Katniss' Favorite, 217
Cornucopia Cake, Golden, 61
Crab Apples, Pickled, Greasy Sae's,
    216
Crabs, in Ocean Creatures and Cocktail
    Sauce, 113
Cranberry(ies)
    Jewels, Sweet Pheasant with, 121
    Stuffed Fowl, Presidential, 112
    Stuffed Portobello Caps, Fruit-and-
        Herb-, 139
    Cream-Filled Cookies, Fancy Capitol,
        195
Cream Sauce, Orange Chicken in, 30

Creamy
    Carrot Soup, Thick and, 18
    Katniss Soup, Roasted, 66
    Mashed Potatoes, 21
    Mushroom Soup, Mixed, 35
Crescent Loaf, District 11's Seeded, 48
Croutons, Toasted Bread, Chestnut and
    Apple Salad with, 131
Cupcakes, President Snow's Snowy
    Rose, 63
Custard
    Cherry, Chocolate-Covered, 104
    Golden Honey, 33

D

Dandelion (Greens)
    in Beef Soup, Greasy Sae's Call It, 13
    Lamb's Neck with Sweet Roots and
        Greens, 138
    Rabbit Stew with Wild Greens, Mrs.
        Everdeen's, 72
    Salad, Hope Springs Eternal, 8
Deceptively Sweet Berry Syrup Soda,
    53
Deer. *See* Venison
Deliciously Simple Grilled Groosling
    Kebabs, 189
Desserts. *See also* Cakes; Cookies;
    Tarts
    Apples, Sautéed, with Brown Sugar
        and Cinnamon, 153
    Cobbler, Blackberry, Prim's, 218
    Custard, Cherry, Chocolate-Covered,
        104
    Custard, Golden Honey, 33
    Fruit Kebabs and a Fountain of
        Chocolate, 124
    Ice Cream, Peppermint, 136
    Pie, Pumpkin, with Slivered Nuts,
        145
    Pudding, Hot Chocolate, Peeta's, 65
    Pudding, Rice, Fresh Orange Vanilla,
        141
Dill Bread, Bittersweet Memories, 94
Disappearing Mints, 120
District Dumplings, 224
District 4 Shellfish in a Spicy Chile
    Sauce, 163
District 4's Loaves and Fishes, 46
District 11's Seeded Crescent Loaf, 48
District 12 Jerky, 76
District 13's Bread, 175
District 13's Hoe Cakes, 213
District 13's Sausage Gravy, 209
Dressing, Bacon, Warm, 8

Dried Fruit. *See* Fruit, Dried
Dry Land Fish Fry, 223
Duck
    Groosling Kebabs, Deliciously
        Simple Grilled, 189
    Groosling Soup with Sweet Root
        Vegetables, Peeta's Healing
        (variation), 51
    Paprika, and Rosemary Tubers with
        Gravy, 89
Dumplings
    District, 224
    Plum, Capitol Lamb Stew with,
        110–111

E

Eat It on the Go Deer Jerky, 220
Egg(s)
    Breakfast Through a Mouthpiece, 126
    Coddled, Glazed Ham Steaks with,
        New Day Dawning, 23
    Sauce, Roasted Rabbit Legs with,
        52
    and Toast, Greasy Sae's, 201

F

Fancy Capitol Cream-Filled Cookies,
    195
Feel Better Fast Bread Soaked in
    Warm Milk, 177
Fence-Roasted Tree Nuts, 130
Fiery Spirits Banana Rum Cake, 38
Fig(s)
    Cookies, Capitol, 199
    in Muffins, Haymitch's Hangover, 90
Finger Licking Chocolate Cake, 22
Finger Thawing Herb Tea, 85
Finnick and Annie's Wedding Cake,
    204
Finnick and Annie's Wedding Cider,
    203
Fish
    Bony, on a Stick, Campfire, 77
    Cakes with Wasabi-Lime Mayo, 101
    Catfish, Fried, Roasted Katniss
        Tubers and, 9
    Catfish Stew with Greens, 6
    Clambake, Authentic Arena, 162
    Cod Chowder, Not From a Can, 194
    Gray Fish and Okra Stew, Slightly
        Slimy But Delicious, 176
    Minnow Hash, Grilled, 239
    Soup, Salty Tears, 41
Flowers, edible, for decoration, 88
Flower-Shaped Rolls, 31

French Toast and Bacon, Buttercup's, 202
Frosting, 63
Fruit-and-Herb-Stuffed Portobello Caps, 139
Fruit(s). See also Berry(ies); specific fruits
    Gelatin, Jewel Colored Mosaic, 155
    Kebabs and a Fountain of Chocolate, 124
Fruit, Dried
    Backpack Treasure, 75
    in Muffins, Haymitch's Hangover, 90
    Stuffed Fowl, Presidential, 112
    Stuffed Portobello Caps, and Herb, 139

G
Gale's Rat on a Stick, 234
Gale's Venison Pot Roast, 211
Game Birds
    Cornish Hens, Stuffed Fowl, Presidential, 112
    Cornish Hens, Stuffed with Oranges over Rice, 102
    Pheasant with Cranberry Jewels, Sweet, 121
    Pigeon, Baked, Katniss', 237
    Quail, Blood Orange, 118–119
Gamemakers' Suckling Pig, 40
Game Meats. See also Rabbit; Venison
    Badger Stew, Greasy Sae's, 238
    Beaver Stew, Hazelle's Authentic, 164
    Groundhog, Baked, Greasy Sae's, 233
    Possum Entrails Stew, Keep You Going, 235
    Possum, Holiday Stuffed, Greasy Sae's, 230
    Raccoon, Roasted, Peeta's Positively Awesome, 231
    Rat on a Stick, Gale's, 234
    Snake Steak, Fried, 236
    Squirrel, Charred Tree Rat, 160
    Squirrel Wings, Fried, Capitol, 232
Gelatin, Jewel-Colored Mosaic, 155
Get You Through 'Til Lunch Hot Breakfast Grain, 172
Glaze, Chocolate, 22
Goat
    Spit-Roasted, 165
    Stew, Goat Trader's, 78
Goat Cheese
    and Apple Tarts, Mellark Bakery's, 55
    Gifts, Prim's, 4
    Toasts with Fresh Apple, 54

Goat Trader's Stew, 78
Golden Cornucopia Cake, 61
Golden Honey Custard, 33
Good for Your Soul Pea Soup, 182
Goose (Chicken) Liver and Puffy Bread, 34
Goose
    Groosling Kebabs, Deliciously Simple Grilled, 189
    Groosling Soup with Sweet Root Vegetables, Peeta's Healing, 51
    Liver, Rich, and Puffy Bread, 73
Gourd and Bean Soup, Greasy Sae's, 86
Grain(s). See also Rice
    Bread
        District 13's, 175
        Multigrain, Peeta's, 91
        Tesserae Hearth, 5
        Whole Wheat Raisin Cinnamon, Mellark's, 144
    Cereal, Tesserae, with Mixed Berries, 60
    Hot Breakfast, Get You Through 'Til Lunch, 172
    and Milk, Hot under the Collar, 180
    Mush, Mom Everdeen's Breakfast of, 71
Gravy
    Blood Orange Quail, 118–119
    Chicken Fried Slop, 192
    with Paprika Duck and Rosemary Tubers, 89
    Red-Eye, and Fried Ham, Greasy Sae's, 215
    Sausage, District 13's, 209
Gray Fish and Okra Stew, Slightly Slimy But Delicious, 176
Greasy Sae's Badger Stew, 238
Greasy Sae's Baked Groundhog, 233
Greasy Sae's Black Walnut Cookies, 212
Greasy Sae's Call It Beef Soup, 13
Greasy Sae's Chicken Fried Slop, 192
Greasy Sae's Eggs and Toast, 201
Greasy Sae's 5-Bean Soup, 221
Greasy Sae's Fried Ham and Red-Eye Gravy, 215
Greasy Sae's Gourd and Bean Soup, 86
Greasy Sae's Holiday Stuffed Possum, 230
Greasy Sae's Pickled Crab Apples, 216
Greasy Sae's Plum Good Lamb Stew, 196
Greasy Sae's Seriously Beef Stew, 193
Greasy Sae's Special Winter Soup, 70

Greasy Sae's Zucchini and Corn Medley, 226
Greens. See also specific greens
    in Beef Soup, Greasy Sae's Call It, 13
    Bitter, with Pea-Sized Tomatoes, 36
    Catfish Stew with, 6
    Lamb's Neck with Sweet Roots and, 138
    Wild, Rabbit Stew with, Mrs. Everdeen's, 72
Green Salad, Fresh, 19
Green Sauce (Pesto), Noodles in, 37
Groosling
    Kebabs, Deliciously Simple Grilled, 189
    Legs, All for Rue, 47
    Soup with Sweet Root Vegetables, Peeta's Healing, 51
Groundhog, Baked, Greasy Sae's, 233

H
Ham
    Cabbage, Boiled, and Burnt Meat, Haymitch-Style, 87
    in Cabbage Casserole, Haymitch Inspired, 147
    Fried, and Red-Eye Gravy, Greasy Sae's, 215
    and Potato Hash, Tigris', 200
    Steaks, Glazed, Coddled Eggs with, New Day Dawning, 23
    Suckling Pig, Snow's, 109
Hash
    Ham and Potato, Tigris', 200
    Minnow, Grilled, 239
Haymitch, Cole Slaw Salad for, 219
Haymitch-Inspired Cabbage Casserole, 147
Haymitch's Hangover Muffins, 90
Haymitch's Pork Chops and Smashed Potatoes, 43
Haymitch-Style Boiled Cabbage and Burnt Meat, 87
Hazelle's Authentic Beaver Stew, 164
Hazelle's Hearty Beaver Stew, 84
Herb Tea, Finger Thawing, 85
Hoe Cakes, District 13's, 213
Homesick Cheese Buns, 108
Honey
    Custard, Golden, 33
    and Spiced Milk, Soothing, 105
    Tea, Soothe My Soul, 92
Hope Springs Eternal Dandelion Salad, 8

Hot Chocolate
    Irresistible, 25
    Pudding, Peeta's, 65
Hot under the Collar Grain and Milk, 180
Hunger Games-themed party menus.
    See Party menus

I

Ice Cream, Peppermint, 136
Irresistible Hot Chocolate, 25
It's Not Really Dog and Rhubarb Stew,
    188

J

Jam, Mrs. Everdeen's Sugar Berry, 58
Jerky
    Deer, Eat It on the Go, 220
    District 12, 76
Jewel-Colored Mosaic Gelatin, 155
Juicy Chocolate Citrus Cake, 150

K

Kale
    Bitter Greens with Pea-Sized
        Tomatoes, 36
    Catfish Stew with Greens, 6
Katniss' Baked Pigeon, 237
Katniss' Favorite Fried Okra, 217
Katniss Mint Tea, 7
Katniss Tubers
    Roasted, and Fried Catfish, 9
    Soup, Creamy Roasted, 66
Kebabs
    Bird, Skewered, 157
    Fruit, and a Fountain of Chocolate,
        124
    Groosling (Goose or Duck),
        Deliciously Simple Grilled, 189
Keep You Going Possum Entrail's Stew,
    235

L

Lamb
    Chops with a Balsamic Plum
        Reduction, 137
    Chops, Tribute, 20
    Neck with Sweet Roots and Greens,
        138
    Puffs, Catching Fire, 154
    Stew, with Dried Plums, Beloved, 42
    Stew, with Plum Dumplings, Capitol,
        110–111
    Stew, Plum Good, Greasy Sae's, 196
Lavender Cookies Fit for a President,
    88

Leek(s)
    Potato Soup, 146
    Rabbit Stew with Wild Greens, Mrs.
        Everdeen's, 72
    Taste of Spring Soup, 115
Lemon Butter Sauce, Baby Vegetables
    in, 122
Lime-Wasabi Mayo, 101
Liver
    Goose (Chicken), and Puffy Bread,
        34
    Goose, Rich, and Puffy Bread, 73
    Pate, Capitol Living, 198
Loaves and Fishes, District 4's, 46

M

Mashed on the Floor Peas, 125
Mayo, Wasabi-Lime, 101
Meat. *See* Beef; Game Meats; Goat;
    Lamb; Pork
Mellark Bakery's Goat Cheese and
    Apple Tarts, 55
Mellark's Cinnamon Bread, 93
Mellark's (Mr.) Farewell Cookies, 15
Mellark's Whole Wheat Raisin
    Cinnamon Bread, 144
Melon
    Fruit Kebabs and a Fountain of
        Chocolate, 124
    Pale Purple, 74
Menus. *See* Party menus
Meringue Mints, Disappearing, 120
Milk
    Bread Soaked in Warm Milk, Feel
        Better Fast, 177
    Grain and, Hot under the Collar, 180
    Honey and Spiced, Soothing, 105
Minnow Hash, Grilled, 239
Mint Tea, Katniss, 7
Mom Everdeen's Breakfast of Mush, 71
Morel Mushrooms, Dry Land Fish Fry,
    223
Mrs. Everdeen's Rabbit Stew with Wild
    Greens, 72
Mrs. Everdeen's Simple Broth, 96
Mrs. Everdeen's Sugar Berry Jam, 58
Muffins
    Cheese Buns, Homesick, 108
    Haymitch's Hangover, 90
    Pepper Jack and Chive, 156
Mush, Mom Everdeen's Breakfast of, 71
Mushier Than Mud Beets, 181
Mushroom(s)
    Dry Land Fish Fry, 223
    foraging for, 34

Groosling Kebabs, Deliciously
    Simple Grilled, 189
Portobello Caps, Fruit-and-Herb-
    Stuffed, 139
Soup, Creamy Mixed, 35
Mustard Sauce, Better Than Nothing
    Bread with Moldy Cheese and,
    197

N

New Day Dawning Coddled Eggs with
    Glazed Ham Steaks, 23
No Manners Needed Chocolate Cake,
    117
Noodles
    Beef Stew, Prim's Hearty, over, 95
    in Green Sauce, 37
    Shellfish in a Spicy Chile Sauce,
        District 4, 163
Not From a Can Cod Chowder, 194
Nut(s). See also specific nuts
    Fence-Roasted Tree Nuts, 130
    Raisin Nut Bread, Burnt, Peeta's, 14
    Slivered, Pumpkin Pie with, 145

O

Oats
    Grain and Milk, Hot under the Collar,
        180
    Tesserae Cereal with Mixed Berries,
        60
Ocean Creatures and Cocktail Sauce,
    113
Okra
    Fried, Katniss' Favorite, 217
    and Gray Fish Stew, Slightly Slimy
        But Delicious, 176
One Fine Spit-Roasted Rabbit, 50
Onion(s)
    and Bean Stew, "Wish There Was
        Meat," 174
    Tiny, Sweet Peas with, 32
Orange(s)
    Chicken in Cream Sauce, 30
    Chocolate Citrus Cake, Juicy, 150
    Coolers, and Sweet Berry, 140
    Cornish Hens Stuffed with, over
        Rice, 102
    in Pork Chops, Haymitch's, and
        Smashed Potatoes, 43
    Preserves, 39
    Quail, Blood Orange, 118–119
    Rice Pudding, Fresh Orange Vanilla,
        141
    Sauce, Chicken with, 151

in Watercress Salad, Sweet Asian, 148
Yams and Plums, Stewed, with Orange Juice, 149
Oysters
Clambake, Authentic Arena, 162
Raw Shellfish, Sweet, 161

P
Pale Purple Melon, 74
Pancakes, Batter Cakes with Thick Orange Preserves, 39
Panem Biscuits, 208
Paprika Duck and Rosemary Tubers with Gravy, 89
Parsley Mashed Potatoes, 123
Party menus
children at the Capitol, 245
cornucopia buffet for adults, 249
cornucopia buffet for kids, 246
deceptively sweet party for kids, 244
dining with President Snow, 250
rustic menu for adventurous teens, 247
teens partying at the Capitol, 248
Pasta. See Noodles
Pastry Puffs, Lamb, Catching Fire, 154
Pate
Goose Liver, Rich, and Puffy Bread, 73
Liver, Capitol Living, 198
Pea(s)
Mashed on the Floor, 125
Soup, Good for Your Soul, 182
Sweet, with Tiny Onions, 32
Pears, Dried Fruits, Backpack Treasure, 75
Peeta's Burnt Raisin Nut Bread, 14
Peeta's Healing Groosling Soup with Sweet Root Vegetables, 51
Peeta's Hot Chocolate Pudding, 65
Peeta's Minced Venison Stew, 179
Peeta's Multigrain Bread, 91
Peeta's Positively Awesome Roasted Raccoon, 231
Peeta's Sweet Breakfast Rolls, 26
Pepper Jack and Chive Muffins, 156
Peppermint
Disappearing Mints, 120
Ice Cream, 136
Pesto (Green Sauce), Noodles in, 37
Pheasant with Cranberry Jewels, Sweet, 121
Pickled Beets, Prim's, 222
Pickled Crab Apples, Greasy Sae's, 216

Pie
Crust, 186
Pumpkin, with Slivered Nuts, 145
Wind in Your Hare, 186
Pigeon, Baked, Katniss', 237
Pineapple, Fruit Kebabs and a Fountain of Chocolate, 124
Plum(s)
Balsamic Reduction, Lamb Chops with a, 137
Dried, Lamb Stew with, Beloved, 42
Dumplings, Capitol Lamb Stew with, 110–111
Lamb Stew, Greasy Sae's Plum Good, 196
Tarts, Tiny, 152
and Yams, Stewed, with Orange Juice, 149
Plutarch's Roasted Turkey Leg, 127
Pork. See also Bacon; Ham; Sausage
Chitterlings, in Greasy Sae's Special Winter Soup, 70
Chops and Smashed Potatoes, Haymitch's, 43
in Liver Pate, Capitol Living, 198
Ribs, Stick to Your, 210
Suckling Pig, Gamemakers', 40
Portobello Caps, Fruit-and-Herb-Stuffed, 139
Possum
Entrails Stew, Keep You Going, 235
Holiday Stuffed, Greasy Sae's, 230
Potato(es)
Biscuits, 225
Breakfast Through a Mouthpiece, 126
in Cabbage, Boiled, and Burnt Meat, Haymitch-Style, 87
in Clambake, Authentic Arena, 162
Dumplings, Plum, Capitol Lamb Stew with, 110–111
in Fish Soup, Salty Tears, 41
Fried, Golden, 24
and Ham Hash, Tigris', 200
Leek Soup, 146
Mashed, Creamy, 21
Mashed, Parsley, 123
in Minnow Hash, Grilled, 239
Smashed, Pork Chops and, Haymitch's, 43
in Venison Pot Roast, Gale's, 211
in Venison Stew with Sweet Roots for Rue, 64
Pot Roast, Venison, Gale's, 211
Poultry. See Chicken; Duck; Game Birds; Goose; Turkey

Preserves, Orange, 39
Presidential Stuffed Fowl, 112
President Snow's Snowy Rose Cupcakes, 63
Prim's Birthday Venison Steaks, 59
Prim's Blackberry Cobbler, 218
Prim's Goat Cheese Gifts, 4
Prim's Hearty Beef Stew, 95
Prim's Pickled Beets, 222
Pudding
Hot Chocolate, Peeta's, 65
Rice, Fresh Orange Vanilla, 141
Puff Pastry
Goose Liver, Rich, and Puffy Bread, 73
Lamb Puffs, Catching Fire, 154
Puffy Bread and Goose (Chicken) Liver, 34
Puffy Bread and Goose Liver, Rich, 73
Pumpkin
Pie with Slivered Nuts, 145
Soup, Savory, with Nuts, 114

Q
Quail, Blood Orange, 118–119

R
Rabbit
Legs, Roasted, with Egg Sauce, 52
Pie, Wind in Your Hare, 186
Spit-Roasted, One Fine, 50
Stew with Wild Greens, Mrs. Everdeen's, 72
in Winter Soup, Greasy Sae's Special, 70
Raccoon, Positively Awesome Roasted, Peeta's, 231
Raisin(s)
Cinnamon Whole Wheat Bread, Mellark's, 144
Grain and Milk, Hot under the Collar, 180
Nut Bread, Peeta's Burnt, 14
Raspberry(ies)
Cereal, Tesserae, with Mixed Berries, 60
Jam, Mrs. Everdeen's Sugar Berry, 58
Soda, Deceptively Sweet Berry Syrup, 53
Soup, Cold, with Fresh Berries, 116
Rat on a Stick, Gale's, 234
Real Bakery Loaf Bread, 12
Red-Eye Gravy and Fried Ham, Greasy Sae's, 215

Rhubarb and It's Not Really Dog Stew, 188
Ribs, Stick to Your, 210
Rice
    Cabbage Casserole, Haymitch Inspired, 147
    Cornish Hens Stuffed with Oranges over, 102
    Pudding, Fresh Orange Vanilla, 141
    Stuffed Fowl, Presidential, 112
Rolls
    Flower-Shaped, 31
    Sweet Breakfast, Peeta's, 26
Rosemary Tubers and Paprika Duck with Gravy, 89
Rue, All for, Groosling Legs, 47
Rue's Cold Carrot and Yam Puree, 142
Rue, Venison Stew with Sweet Roots for, 64
Rum Banana Cake, Fiery Spirits, 38

S
Salads
    Chestnut and Apple, with Toasted Bread Croutons, 131
    Cole Slaw, for Haymitch, 219
    Dandelion, Hope Springs Eternal, 8
    Green, Fresh, 19
    Watercress, Sweet Asian, 148
    Watercress and Almond, 103
Salty Tears Fish Soup, 41
Sauces. *See also* Gravy
    Balsamic Plum Reduction, Lamb Chops with a, 137
    Chile, Spicy, Shellfish in a, District 4, 163
    Cocktail, 113
    Cream, Orange Chicken in, 30
    Egg, Roasted Rabbit Legs with, 52
    Green (Pesto), Noodles in, 37
    Lemon Butter, Baby Vegetables in, 122
    Mustard, Better Than Nothing Bread with Moldy Cheese and, 197
    Orange, Chicken with, 151
    Wasabi-Lime Mayo, 101
Sausage
    Breakfast Through a Mouthpiece, 126
    Gravy, District 13's, 209
Say It Isn't So Bread and Cabbage, 178
Seafood. *See* Fish; Shellfish
Seeded Crescent Loaf, District 11's, 48
Shellfish
    Clambake, Authentic Arena, 162

Ocean Creatures and Cocktail Sauce, 113
    in a Spicy Chile Sauce, District 4, 163
    Sweet Raw, 161
Shrimp
    deveining, 113
    in Ocean Creatures and Cocktail Sauce, 113
Silent, Cold Soup of Beet Puree, 100
Skewers
    Bird, Skewered, 157
    Bony Fish on a Stick, Campfire, 77
    Burnt "Tree Rat" for the Timid, 132
    Fruit Kebabs and a Fountain of Chocolate, 124
    Groosling Kebabs (Goose or Duck), Deliciously Simple Grilled, 189
    Rat on a Stick, Gale's, 234
    Slightly Slimy But Delicious Gray Fish and Okra Stew, 176
    Smelt, Bony Fish on a Stick, Campfire, 77
Snail Scampi, Fried, 240
Snake Steak, Fried, 236
Snow's Suckling Pig, 109
Snowy Rose Cupcakes, President Snow's, 63
Soda, Berry Syrup, Deceptively Sweet, 53
Soothe My Soul Tea, 92
Soothing Honey and Spiced Milk, 105
Soups. *See also* Broth
    Bean, 5-, Greasy Sae's, 221
    Beef, Greasy Sae's Call It, 13
    of Beet Puree, Silent, Cold, 100
    Carrot, Thick and Creamy, 18
    Cod Chowder, Not From a Can, 194
    cold, 100
    Fish, Salty Tears, 41
    Gourd and Bean, Greasy Sae's, 86
    Gray Fish and Okra Stew, Slightly Slimy But Delicious, 176
    Groosling, with Sweet Root Vegetables, Peeta's Healing, 51
    Katniss, Creamy Roasted, 66
    Mushroom, Creamy Mixed, 35
    Pea, Good for Your Soul, 182
    Potato Leek, 146
    Pumpkin, Savory, with Nuts, 114
    Raspberry, Cold, with Fresh Berries, 116
    Taste of Spring, 115
    Winter, Greasy Sae's Special, 70
Spice Cookies, Mr. Mellark's Farewell, 15

Spinach
    Catfish Stew with Greens, 6
    Green Salad, Fresh, 19
Spit-Roasted
    Goat, 165
    Rabbit, One Fine, 50
Split Pea Soup, Good for Your Soul, 182
Squash
    Badger Stew, Greasy Sae's, 238
    Gourd and Bean Soup, Greasy Sae's, 86
    in Lamb Stew with Plum Dumplings, Capitol, 110–111
Squirrel(s)
    Charred Tree Rat, 160
    Fried Wings, Capitol, 232
Stews
    Badger, Greasy Sae's, 238
    Bean and Onion, "Wish There Was Meat," 174
    Beaver (Beef), Hazelle's Hearty, 84
    Beaver Hazelle's Authentic, 164
    Beef, Greasy Sae's Seriously, 193
    Beef, Prim's Hearty, 95
    Catfish, with Greens, 6
    Goat, Goat Trader's, 78
    Gray Fish and Okra, Slightly Slimy But Delicious, 176
    It's Not Really Dog and Rhubarb, 188
    Lamb, with Dried Plums, Beloved, 42
    Lamb, with Plum Dumplings, Capitol, 110–111
    Lamb, Plum Good, Greasy Sae's, 196
    Possum Entrails, Keep You Going, 235
    Rabbit, with Wild Greens, Mrs. Everdeen's, 72
    Venison, Minced, Peeta's, 179
    Venison with Sweet Roots for Rue, 64
Stick to Your Ribs, 210
Stock, homemade, 164
Strawberries, Mrs. Everdeen's Sugar Berry Jam, 58
Suckling Pig
    Gamemakers', 40
    Snow's, 109
Sweet Peas with Tiny Onions, 32
Sweet Potato(es). *See also* Yam(s)
    in Groosling Soup with Sweet Root Vegetables, Peeta's Healing, 51
    Lamb's Neck with Sweet Roots and Greens, 138
Sweet Raw Shellfish, 161
Syrup, Deceptively Sweet Berry, 53

T

Tarts
  Apple, Easy, 143
  Goat Cheese and Apple, Mellark
    Bakery's, 55
  Plum, Tiny, 152
  rustic, 152
Taste of Spring Soup, 115
Tea
  Herb, Finger Thawing, 85
  Mint, Katniss, 7
  Soothe My Soul, 92
Tesserae Cereal with Mixed Berries, 60
Tesserae Hearth Bread, 5
Thick and Creamy Carrot Soup, 18
Tigris' Ham and Potato Hash, 200
Tiny Plum Tarts, 152
Toast(s)
  Croutons, Toasted Bread, Chestnut
    and Apple Salad with, 131
  Eggs and, Greasy Sae's, 201
  French Toast and Bacon,
    Buttercup's, 202
  Goat Cheese, with Fresh Apple, 54
  Tomatoes, Pea-Sized, Bitter Greens
    with, 36
Tree Rat, Charred, 160
Tribute Lamb Chops, 20
Trout, Gray Fish and Okra Stew,
    Slightly Slimy But Delicious,
    176
Tubers
  Roasted Katniss, and Fried Catfish, 9
  Rosemary, and Paprika Duck with
    Gravy, 89
Turkey
  Groosling Legs, All for Rue, 47
  Roasted, Crispy Juicy, 187
  Roasted Leg, Plutarch's, 127

Turnips
  in Groosling Soup with Sweet Root
    Vegetables, Peeta's Healing, 51
  in It's Not Really Dog and Rhubarb
    Stew, 188
  Mashed Breakfast, Distict 13's, 173

V

Vegetables. See also Greens; specific
    vegetables
  Baby, in Lemon Butter Sauce, 122
  Soup, Taste of Spring, 115
  Sweet Root, Groosling Soup with,
    Peeta's Healing, 51
  Sweet Roots and Greens, Lamb's
    Neck with, 138
  Sweet Roots for Rue, Venison Stew
    with, 64
Venison
  Jerky, Deer, Eat It on the Go, 220
  Jerky, District 12, 76
  Pot Roast, Gale's, 211
  Ribs, Stick to Your, 210
  steaks, cooking, 76
  Steaks, Prim's Birthday, 59
  Stew, It's Not Really Dog and
    Rhubarb, 188
  Stew, Minced, Peeta's, 179
  Stew with Sweet Roots for Rue, 64

W

Walnut(s)
  Black, Cookies, Greasy Sae's, 212
  Slivered, Pumpkin Pie with, 145
Wasabi-Lime Mayo, 101
Watercress
  in Beef Soup, Greasy Sae's Call It, 13
  Lamb's Neck with Sweet Roots and
    Greens, 138

Salad, and Almond, 103
Salad, Sweet Asian, 148
Wedding Cake, Finnick and Annie's,
    204
Wedding Cider, Finnick and Annie's,
    203
Whole Wheat Raisin Cinnamon Bread,
    Mellark's, 144
Wind in Your Hare Pie, 186
"Wish There Was Meat" Bean and
    Onion Stew, 174

Y

Yam(s). See also Sweet Potato(es)
  and Carrot Puree, Cold, Rue's, 142
  and Plums, Stewed, with Orange
    Juice, 149
Yucca
  Roasted Katniss Tubers and Fried
    Catfish, 9
  Rosemary Tubers and Paprika Duck
    with Gravy, 89
  Soup, Creamy Roasted Katniss, 66

Z

Zucchini and Corn Medley, Greasy
    Sae's, 226

CPSIA information can be obtained at www.ICGtesting.com
Printed in the USA
LVOW091416191212

312443LV00009B/84/P